Women Workers in the First World War

THE BRITISH EXPERIENCE

GAIL BRAYBON

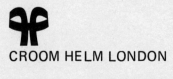

CROOM HELM LONDON

BARNES & NOBLE BOOKS
TOTOWA, NEW JERSEY

© 1981 Gail Braybon
Croom Helm Ltd, 2-10 St John's Road, London SW11

British Library Cataloguing in Publication Data

Braybon, Gail
   Women workers in the First World War.
   1. European War, 1914-1918 — Women's work
   2. Women — Employment — Great Britain —
   History — 20th century
   3. Labour and labouring classes — Great
   Britain — History — 20th century
   I. Title
   331.4'0941   D639.W7   80-41178
   ISBN 0-7099-0603-X

First published in the USA 1981 by
BARNES & NOBLE BOOKS
81 ADAMS DRIVE
TOTOWA, New Jersey, 07512

ISBN 0-389-20100-6

Reproduced from copy supplied
printed and bound in Great Britain
by Billing and Sons Limited
Guildford, London, Oxford, Worcester

To:
My parents, my dogs, Alan and my friends

CONTENTS

ACKNOWLEDGEMENTS

My thanks go to all those who have read and commented on the manuscript of this book, and to the people with whom I have discussed particular important issues, including Antonia Ineson, Penny Summerfield and Stephen Yeo. I would also like to express my gratitude to staff of the various libraries I have visited, and to the Twenty Seven Foundation, which provided me with a grant for travelling expenses.

PREFACE

This book does not pretend to be a full history of women's work during the First World War. To begin with, I am mostly concerned with the position of working-class women, and thus there is no information on the work of VADs, members of the Land Army, clerks or civil servants, who were primarily middle-class — although it should be evident that many comments made by contemporaries about women's work and their domestic role were aimed at women in general. In addition, although there is some description of women's industrial work, my major interest is in the public and semi-public debates which revolved around such work. What I am trying to show is the remarkable consistency of male attitudes towards women's work, even in the exceptional time of war, and the way in which such attitudes affected the women themselves.

My work here is a development of an MPhil thesis, and although I have, in the last two years, been able to widen the scope of my work considerably, I have still not been able to use all the sources I would have liked, particularly material in the PRO and Imperial War Museum. I have not been funded in my continuing research, and this has been a handicap: it is, indeed, the main reason why I cannot expand this book further. I am very grateful to the Twenty Seven Foundation for the help with travelling expenses during the last few years; without such aid the book would certainly never have been written. Critics of this work will notice many omissions in the source material; I have not been able to do any local studies, which I feel would have been very useful, or follow through union policy in detail between 1914 and 1922, or look at the approach of suffragettes and suffragists as fully as I would like to have done. Although some work has been done in these fields by other writers, there is still much more for historians to do. This book has to be seen as a broad study, and one which has incorporated as many different kinds of source material as possible. I have used government reports and the evidence presented to wartime committees, books of the time, trade union and trade journals, some feminist journals, and newspapers of all kinds. Attitudes towards women's industrial work and opinions about their domestic roles were expressed readily in these, and they represent the view of a broad cross-section of society; these attitudes are what concern me here, as they had a devastating effect upon working-class women after the war, when the public applause for their 'marvellous work' died away.

In the following chapters, I shall show the way in which the general expectations that women's energies and time should be spent on homes, husbands and children dominated discussions about the desirability of paid work for them, the suitability of certain jobs, and their capabilities as workers. These ideas existed at all levels of society, and the importance of this should be appreciated. I have been criticised for concentrating on women's oppression by some of those who are more concerned about the oppression of the working class in general, and who think that by describing the prejudice of workmen and unions towards women workers I am ignoring the fact that men's behaviour was influenced by their fear of cheap female labour displacing them. I am a socialist as well as a feminist, and appreciate this point, but I see this matter as being more complex than do many labour historians. The following statements sum up my views, and will be elaborated upon during the book.

(1)   The patriarchal system coexists with the capitalist system; the working class have been exploited by the latter, but women have also been oppressed by men of their own or other classes in a multitude of ways.

(2)   The ready acceptance by working-class men of women's lower status, and of strictly defined sex roles at home and work, has bolstered up capitalism and contributed to men's own economic vulnerability. Men who did not wish their wives to work accepted the existence of a cheap female labour force; members of this labour force took low-paid, short-term jobs with the expectation of leaving work on marriage, or were driven to take such work in desperation. This pool of labour was a danger to male workers, yet many men were reluctant to work towards equal pay and equal job opportunities, as such action meant the tacit acceptance of the idea that women need not be defined primarily as wives and mothers.

(3)   The sexual division of labour has also encouraged working-class men to fight for higher male wages *rather than* shorter hours or better conditions for all, and to accept higher risks at work. This fight has been waged on the assumption that women need less money when working, that they will be dependent upon men for most of their lives, and that they will perform all domestic tasks and look after the children (whether or not they are doing paid work themselves), thus sparing the exhausted male worker such chores.

As working-class women were invariably worse off than any other section of the population under this economic system, whether or not they were wage-earners, I make no excuses for wishing to examine the rhetoric and action used to keep them in their 'proper place'. Labour historians have examined the nature of men's oppression; I hope to throw some light on that of working-class women. They can be seen as a coherent group, whether or not they were full-time wage-earners for life, since all of them were affected in some way by the assumptions about women's role in society. Much of this book is concerned with the way in which attitudes towards them influenced their lives as paid workers, as most working-class women were employed for at least part of their lives, but in addition the importance of their unpaid domestic work has to be taken into account. It was this which was used to limit their job opportunities and wages, and this which made their lives harder.

There is another point which I would like to clarify. In the following pages I make much of the importance for women of the right to paid work. In many ways there is nothing wonderful about the right to work (hence the slogans which went up around Paris in 1968, 'Never Work'), as it simply means the right to sell your time and your labour for an inadequate sum of money. But women always worked; it was simply a matter of whether they were doing *paid* work or unpaid, and whether they were forced into the ghetto of low-paid jobs or allowed to enter other trades. Women before and after the war were often obliged to depend upon men for financial support or work at rates few men would have accepted; in this context the 'right to work' and the right to enter men's trades were important indeed.

Finally, it should be obvious that I see the evidence in this book as being relevant to the present. A study of women's position during the First World War isolates one phase of a continuum. Research (undertaken by Penny Summerfield, and to be published shortly) indicates that even during the Second World War, when, it is popularly assumed, women were allowed into men's jobs *en masse*, the assumption that a woman's first responsibility was to her home and family remained remarkably resilient, and acted as a brake on the opening up of opportunities for women. The demand for women's labour during the two wars may suggest that at this time, if no other, views of women's position and role might change — such has been the conviction of many a social historian when describing the granting of women's suffrage. Yet in fact views of women remained consistent during the war. Perhaps traditionalist views were even encouraged by the events of 1914 to 1918. By the end of the war there was a strong desire to get back to the 'normality' or 'stability' of peacetime, and fears about sudden change were fuelled by the October Russian Revolution — with all this symbolised for the position of women in Russia — and by the seeming reluctance of women in England to abandon their wartime jobs and 'go home'. Working-class women wage-earners in the 1920s had to face far more hostility than they had before the war. The fact that women did *not* escape from the classic female trades is important, and many of the features which characterised the position of working-class women in industry then still exist today.

1 WOMEN'S POSITION IN THE LABOUR FORCE BEFORE 1914

No analysis of women's work during the First World War would be complete without some description of the conditions and attitudes which existed before 1914. Obviously I can only touch upon certain aspects of women's work here — other writers have covered the nineteenth century in far more depth[1] — but in this chapter I want to do two things: first, to establish the nature of women's industrial work before the war and, secondly, to give some idea of prevailing attitudes towards women as workers. The years between 1890 and 1914 concern me most, but I shall give a fairly brief description of women's work in earlier years, as the pattern of labour which existed by the turn of the century was established by the Industrial Revolution. Similarly, the feelings expressed about 'women's role' in the 1900s had their roots in Victorian ideas about suitable work, and the duties of wives and mothers. Although this is very much a background chapter, certain features of particular relevance to later chapters should become clear, particularly the close association between job opportunities open to working-class women and ideas about Women's Role in society.

The Industrial Revolution and its Effects

The Industrial Revolution had a profound effect upon the nature of women's paid work and their role in the home. The development of the factory system led to the separation of 'home' and 'work' for those drawn into the new industries. In earlier years much industrial work was done in the homes of the workers: carding, spinning and weaving of wool and cotton, knitting, glove making, etc., were done by men, women and children, at the hours they chose. Such work was often interspersed with agricultural labour for local farmers, or work upon the cottagers' own gardens or common land. Many families thus had a varied source of income, and the whole family was a productive unit, producing goods for its own consumption and for sale to others. Typically, in the textile industry the wages earned by the whole family were paid to the man, as the 'head' of the family, even though wives and children worked just as hard. Different processes were performed by men, women and

15

children under the same roof, and they were paid a 'family wage'.

The Industrial Revolution took place during the Agrarian Revolution — which involved the enclosure of common land and the modernisation of farms — and thus male and female workers in all areas found their land disappearing, while those in the textile industry were faced with competition from powered machinery.[3] Textiles lay at the heart of the Industrial Revolution; first cotton spinning, then carding and weaving went into the factory. Although handworkers attempted for a while to compete, this was impossible as machinery became more sophisticated. Wool saw less speedy changes and many other hand industries remained, but cotton had set the pace, and factory work was regarded as increasingly normal.

A completely different pattern of life was established for both male and female workers in the new industries, and outside. Deprived of additional income from common land, and of work in domestic industries, those in many areas became dependent upon labouring full-time for farmers. Those in the emergent textile towns had to adjust to life in the factory. The cotton industry had employed many women in the home; it now employed them in weaving sheds and card rooms, and they were often preferred, with children, to men. Even at this early stage of industrialisation they were said to be more docile and co-operative and more amenable to the discipline of the factory, which many men resisted bitterly. They were also cheaper to employ than men. The old idea of the 'family wage', which had never been appropriate to single women living alone, even in the pre-industrial age, was adapted to fit the changing circumstances. Women were paid less than men because it was assumed that they were living with husbands or fathers who were also working. Working men increasingly felt that women were taking jobs which should have gone to men, and they argued that as women were classed as dependants, men's employment should be given priority. Employers were reluctant to accept this philosophy to begin with, eager though they were to exploit the idea that women required less money, but the developing labour organisations and trade unions took up the cause of working-class men, rather than women, and they were quite prepared to press for the exclusion of women from certain jobs, partly for economic reasons, partly for reasons which will be discussed shortly.

By the mid-nineteenth century women made up the bulk of power-loom weavers, and were seen as natural recruits for any other mechanised industries. They were also being employed as domestic servants in ever increasing numbers — far more women than men were servants throughout the century⌋ At the same time, they were being withdrawn from mining, which was now considered to be unsuitable work for them — although many women did hard and heavy work in agriculture at lower wages, and there remained thousands of women who still worked long and tedious hours in cottage industries and aroused little attention from middle-class investigators (with the notable exception of the handloom weavers). The pattern of employment for men, women and children which existed in 1914 was established during the second half of the nineteenth century⌈Men and women in the factory trades went out to work, leaving their homes for more than a dozen hours a day, were usually paid in cash, and bought food, clothes and fuel with these wages, where once they had grown food, made clothes and cut wood. The house was no longer the centre of industry, and no longer the place where goods were produced for the consumption of the family⌋ Running a home, which had once been a full-time task, and included care of garden and animals, now became a matter of cleaning, cooking and child care. Child care meant looking after children who had once been occupied in domestic industry themselves; formerly men and women could supervise their children's activities while they were all working; as adults now went out to work, and children were steadily withdrawn from the factories and mines which had been so eager to employ them in the early days of industrialisation, it was clear that somebody had to take care of them. Although the development of state education ensured that they would be supervised for part of the day, schooldays were shorter than workdays, children did not start until the age of four or five,[4] and they went home at lunch-time⌊ It was assumed that women, those who had always organised home life, should stay at home to look after the children.⌋

The flourishing factory system affected the labour of both sexes, but the repercussions were different for men and women. Women were established as quick, docile workers, ideal for machine minding, but they were also seen increasingly as men's competitors. They found themselves capable of earning independently (instead of earning as part of the family unit), but also encountered the belief that they were taking work away from men by working for lower wages, and that they should, if married, retire to look after their children. Women had not given up paid work on marriage in pre-industrial times; those who worked in agriculture or in the hand industries had been expected to help maintain the family. But attitudes were changing as society changed. This was partly because children had to be looked after by an 'unoccupied' adult. It was also because men saw the retreat of married women from paid work as improving their own chances of finding and holding work. But there was another factor in operation as well. The new middle classes did not approve of married women working. To them a leisured wife was a sign of a man's success — alone, he was making enough money to keep his family in comfort. Throughout the first sixty or so years of the nineteenth century, the number of middle-class men and women was increasing, and their standard of living rose steadily. The money they acquired went on houses, possessions, large families and servants. Middle-class women were withdrawn not only from paid labour, but from many of the domestic tasks which had occupied their mothers and grandmothers. Their role was to devote themselves to their husbands, and, above all, to their children: motherhood was 'the consummation of the world's joy to a true woman',[5] or, as Frances Power Cobbe put it: 'the great and paramount duties of a mother and wife once adopted, every other interest sinks, by the beneficent laws of our nature, into a subordinate place in normally constituted minds.'[6] The home became the middle-class man's retreat from the world of business and competition, and the wife who presided over this retreat was not to be sullied by paid work herself. Domestic work was also unsuitable; she was supposed to spend her time educating her children while servants performed the menial tasks. Large numbers of cheap servants were vital to this world.

What, it may be asked, has this scheme of things to do with the domestic lives of the working classes? In many ways it was entirely inappropriate. Although working men were generally paid more than women, this wage alone was seldom enough to support families in any degree of comfort. A skilled man might be able to support a wife and a number of children, but well-paid skilled men were in the minority. In any case, even the most steady workman could find himself laid off or ill, and the only aid the state offered was in the workhouse. A family dependent upon a single wage-earner was very vulnerable. For those working-class women who did give up work on marriage, life was very different from the middle-class ideal. They could not devote themselves to the moral education of their children as they had far too much domestic work to do. This work was often made harder by the fact that only one wage was coming in — cheaper food was bought, more clothes had to be altered or mended, accommodation was worse, washing was done at home instead of being sent to the laundry. Many married women were sacked from factory work when they married, or when their first child arrived, but found that they had to take in washing or sewing or go out cleaning in order to make ends meet.

But the concept of the 'idle' wife was increasingly influential. Working

women were sacked on marriage simply because a number of manufacturers also believed that they should be at home looking after homes
and husbands. Pressure groups forced Parliament to consider what was
'suitable' work for women who were, or would become, wives and
mothers — and governments which were usually reluctant to interfere
at all in industry nevertheless passed Factory Acts limiting women's
labour. Middle-class authors and investigators had much power when
backed by an outraged electorate. Wanda Neff described this influence
in her book *Victorian Working Women*:

> But even while economists and the manufacturers were satisfied with
> the general status of women in the textile factories, other forces
> entered the question. The sentimental prejudices of the average
> Englishman were arraigned against a system which, in his opinion,
> attacked the institution of the home, ranked by him above scientific
> theories or private fortunes . . . All women were regarded in the first
> half of the nineteenth century solely as potential mothers. The worker
> with her own earnings was, accordingly, an affront against nature
> and the protective instincts of man. That the family was affected by
> the labour of girls and women in the mills was a consideration that
> raised general concern. The question of the health of human beings
> who were entrusted with the responsibility of the next generation,
> the conflict of factory work and long hours with domestic life and
> with a mother's care of her home and children, the moral and spirit-
> ual degradation which might result from the employment of females
> outside their homes — with all this most of the literature dealing
> with the new industrial age was primarily concerned.[7]

This ideology of women and the home had a more insidious influence
also. Skilled working men aspired to middle-class respectability. For
them too a non-working wife became a status symbol, and they readily
adopted the idea that wives should devote themselves to the comfort
of husbands and children. Many trade unionists, fighting for better
wages and more secure employment, also adopted this ideology. A
non-working wife seemed to be the answer to many problems. As she
withdrew from the work-force she ceased to compete with men; she
provided a comfortable retreat for the hard-working man; she did all
the domestic chores; she kept the children from harm. More and more
she appeared to be a 'right' that the working man could aspire to, and
even a symbol of the working class's struggle against capitalism. When
all men earned good wages, their wives need work no longer.

Although women were theoretically withdrawn from underground mining during the nineteenth century, and restrictions on night work and long hours were adopted in the new factory trades, many married women continued to work, in spite of social pressure not to. A large number of them were *hidden* workers — those who did paid work in their homes for atrocious wages, or worked a few hours a day as charwomen. Others worked for occasional spells, when the family particularly needed the money, or returned to work when widowed. Only in the cotton and pottery industries did many women continue to go *out* to work after marriage on a regular basis. These worked under the close scrutiny of society: MPs, novelists, philanthropists, all took it upon themselves to study the ill-effects of such work upon homes, husbands and children. To begin with, this concern often stemmed from a general distaste for the effects of the factory system upon established life, but increasingly it became centred upon women. It is worth looking at views of working-class women's work in some detail here, since they have elements in common with attitudes expressed in the early twentieth century, and even during the First World War. Two industries in particular attracted attention in the 1830s and 1840s; one was mining, which many considered was unsuitable for all women; the other was cotton-weaving, which critics believed should not be done by married women — debates on the cotton workers continued throughout the century.

Mining was hard, dirty and dangerous work for both sexes and all age groups. Not surprisingly, many people felt that children should be withdrawn from such work — it stunted their growth, led to deformities, and imposed heavy work and long hours on those who were least able to protest. But much attention was also paid to the work of women in the mines. This was partly because it was felt that such labour was a harsh burden on those who were physically weaker than men, and that it might damage their health and childbearing capacity. It was also because of the possible effect of the working conditions upon women's behaviour and their social role. One Factory Commissioner wrote:

> They are to be found alike vulgar in manner and obscene in language: but who can feel surprised at their debased condition when they are known to be constantly associated, and associated only, with men and boys, living and labouring in a state of disgusting nakedness and brutality [8]

Observers may have been genuinely concerned about the harshness of the work, but few can doubt that the fact that half-naked men and women worked together in the darkness shocked them at least as much, if not more. In addition, women's work was supposed to destroy the comfort of the home. They returned to their houses in the evenings, blackened and exhausted, and reluctant to do domestic work and cook proper meals. They thus failed to be caring wives, and were seen as playing a part in the brutalisation of their husbands. As the writers of the Report on Mines expressed it:

> Give to the Collier the comforts of a clean and cheerful home, and the companionship of a sober and decently-educated female, not degraded to brute labour by working in the pits; let her attend to a mother's and housewife's duties; and you will soon change the moral condition of the collier.[9]

One can see again evidence of the strongly held feeling that women should be the guiding light of the home. Lord Shaftesbury was quite happy to exploit further the horror aroused by the descriptions of women's work, in his speeches to Parliament:

> They know nothing that they ought to know ... they are rendered unfit for the duties of women by overwork, and become utterly demoralized. In the male the moral effects of the system are very sad, but in the female they are infinitely worse, not alone upon themselves, but upon their families, upon society, and, I may add, upon the country itself. It is bad enough if you corrupt the man, but if you corrupt the woman, you poison the waters of life at the very fountain.[10]

This was an all too common theme throughout the nineteenth century; not only were women seen as being more susceptible to physical injury, they were also believed to succumb more readily to moral corruption (which then expressed itself in the form of bad language, promiscuity, profanity, etc., all of which were classed as equally dangerous to society). The state of their physical health was said to be more important than that of men, because of their childbearing role, and ironically they were supposed to remain men's moral superiors − a source of guidance to husbands and children alike.[11]

The result of the furore over women in the mines was legislation to ban them from working underground. Unfortunately, no alternative work was offered to them, and families found their incomes cut drastically, while single women faced starvation. The middle-class reformers did nothing about this unfortunate state of affairs. Two additional points can be made. Mining was hard work, but wages in this industry were much higher than those of many classic 'women's trades'. Women miners could afford to eat better food than the women in more 'suitable' trades. In addition, it is an interesting fact that although women were removed from the pits by the Mines Act, boys over the age of 11 were still employed. One has to wonder now whether a twenty-year-old woman or a twelve-year-old boy suffered the more from gruelling pit work. Middle-class reformers reacted to bad conditions by *banning women from the work* instead of calling for improvements for men and women alike. This response became typical, and was adopted by later trade unionists as well.

Women's work in the cotton mills did not cause quite such an outrage, although there were plenty, like Shaftesbury, who exaggerated the harshness of the work or the unpleasantness of factory conditions in order to hammer home their points about the ill effects of such labour. Weaving and carding were not exceptionally hard work, and no one could stir up public anger by producing etchings of half-naked workers, as they had done during debates about women miners. Nevertheless, many saw the work as being particularly harmful for married women, who would neglect home, husband and babies, and break up the family. As Lord Shaftesbury (by this time Lord Ashley) put it:

> You are poisoning the very sources of order and happiness and virtue; you are tearing up root and branch all relations of families to one another; you are annulling, as it were, the institution of domestic life decreed by Providence Himself, the wisest and kindest of all earthly ordinances, the mainstay of peace and virtue and therein of national security.[12]

Or, to quote a factory inspector:

> we will not see that female labour in factories, even though it be necessary, is at variance with domestic teaching, and that, for the sake of the wages it brings, everything that is good and holy in the female character is often being sacrificed.[13]

Married women's work was supposed to lead to poor housewifery — although none of the critics stopped to wonder about the general standards of working-class housewifery, and the adverse effects of poverty, poor housing, lack of good food — and to promiscuity. Women's relatively high earning capacity was also blamed for early 'improvident' marriages, and for the 'demoralisation' of husbands, who sought to live off their wives' earnings instead of fulfilling their true role as breadwinners.[14] Margaret Hewett has neatly demolished these claims in her book *Wives and Mothers in Victorian Industry*, showing that marriage occurred little earlier amongst cotton operatives than amongst any other members of the working class, and that most women's husbands in this area did work full time as well. She draws attention to the one important effect such work did have for married women, however; infant mortality rates were higher amongst those who worked after marriage in the cotton towns than amongst those who retired to look after young children, because the babies had to be weaned early and were therefore more susceptible to disease. (It must be added that when families were poor enough, the existence of a non-working wife might not reduce infant mortality, since poverty was also responsible for death.) This was a problem all working wives encountered, and was not peculiar to the cotton industry — and the answer lay in crèches, nurseries and hygienic infant foods, not the withdrawal of women from the factory. Yet the pressure was for the withdrawal of wives from industry, rather than for the provision of adequate child-care facilities. These feelings often lay behind demands for shorter hours and no night work for women: if they could not be withdrawn from work they could at least be forced to spend more time in the home. The Short Time Committees set up to press for the ten-hour day often contained many who would have preferred to see married women removed from the cotton industry altogether, since 'the home, its cares and employment, is the woman's true sphere'.[15]

The 1844 Factory Act reduced the hours women could work in the cotton trade, and banned night work. Men were still allowed to work longer hours, as this was not supposed to damage the quality of home life. Women apparently used their new-found 'leisure' to do more housework, and many married women continued to work through their pregnancies and take the minimum amount of time off for childbirth. They could not afford to leave work for long, and many of them did not want to, appreciating the independence their wages gave them. Of course, women in other trades continued to work for long hours, and throughout the night if necessary: they worked in 'suitable' trades, like millinery or dressmaking, and were not venturing out into the dangerous, unsupervised land of the factory. As Wanda Neff points out, many of the criticisms of textile workers in particular stemmed from the fact that they were economically independent: wives could support themselves,

daughters could move away from home if they so chose. This appeared
to be a serious threat to the family.

Women and Work on the Eve of War

The Industrial Revolution created the pattern of men's and women's
employment, and as the nineteenth century passed certain trades declined while others were industrialised. The preoccupation with women's
domestic role remained, but the nature of the concern changed slightly
as time went on.

By the 1890s the factory system was accepted; there were no longer
doubts about its necessity. But the importance of women's work and its
effects upon society were now considered in another kind of investigation. There was a growing interest amongst MPs, charitable organisations,
philanthropists and the emergent socialist-labour movement in the
nature of poverty, which had clearly not been eliminated by industrialisation (as some believers in *laissez-faire* had claimed would happen).
According to the surveys of Booth and Rowntree,[16] some 30 per cent
of the population lived in poverty, and it became increasingly evident
that sickness, old age and low or irregular earnings caused this, not any
tendency to immorality or idleness on the part of individuals. Much
attention was therefore paid to the structure of men's and women's
employment, and it was all too evident that women were in many of
the worst-paid trades, were ill unionised, and were adversely affected
in industry by the assumption that they would leave on marriage. The
House of Lords Select Committee on Sweating, set up in 1886, produced
volumes of evidence on the exploitation of the women who did 'out
work' or 'home work' — the making of goods in their own homes — and
this, together with Booth's survey of London, showed the connection
between women's low-paid labour and the male casual labour market
in cities which did not offer regular work to either sex (particularly
London itself).[17] The Royal Commission on Labour requested reports
from the 'Lady Commissioners' on women's employment around the
country in the 1890s,[18] and received evidence of low pay, poor conditions and few opportunities for anything other than unskilled or semi-
skilled work. The reports showed that, apart from the cotton-weaving
industry in Lancashire, and isolated instances in particular factories,
women *always* got lower wages than men, on similar work.

The 1900s saw more evidence of women's dreary jobs, and also
further analysis of the reasons for their low position in the labour

market, together with suggested courses of action which could be taken to improve matters. In 1906 Edward Cadbury's book *Women's Work and Wages*,[19] a sympathetic study of women in Birmingham, was published, and at the same time yet another committee on sweated labour (the Select Committee on Homework)[20] was sitting, the reports of which advocated the provision of Trade Boards to establish minimum wages in the lowest-paid industries. Just after the war began, books by B.L. Hutchins and Clementina Black came out, giving information about the position of women workers in 1914.[21]

These key texts of the period, together with census reports, and backed up by other books and periodicals, gave a very full picture of both working-class women's work and society's attitude to it — while the irony of the bourgeois Victorian ideal of womanhood became increasingly evident. Many of the most unpleasant and low-paid jobs were done by women, and the most exploitative were done by married women who had no better jobs to turn to.

The 1901 census revealed that 83.7 per cent of males over ten years old were classed as 'occupied', while only 31.6 per cent of females were, which is broken down to 52.3 per cent of single women over ten, and 13.2 per cent of married or widowed women over ten. The figures show that throughout the two decades preceding the war an increasing number of young single girls were going out to work (obviously the increase was partly due to the growing acceptance of the idea that middle-class girls might have a job before marriage), but that married women were far less likely to have a job. However, it is not true to say that married women nation-wide did not work. The proportion who did varied from area to area. Where there was factory or outwork available, women frequently continued to work after marriage. The writers of the general report of the 1901 census isolated the areas where the highest proportions of married and widowed women were working. The percentages were as follows: in Redditch, a needle, pin and fishing-tackle producing area, 43.3 per cent of the occupied female labour force were married or widowed. The equivalent figures for other such towns were: Great Harward (a cotton-weaving town), 41.7 per cent; Nantwich (a tailoring area), 40.1 per cent; Luton (a straw-hat-making area), 40.0 per cent; Darwen (a cotton town), 31.1 per cent; and Barnoldswick (a cotton town), 38.6 per cent. Perhaps more significantly, if the figures are broken down by age group, in the county borough of Blackburn (a cotton area) the percentage of married and widowed women at work between the ages of 20 and 25 was 66.5 per cent, and this only dropped to 53.5 per cent in the 25-30 age group.[22] In addition, statistics did not reveal much of women's home work, nor allow for the casual nature of many wives' jobs.

‹ In the areas where many married women did do outside industrial work it was by now customary and locally acceptable to many (although not necessarily to the government or philanthropic writers who came from the outside to investigate the situation).(In areas where some married women worked it was a talking point, and in those where there was hardly any industry available for women (as, for example, in many mining areas), it was classed as highly undesirable, and notions of 'a woman's place is in the home' were very strong. It was a convenient philosophy there, and one which the women themselves had no chance of acting against.)

‹ The most important trades for women were, throughout these years (as earlier in the century), domestic service, tailoring and clothing, and textiles. Domestic service involved mostly single women, and was, by the beginning of the twentieth century, becoming increasingly unpopular. Census figures show that a declining number of girls chose to go into service,[23] but on the eve of the war there were nevertheless 1,734,040 female servants (there were only 387,677 males): it was still the largest single trade for women) Its growing unpopularity was shown by the declining proportion of women who did enter the industry, and working-class girls' own feelings can be gathered from other sources. For example, factory girls expressed their distaste for the long hours, lack of privacy and lack of freedom which servants had to endure,[24] and many women who went into war work during 1914-18 came from service and were glad to leave it behind. By both masters and mistresses it was taken for granted that their servants were always on call, had no regular free time, had to live in (accepting whatever standard of food and lodging was offered), and were to have no male 'followers'. All this was in total contrast to the lives of the factory girls, which involved hard work for a limited number of hours, followed by freedom to do what one chose in the evenings — even Clara Collet, a Lady Commissioner for the Royal Commission on Labour, and one of the surveyors for Booth's study of London labour, could not resist expressing admiration for the liveliness and brightness of the decked-out factory girls of London.

‹ The clothing industry was another old-established trade, but one which was being affected by the increasing use of machinery — especially the sewing machine.)The *Report* of the Select Committee on Sweating, Booth's survey of London, the Royal Commission on Labour and other sources established that 'high-class tailoring' was dominated by men, and women were confined to less skilled and lower-paid work. Many women in the clothing trades still worked not in workshops or factories but at home, as outworkers or homeworkers, getting their work through a middleman. Not only did they pay for their own heat, light, thread and equipment, they were paid pitifully low rates for goods which were frequently sold at far higher prices. The *Fifth Report* of the Select Committee on Sweating,[25] for example, quoted the rate paid for a good-quality coat as being 4s 6d per garment; these were later sold at £2 2s in the shops. Miss Orme, in the *Report on the Conditions of Work in Scotland*, relayed the experience of Witness 262, the wife of an iron worker:

> She is paid 7d a dozen for pressing and putting on buttons on boys' trousers; by working from 6a.m. to 6p.m. she can do 2 dozen, 1s 2d. For this, coal (extra being needed for heating irons) costs her 2½d per day and sticks ½d. She also pays 2d to a girl for carrying the work to and from the workshop . . . thus leaving a profit of 9d.[26]

Both married and single women worked in the clothing trades, but the majority of the former were home workers; home work was convenient for those who looked after children, sick husbands or aged parents. Women who most needed money were most exploited, as middlemen were free to cut rates arbitrarily: the competition for work was so intense that there were always people ready to work for lower rates. Clothing workers were not, of course, the only outworkers; women also worked at home making boxes, artificial flowers and other small goods, and evidence of the bad conditions shocked newspapers and public in the 1880s and 1890s.[27] By 1910 the government had decided to set up Trade Boards, as suggested by the 1907-8 Select Committee on Homework, which would set a minimum rate of payment for some of the low-paid trades. At the outbreak of the war some of these, made up of employers, trade unionists and employees, were in operation, but home work was still the area where wages were lowest. It was, in fact, a legacy of the old domestic industries, but although it enabled women to stay at home while they worked, it often put them in competition with people in workshops with superior machinery, or with cheap foreign imports. Like the domestic workers earlier in the Industrial Revolution, the frame-work knitters or the handloom weavers who competed with the new factories, they were scattered, disorganised and sufficiently near to destitution to accept what rates they could get. The position of employers was actually strengthened by the fact that most of the outworkers were *married* women — they often needed money desperately, as many of them were the wives of casual labourers and low-paid men, or were widows, and, because of the prevailing mood against married women working outside the home, they had no other jobs to go to. The Lady Commissioners, and others, noted that where factory work was easily available home work was less common, and certainly no single girl took up homework if she could get into a factory — unless, of course, her family had pretensions to a higher status, and she did needlework at home rather than associate with rough factory girls. Such a woman was a dreaded figure, the 'pocket money worker', who accepted low rates because she was supported by husband or father and did not need to feed, clothe or house herself.[28]

The third largest user of women's labour was the textile industry, the oldest factory industry. In the cotton trade women had a chance to learn a skill and earn good wages; they were also still allowed to stay on after marriage, unlike so many other factory workers — the women at Cadbury's Bournville factories, for example, were automatically dismissed on marriage, as the Lady Commissioners approvingly pointed out.[29]

It is probably true to say that the women weavers of Lancashire were by this time the elite amongst women workers — and they knew it.[30] In weaving, men and women earned equal piece rates, and the latter's ability to earn on an equal footing with men had meant that they maintained a noticeable degree of independence. Lancashire women had a pride in their work and status which no other women workers could imagine. However, there are two other points to be made about the cotton industry: the first is that by the end of the nineteenth century, the weavers' wages, although high for women, were low for men — in other, male-dominated industries the rates were often higher, and this leads one to wonder whether women's presence did in fact keep rates down, as some commentators of the time suggested. The other point to note is that although women were acceptable in the weaving sheds they were certainly not allowed on to other processes like mule-spinning, which had been established as a trade for men and boys, and there was no suggestion that women might learn this skilled and tiring work.[31]

Apart from domestic service, the clothing trades and textiles (silk and wool as well as cotton, though fewer women were employed here), women were employed in other jobs, but in smaller numbers: they dominated the laundry trade, and there were thousands of charwomen (mostly married); they made up part of the labour force in the metal trades, particularly in Birmingham and the Midlands; their numbers were growing in food, drink and tobacco, pottery and china; they were increasingly employed in the retail trade. But in all industries they were on a lower class of jobs, and they received far lower wages in general, even where the work done by men and women was similar – while, of course, they really had two jobs, for when they returned home, or in between spells of outwork, they had housework, cooking and child care, the tasks of their 'true role'.

Women's role at home as wives and mothers preoccupied the observers of the 1890s and 1900s, as it had done earlier in the century. The reports of their wage labour reveal not only the views held by employers and workmen on the subject of women's home and work duties, but the preconceptions of the writers. There were debates throughout these years about how to improve conditions for outworkers, and whether to introduce a minimum wage, debates which thus treated women's labour as an industrial problem, but there were also still discussions about whether to 'ban married women's work', and introduce further restrictions on the trades and hours women might work. Behind such ideas lay the continuing conviction that married women belonged at home, and that women in general, as bearers of the race, were weaker and should be protected. These moral and physical considerations were always bound up with the industrial ones, and no matter how sympathetic the observer, he or she felt obliged to discuss the question of whether married women were morally or physically damaging their husbands and children by venturing outside the home.

The books, reports and papers about working-class women reveal the range of prejudices about women's industrial capabilities and moral duties. Attitudes were complex, and opinions often not overtly stated, but particular ideals nevertheless suffused much that was written. Although one encapsulates attitudes at the risk of over-simplifying them, it is essential for one to have some understanding of the kind of approach adopted by government, employers, press and middle-class public towards working-class women before the war in order to comprehend the response to women's work between 1914 and 1918. Opinions about women's role in industry (and ideas about wifehood and motherhood) were descendants of the well established notions of women's role and capabilities in the years immediately before 1914, and were themselves a development of earlier concerns.

For the sake of brevity and simplicity I shall here divide the major preoccupations into three separate categories, although in fact they are interwoven, as they had been before; they are: the problems of women in industry (wages, status, training, etc.); the interaction of women and the home (e.g. should married women work?); and the health of women workers (the physical effect of labour, the need for further restrictions on hours, etc.).

Women in Industry

The drawbacks of women's labour were very obvious by the 1890s, and have been described in the preceding pages — they were low status and low pay. What emerged, however, from the studies of the time was that employers, male-dominated unions and working men alike *expected* women to be unambitious and apathetic about work, and were not concerned with enlarging women's opportunities.

The best trades were held by men, and they intended to keep them. The excuses were varied; it was claimed that women were uninterested in doing skilled work, that they were incapable of skilled work, and that they did not *deserve* to learn skilled work, as they would marry, and leave. Unions and men were, in fact, convinced that women needed less money and status because their primary duties were to be those of wives and mothers, while men acted as breadwinners. This attitude of course fitted in very well with the ideal of womanhood as promoted by the middle class. However, it did leave male workers in something of a dilemma as men in factory work had realised earlier on in the century — if women were to be paid less money by virtue of their sex they could be brought in by employers to undercut men. This had happened in some industries when new machinery, requiring less skill on the part of the operative, was introduced, and it was happening in engineering, where unskilled men were also a threat.[32] But in reality the development was less common than was believed, and the introduction of machinery could reduce women's employment instead, as happened in the lace industry during these two decades, where women's dominance was being steadily eroded. The solution appeared to be for men's unions to demand equal pay (which happened, for example, in a tailoring shop in Glasgow cited by the Royal Commission on Labour).[33] This kept women's competition to a minimum in the trades which were strongly unionised, but went against all the principles of masculine superiority at work and the belief that male breadwinners should earn more money. Alternatively women could be excluded altogether (once again by the strongest unions), so that employers were never given the chance to use them at lower wages. This latter was the most convenient solution for those male workers who could manage it, and it fitted in with many employers' own prejudices against women. They too believed that women were only capable of doing less skilled work, were uninterested in their trade, and were not worth training if they were only to stay until marriage.[34] Many (as described by the Royal Commission on Labour, the employer Edward Cadbury, and the feminists Hutchins and Black), dismissed women on marriage, and prided themselves on sending women back to their husbands' homes. If the dismissed wives took in home work at half the factory rate that did not of course trouble them.

Unions, men and employers had a low opinion of women's industrial capabilities, and little desire to find out if they could do better or if they wished to earn more. Most of them expressed the belief that women were dependants, did not deserve good money (unless they were in direct competition with men, when unions and employers had different ideas about the necessity of equal pay), and were inherently less skilful than men. Most commentators accepted by the 1900s that such beliefs were largely a matter of 'custom', and that this rested on the idea that men were paid a family wage and that woman's place was in the home; the factory or workplace was merely an interlude between childhood and wifehood.

Edward Cadbury grasped many of the implications of women's existing position in the labour market when he wrote:

> quite apart from any questions of skill and better work on the part of men, a woman worker receives less just because she is a woman ... it is taken for granted that a woman ought to receive less than a man ... Women's wages are at an inferior level because they accept the inferior position and take it for granted. Women accept this lower, dependant position just because they have always been used to it, and from a want of education on broader lines.[35]

In *Women's Work and Wages* he placed women's employment disabilities in a wider context: 'The reason for this inferiority of women, as compared to men workers, seems to be the same reason that accounts for their subjection and inferiority in other lines, such as politics and education.'[36] He thus recognised the important interaction of women's industrial and social roles, and the effect of women's poor status upon their own view of themselves. But even he, for all his sympathy, could not face up to the full implications of all this. He pitied married women who were forced out to work, but he thought that work for wives was undesirable in itself. He envisaged education and training schemes to improve women's job prospects and wages, yet it did not occur to him that he should tackle the basic premiss which affected women's lives — he did not think of attacking the idea that women were first and foremost wives and mothers, and only secondly individuals in their own right. The influence of 'custom' showed itself in all classes. Prospects and wages remained poor as long as it did.

The Interaction of Woman and the Home

Cadbury was simply reflecting the ideas and ideals of his time — ones which were accepted to a greater or lesser degree by unions and employers, and by nearly all the others who studied women and their work. Whereas investigations of male workers in industry most certainly did not cover men's treatment of their wives and children, or the condition of the homes they lived in, or the effect of their trade on their potential fatherhood, those concerning women *did* look at the interaction of work, home and family in much the same manner as earlier investigations, though the tone was less hysterical. This is true from the *Reports of the Lady Commissioners* in 1894 right through to the books of Hutchins and Black which were published just after the war began. Lady Bell, in her study of Middlesborough in 1907, summed up the idea behind this obsession with working-class women's whole lives:

> It is no doubt an obvious platitude to say this, but it cannot be too often repeated in these days when we are consciously, anxiously, unavailingly, trying to prevent the much discussed deterioration of the race. The pivot of the whole situation is the woman, the wife of the workman and the mother of his children.[37]

Hence the morals of the factory girls were always under analysis — loose morals were put down, by the Lady Commissioners, to bad language and mixed toilets, and others commented in a similar fashion on the adverse effects of swearing and mixed workshops. The Victorian dislike of places where the sexes worked together remained. One of the reasons put forward for not employing married women in factories was that their talk might corrupt young unmarried girls — a curious attitude, in view of the way the sanctity of motherhood was discussed elsewhere. But the main concern amongst those who analysed the effect of work on home life or morals was the behaviour of working-class wives, as it had always been in the nineteenth century. As I have said, working-class men and women themselves had varied views about the desirability of married women working, and these depended upon their own financial needs — they might be in competition with married women for work (as was claimed by indignant witnesses before the Royal Commission[38]), or alternatively feel secure enough to sympathise with women whose husbands did not earn enough and so had to work — and views also varied according to the availability of factory work in the area. Many of them appear to have disagreed with the idea of wives working in principle but accepted it in practice. Married women who worked objected strongly to the idea that their freedom to take jobs should be curtailed.[39]

There was little such ambiguity in the feelings of most of the middle-class investigators of women's work, however: as far as they were concerned, married women belonged at home, not at work, and their primary duty was to husbands and children. The exceptions to these writers were feminists like B.L. Hutchins and Clementina Black, but even they felt the need to justify women's work at least partly by saying that it did not adversely affect their roles as wives and mothers.

A few quotations will give some idea of the way this aspect of women's lives was dragged in at every opportunity. Clara Collet, writing for Charles Booth's survey of London, commented on the poor and irregular wages of homeworkers, then added: 'Wherever the home-workers are being supported by their husbands, *as they ought to be* [my emphasis], this irregularity is in itself a slight evil.'[40] Later, as a Lady Commissioner, she stated that: 'The employment in factories and workshops of married women whose husbands are well able to support them seemed to me to be one of the worst features in the industrial life of Birmingham.'[41] This statement is all the more disturbing, considering Clara Collet's own knowledge of the dreadful conditions women, single and married, put up with around the country in many trades, and also in view of her own appreciation of *why* women wanted to work for reasons besides money:

> After marriage they miss not only the cheerful society (for it is cheerful) of the factory, but also the steady work to which they have been accustomed, and for both reasons many of them persist in going to the factory. They are not, generally speaking, engaged in work which would otherwise be done by men, and therefore there seems remarkably little of the opposition to married women's labour invariably displayed by men when they consider their own labour is being displaced by women, *but the evils exist none the less* [my emphasis].[42]

What 'evils'? The evil of not staying at home where a wife belonged, even if there were no children. May Abraham, another Lady Commissioner, echoed such disapproval in her reports on Yorkshire and Lancashire, and reported triumphantly that Huddersfield was strongly against married women working.[43]

The reasons given for the objections are all too familiar to anyone who has read what the early Victorians had to say on the subject. It was still claimed that working wives neglected their husbands and children; the former were supposed to be driven to drink, or to be 'demoralised', and throw up their jobs to live on their wives' earnings — as the representatives of one firm claimed in evidence to the Royal Commission on Labour, in words all too similar to those of earlier critics of the factory system: 'in many cases within their knowledge the women were forced into the mill at the instance of idle and worthless husbands, who preferred to live on the earnings of their wives.'[44] Ramsay MacDonald, a decade later, expressed similar beliefs in *Women in the Printing Trades*,[45] and even the writers of the *General Report* on the 1901 census felt obliged to give a paragraph to this undesirable feature of women's work:

> Most of these women are employed away from their homes in cotton factories, and consequently are unable to give proper care to their children. The inevitable neglect from which these latter must suffer in their earliest years cannot be regarded as suitable preparation for their own premature employment as wage earners.[46]

It seems that working-class women were even to be blamed for the society which demanded that children work from an early age: certainly it did not occur to these authors that a woman's own income might *save* children from the necessity of early wage labour, any more than it occurred to many others who condemned mothers for 'deserting' their children that the extra money so earned might give the children extra comforts.

This point was taken up in 1915, when it was well established that women did work because the family needed the income for survival. Clementina Black reminded her readers that any other reasons beside dire necessity were still unacceptable.

> It is a general opinion and especially, perhaps, among persons of the middle class, that the working for money of married women is to be deplored. That such work is sometimes made necessary by poverty will be conceded, and wives who earn because they must are to be pitied: while wives who earn not for their own or their children's bread, but rather for the butter to it, are regarded as at least somewhat blameworthy.[47]

However, in succeeding chapters of Black's book it becomes obvious that she is defending not simply women's right to work as individuals (which she does), but also the standard of their work as wives and mothers. The contributors to her book describe the conditions under which married women work, and then add what good and efficient housekeepers they are. In other words, these supporters of working women's rights used the same yardstick as their opponents — they analysed the relative success of woman's work at home, and accepted that this must be women's rather than men's responsibility. B.L. Hutchins wrote:

> The tragedy of the domesticated woman who is driven abroad to earn has been amply demonstrated above. But all women are not of the same type. The mother who prefers to work may have quite as much mother love, and although clinging less to home, may very likely have a wider knowledge of life, a keener sense of citizenship, than the domesticated woman, and thus possibly make up to her children in one way what she lacks in another.[48]

This is a defensive statement, and it is designed to counter existing claims about working wives' failings rather than promote the idea of woman's right, as an individual, to work outside the home.

The Health and Welfare of Women Workers

Since 1900 'the health of the race' had become an increasingly important concern, particularly because of the high number of working-class recruits who appeared to be unfit for service during the Boer War. This intensified the concern which had long existed about the physical effects of work upon mothers and children. There were fears that in future Britain's young men would be poor fighters for England, and in spite of all the other causes of physical illness or weakness (poverty, overcrowding, malnutrition) it became a widely held belief that working-class mothers were at least partly to blame for this poor state of things.[49]

By the 1890s it had been accepted that the state had the right to interfere in industry for the benefit of the workers' health to an ever greater extent. But the tradition established by the first Factory Acts was maintained in the 1890s and 1900s: the law was primarily designed to protect not men, but the 'weaker' members of society, women and children. Women were still grouped with children whose vulnerability is obvious, because they too were supposed to be unorganised, weak and exploitable.

It is true that women were to be found in the least unionised trades, and that they tolerated bad conditions and low pay, but whether Factory Acts were the answer to such problems was another matter. The 1890s and 1900s saw a running disagreement between those who felt women workers should be treated as a special case, and others who felt that this approach handicapped their position in the labour market and society. The former included some who had a genuine desire to help women, but also those who would have been pleased to see women tightly confined to 'women's trades', and working wives withdrawn from the labour market altogether. Those who feared for the possible effects of further protective legislation included feminists who suspected the motives of many who pressed so hard for restrictive laws, and their attitude was epitomised by the books of Helen Blackburn, who wrote one with Jessie Boucherett, *The Condition of Women and the Factory Acts*,[50] and another with Nora Vynne, *Women Under the Factory Act*.[51] There was a degree of self-help philosophy in their objections. When they wrote, for example, 'The kindly legislator who wishes to protect women because they are helpless and ignorant only makes that helplessness greater by treating them as hopelessly helpless,'[52] the idea in mind was that those who were aided or protected by the state became incapable of standing on their own two feet, and their belief that women needed to take risks with their health in order to earn money may seem callous. Such writers maintained their objections throughout this period, although amongst many other feminist writers the idea that women needed special protection because they were liable to particular forms of exploitation became increasingly acceptable. In 1903, Vynne and Blackburn were writing:

> The greatest danger, though not the most immediate, lies in its tendency to treat the workers as if they had no duties, as if, like mere animals incapable of taking care of themselves they must be perpetually taken care of; or even as lower than animals, for those at least have instincts which keep them from what is dangerous to themselves.[53]

For the other side, B.L. Hutchins, a feminist herself, responded:

> The social conscience has travelled beyond the point at which exhausting soulless toil is regarded as a 'virtue', It recognises the danger of intolerable strain both to the women themselves and to their actual and possible offspring, and it sees in the frantic efforts of the

unorganised, unskilled woman to work for impossible hours, to undersell her competitors and lower both her and their standard of life, an 'offence' which, however pardonable in an individual, must in a member of society, by some means, be controlled or prevented for the general good.[54]

Hutchins' view was a logical and sympathetic one, but the feelings of the anti-protectionists are understandable, particularly in view of the nature of earlier Factory Acts: protective legislation did maintain the idea that women were not men's industrial equals, and in spite of the claim by many supporters of protection that such measures would in due course be extended to men, this never happened in full. Nor were the trade unionists who backed the Factory Acts necessarily reliable allies for women workers, since they were prepared to use them to displace women. Even Lady Dilke, a campaigner against home work, who fought for women's equal participation in trade unions, nevertheless wrote of her campaign in the 1890s:

> yet we do this, feeling, many of us, day by day more strongly, that our place, the place of the women of the land, is not here, but at the hearth . . . the homes of England are at stake; we are fighting for the manhood of her men, for the health of her women, for the future of her little children.[55]

One of her arguments against home work was that it destroyed the sanctity of the home; of the women chain-makers (who worked at forges in their own homes) of Cradley Heath she wrote: 'It is difficult indeed to recognise in the being who stands grimy and half-naked at the forge, her whose motherly perfection should make of the home a place of peace.'[56] Such comments show how firmly entrenched in the minds of *even* those who fought for political and industrial rights for women, notions of noble motherhood, physical vulnerability, and duty to husband and children were; all these aspects invariably arose when there were discussions about the health and welfare of women workers.

The dilemma of how far to 'protect' women in industry has not been solved today, and certainly was not a clear-cut issue by 1914. The 1900s saw arguments similar to those of earlier years about the need to guard women or allow them to organise and protect themselves — but in addition the 'health of the race' had become a topic of paramount importance, and the words became a catch-phrase for the widespread concern over the apparent decline in the health of the working classes, which had been stimulated by the fact that a high proportion of working-class volunteers for the Boer War proved to be unfit for service. Whether or not the nation's health was really significantly worse in the 1900s than in the 1800s is not a matter for debate here: the fact is that people believed it was, and so there emerged ideas for new schemes for reducing the rate of mortality and morbidity amongst children, including the provision of baby clinics and school meals. Fears also encouraged the idea that working-class mothers should have access to midwives and maternity hospitals, and should possibly have maternity grants; also, unfortunately, they fuelled the notion that women should not do factory work, as working wives were often held to be to blame for weak children — by working through pregnancy and by neglecting babies after birth. It was widely believed that infant mortality was highest amongst mothers who worked outside the home, and although women's defenders pointed out the adverse effects of general poverty, poor living conditions and lack of child-care facilities, many people, from all classes, still chose to maintain that the answer lay in banning married women's work — 'for the sake of the nation'.

There is little doubt about the fact that working-class women before the war really were plagued by ill health, and that this made their lives more difficult, as well as affecting the health of their children. But the aspect seldom explored by those who commented upon this state of affairs was the effect of frequent pregnancies upon women. To read *Maternity*,[57] a book of letters gathered together by the Women's Co-operative Guild, is to read about a constant struggle against exhaustion and sickness. The women themselves knew that they were worn out by a succession of births and miscarriages, and weakened not only by poor diet, but by the heavy domestic labour done around the home, which most of them found far more exhausting than factory work. They said, both directly and indirectly, that both men and women needed a greater degree of knowledge about sex, and that birth control was essential to women's health and happiness. They also expressed a weary resentment of the fact that husbands insisted on maintaining a sexual relationship, even though they knew that further pregnancies would exhaust their wives, and that they could not afford to have more children; they had no doubts about the harmful effect of getting up and caring for the house and family immediately after childbirth. In other words, precisely those tasks which were seen by many as being women's most noble duties — childbearing, child-rearing and housework — were those which had an adverse effect upon their health, yet this fact was barely discussed in public, and birth control was still a taboo subject. It was easier to blame industrial work for women's health problems than look into the subject in more depth. Similarly, crèches and nursery schools were still not popular, as they appeared to further the break-up of the family, and would cost the state more money.

Conclusion

It may be seen by now that although to a certain extent arguments to do with women's industrial role, women's home role and women's physical health can be dealt with separately, ultimately they are all interconnected, and all revolve around the same idea of women's place in society, as developed by the circumstances of the Industrial Revolution. Women were born to be wives and mothers, and working-class girls who earned their own living were supposed to accept that once they were married their place was at home where their duty was to tend to husbands and bear healthy children.

Their position in the labour force was dominated by the effect of these ideas — many of them were indeed 'meantime' workers who expected to leave on marriage: others were obliged to leave whether they wanted to or not. Consequently they could not enter into long apprenticeships or develop skills over a period of years, and logically enough their interest in their work was seldom great. Any ambitions in industry were pointless, since there were no opportunities for women who did not wish to marry and leave work. These facts of life were accepted by employers, unions and other observers. While some men from all these groups regretted women's low wages and poor opportunities, and suggested better training facilities and fairer wages, they nevertheless accepted that in due course women would become dependent wives, and believed that no 'normal' woman would be interested in a career involving skilled work: unions spent more time keeping women out of men's work than considering how their position might be improved.

Similarly, nearly all observers, government, philanthropic or otherwise, accepted that no analysis of women's position in the labour market was complete without a look at how they kept their homes, whether their husbands were fed on time, and whether their children were neglected, and throughout this period the criteria for physical health remained whether working women were fit to bear healthy children. The attitude on nearly all sides was patronising, and invariably sympathy was paternal (as with Cadbury), while criticism was tinged with contempt: how, people asked, can we help these incapable women? How can we teach them to organise at work, keep their homes tidy, look after their babies better? Unfortunately, many working-class men, particularly those who were skilled and had jobs to 'protect', could no better understand the pressures and restrictions experienced by working women than could middle-class employers or government officials, and few middle-class women tried to really understand the feelings of working-class women about work or motherhood. Although they remained perhaps more reliable allies than many male trade unionists, they too often had ideas about feminine respectability and the nobility of motherhood. At no time could working-class women depend upon any other pressure groups in society to stand up for their right to work in whatever trade they chose.

In 1910, Anna Martin, one of those feminists who did commit herself to the idea that working-class women must have more independence, wrote with some bitterness:

In the eyes of most people the workman's wife is a creature of limited intelligence and capacity, who neither has, nor ought to have, any desires outside her own four walls. She is not so much an individual, with interests and opinions and will of her own, as a humble appanage of husband and children.[58]

The same words held true in 1914, when England went to war. Those who were discriminated against by virtue of both sex and class were at the bottom of society's ladder.

Notes

1. Wanda Neff, *Victorian Working Women* (Allen & Unwin, 1929); Ivy Pinchbeck, *Women Workers and the Industrial Revolution* (Routledge, 1930); Margaret Hewett, *Wives and Mothers in Victorian Industry* (Rockcliff, 1958); B.L. Hutchins, *Women in Modern Industry* (Bell & Sons, 1915); Barbara Drake, *Women in Trade Unions* (Labour Research Department, 1921).
2. See in particular Pinchbeck, *Women Workers*.
3. The different rates of industrialisation affected workers in different ways. As well as Pinchbeck, *Women Workers*, see M. Thomis, *The Luddites* (David & Charles, 1970), for an interesting discussion of workers' responses to the threat of machinery owned by large manufacturers.
4. Although parents sometimes managed to get them accepted at an earlier age; the schools virtually acted as childminders in such cases.
5. J.A. & Olive Banks, *Feminism and Family Planning* (Liverpool University Press, 1969), p. 61.
6. Quoted in Banks, *Feminism and Family Planning*. Frances Power Cobbe

was a feminist, but as the Banks point out, this did not mean that she rejected conventional ideas of married women's duties. The mid-nineteenth-century feminist movement was largely concerned with widening opportunities for single women.

7. Neff, *Victorian Working Women*, pp. 36-7.

8. Pinchbeck, *Women Workers*, p. 262.

9. Ibid., p. 263.

10. Ibid., p. 267; 7 June 1842.

11. Yet this moral 'superiority' was born of innocence and simplicity. At the same time, the wife was subject to the husband, who was still classed as the head of the family.

12. Hewett, *Wives and Mothers*, p. 49; 1847.

13. Ibid., p. 50.

14. Ibid., Ch. 4.

15. Ibid., Ch. 3 and p. 23.

16. Charles Booth, *Survey of London Life and Labour* (Macmillan, 1890s); Seebohm Rowntree, *Poverty: A Study of Town Life* (Macmillan & Co., 1901).

17. Outwork was often associated with the partial mechanisation of a trade, when handworkers worked in competition with those on machines in workshops, but not always. In London during the 1880s to the First World War, for example, most dextrous work, like making boxes, trimming hats, etc., could not have been done by machine. Wives often took in the work because of the irregularity of their husbands' earnings, in turn the result of the casual labour market at this time.

18. Royal Commission on Labour, *Reports by Lady Commissioners on Conditions of Women's Work*, including those in London, Luton and Bristol, Birmingham, Liverpool, Yorkshire, Lancashire and Cheshire, the Provinces and Scotland (1894).

19. E. Cadbury, M.C. Matheson & G. Shann, *Women's Work and Wages* (T. Fisher Unwin, 1909).

20. Select Committee on Home Work, *Reports*, 1907-8.

21. Hutchins, *Women in Modern Industry*; Clementina Black, *Married Women's Work* (Bell & Sons, 1915).

22. Census, 1901. See also the excellent discussion of married women's work in *History Workshop* (Autumn 1979), by Sally Alexander, Anna Davin and Eve Hostettler, 'Labouring Women'.

23. Census, 1911, vol. X, *Occupations and Industries* (published 1914).

24. See for example C. Collet in Booth, *Life and Labour*; also C.V. Butler, *Domestic Service* (Bell & Sons, 1916).

25. House of Lords, Select Committee on Sweating, *Fifth Report*, 1890.

26. Royal Commission on Labour, *Reports of the Lady Commissioners*, p. 272.

27. So did the idea that disease might be carried into the houses of the poor who made goods for the rich!

28. Royal Commission on Labour. The 'pocket money worker' was much discussed. She was resented by men, who saw her as a symbol of cheap female labour, and by women who depended upon their earnings. It is not possible to even guess how many 'pocket money workers' there were, or indeed if they really existed, since many women who were ostensibly 'dependants' made very important contributions to the family income, even when earning very low wages. See also Clara Collet's descriptions in Booth's survey, and sections on Scotland (Tailoring Trade and Umbrella Covering) and Yorkshire Textile trades in the Royal Commission on Labour, *Reports of Lady Commissioners*.

29. Royal Commission on Labour, Clara Collet on Birmingham, Walsall, Dudley and the Staffordshire Potteries.

30. *Oral History*, vol. 5, no. 2 (Autumn 1977), Jill Liddington, 'Working

Women in the North West', II.

31. Women were to be increasingly employed on ringspinning, a lighter and less skilled process, which did not require workers to set their own tools. For full discussion of the difference between the two, see J. Jewkes & E.M. Gray, *Wages and Labour in the Lancashire Cotton Spinning Industry* (Manchester University Press, 1934).

32. J.B. Jefferys, *The Story of the Engineers* (Lawrence & Wishart, 1945).

33. Royal Commission on Labour, Miss Orme, on Conditions of Work in Scotland.

34. Many employers did use women, of course, but for 'women's trades', and on the assumption that they would do unskilled or semi-skilled work, would be cheap, etc. Most employers of 'skilled' labour would not have dreamed of trying to use women, no matter how little they could be paid: they did not believe that women were capable of doing the work, or that they would stay for long. Normally, it is only when processes are undergoing change for technological reasons that women are a danger to *skilled* men; the majority of skilled workmen before the war were simply not threatened by an influx of female labour. Even those who employed women often disapproved of married women working. Thus one Huddersfield employer said, 'a great deal of unhappiness and drunkenness in working families arose from the wives being in the mills and from the consequent dirtiness and untidiness of their homes" (Royal Commission on Labour, May Abraham on the Conditions of Work in the Textile Industries of Yorkshire, p. 102). Miss Orme, in her report on Scotland, wrote that 'This firm, and the majority of others consulted, stated that they did as much as possible to discourage the employment of married women.' Such words sound very similar to those spoken earlier in the century, though it is still worth noting that those who employed women at the lowest rates had no scruples about employing wives.

35. E. Cadbury & G. Shann, *Sweating* (Headley Bros., 1907), p. 77.

36. Cadbury, Matheson & Shann, *Women's Work and Wages*, p. 137.

37. Lady Bell, *At the Works* (Arnold, 1907), p. 171.

38. Many of the witnesses were unmarried women – see note 28.

39. Royal Commission on Labour, Yorkshire Textiles. See also Black, *Married Women's Work*, p. 195.

40. Booth, *Life and Labour*, vol. IV, p. 304.

41. Royal Commission on Labour, Conditions of Work in Birmingham, p. 53.

42. Ibid.

43. See note 34.

44. Royal Commission on Labour, Report on Scotland, p. 306.

45. Royal Commission on Labour, section on Tailoring; also, Ramsay Macdonald, *Women in the Printing Trades* (King & Sons, 1904).

46. 1901 Census, *General Report* (published 1904), p. 81.

47. Black, *Married Women's Work*, p. 1.

48. Ibid., chapter by Hutchins, p. 143.

49. See Anna Davin, 'Imperialism and Motherhood', *History Workshop* (Spring 1978).

50. J. Boucherett & H. Blackburn, *The Condition of Women and the Factory Acts* (Elliot Stock, 1896).

51. N. Vynne & H. Blackburn, *Women under the Factory Act* (Williams & Norgate, 1903).

52. Boucherett & Blackburn, *The Condition of Women*, p. 75

53. Vynne & Blackburn, *Women under the Factory Act*, p. 114

54. B.L. Hutchins & A. Harrison, *A History of Factory Legislation* (King, 1925), p. 185.

55. Lady Dilke, *Trade Unions for Women* (1891, pamphlet), p. 12.

56. Ibid.
57. Margaret Llewellyn Davies (ed.), *Maternity* (reprinted Virago, 1979).
58. Anna Martin, 'The Married Working Woman', in *Nineteenth Century & After* (1910).

2 THE NEED FOR WOMEN'S LABOUR IN THE FIRST WORLD WAR

An Outline of the Expansion of Women's Labour

The immediate effect of the outbreak of war was a drastic increase in unemployment, and many of the industries worst hit were those which, in peacetime, employed large numbers of women. As an economy measure wealthy households dismissed servants, and cut their orders to 'luxury' trades like jewellery, millinery or dressmaking; women employed as fish-gutters found themselves out of work as the fishing fleets withdrew from areas patrolled by German ships; many industries, including the cotton trade, contracted as employers and clients hesitated, awaiting developments in the war and in the economy. One contemporary author, I.O. Andrews, estimated that 44.4 per cent of all women workers were unemployed for a brief time in September 1914,[1] and the Central Committee on Women's Employment (a labour body) issued figures on unemployment and short-time working which revealed the full extent of the problem that autumn. In dressmaking, only 34 per cent of women workers in large firms were working full-time, and 31 per cent of women in small firms; in boots and shoes a mere 13 per cent of women workers were in full-time work, and the equivalent percentages for other trades were: printing and books, 26 per cent; jam and sweets, 39 per cent; furnishing and upholstery, 18½ per cent; furs and skins, 33 per cent.[2]

The position of women was considered to be serious, and at this time industry, government and unions had no idea that within weeks there would be a labour shortage. Efforts were put into organising some form of relief work for the female unemployed: 'Queen Mary's Work Fund' was set up, followed by 'Queen Mary's Workrooms', which were to be administered by the Central Committee for Women's Employment, itself set up on 20 August by such stalwarts of the labour movement as Mary Macarthur, Susan Lawrence, Margaret Bondfield and Marion Phillips, to mitigate the worst effects of unemployment by providing needlework for women who had been laid off. Sylvia Pankhurst pointed out that the wages paid at the sewing workrooms were only 10s a week, which was virtually a sweated rate, but the aim was to provide as many women as possible with some form of subsistence without the taint of charity,[3] while the Committee continued to press for the early placing of government clothing and supplies contracts with industry.

Many of the traditional 'women's trades' — cotton, linen, silk, lace, tailoring, dressmaking, millinery, hat-making, pottery and fish-gutting — did not speedily recover,[4] but the irony was that even by November 1914 there was a labour shortage in some sections of industry. Men too had been unemployed in the chaotic months of August and September, including skilled engineers, and many of them enlisted. As the engineering and chemical industries began to expand munitions production, it soon emerged that there was a shortage of skilled labour. The problem became increasingly evident in 1915.[5]

During the winter and spring of 1914-15 government contracts did give employment to many women, as industries which traditionally employed them expanded to supply the troops with equipment: the leather, hosiery, boot, kitbag, medical dressing and tailoring industries all took on more women,[6] but such extra labour was for jobs which were usually regarded as women's in peacetime. Very few women were, at this time, employed on work normally done by men in any industry, and the engineering industry, although short of labour, was loath to employ women — for reasons which will be discussed later. By 1915, however, women were being employed in non-industrial jobs which were new to them: they replaced men in offices and in the transport system, where custom rather than skill had led to the notion that these were men's trades. I.O. Andrews pointed out the effect of this:

> In these lines from the first women took men's places, and, as the public came into daily contact with women clerks in banks and business offices, postal employés, employés in shops and on delivery vans, tram conductors and ticket collectors, there probably arose an exaggerated idea of the extent to which women did 'men's work' during the first year of the war.[7]

As men enlisted, women were indeed employed as van drivers, window-cleaners, shop assistants, etc., but they were often informally taking the places of husbands, fathers or brothers: major industries remained wary about using them, unions remained worried about the effect of female labour on wages and security, and the women themselves were given little opportunity for training.

'Substitution', the extensive use of women in place of men, in industry really began in the summer of 1915 on a limited scale. (Full discussion on the nature of substitution, which jobs women worked on, and how successful they were will be found in Chapter 3.) Women were being employed in the munitions industry in quite large numbers by August 1915, but on jobs like shell-filling (which they had done before the war) or on processes formerly deemed just above their capabilities. They were confined to simple repetition work for the most part.[8] But once the terms of substitution became established, and unions and employers came to grudging agreement about the use of women in many industries, the expansion of women's labour began in earnest. In March 1915 there was still a surplus of unemployed women[9] and the government was sufficiently concerned to launch a national scheme for the registration of women who wanted paid work; the rush of women into engineering and explosives began in the autumn of 1915[10] and by 1916 there was actually a shortage of female labour in the textile and clothing trades, as women moved into more lucrative munitions work.[11] This rapid expansion in munitions continued in 1916 and 1917, and women also increasingly replaced men in private, non-munitions industries, like grain milling, sugar refining, brewing, building, surface mining and ship-yards. London dressmakers found it so hard to get female apprentices by 1917, because of the competition offered by other industries, that they contacted the LCC and labour exchanges with a view to planning shorter, more regular hours for their workers — the first time such trades had ever been driven to consider improvements. In 1917, the *Labour Gazette* estimated that 1 in 3 working women was 'replacing' a male worker in industry.[12]

The background to this expansion was the introduction of conscription for men in January 1916. At first there were many exemptions — older and married men were not called up, nor were skilled workers in munitions industries. But as casualties increased abroad, and women's industrial capabilities became more evident to the government at home, the blanket exemption of skilled men from conscription by union was withdrawn and the Manpower Bill was passed in February 1918, cancelling all previous exemptions; from that time all munitions workers (male) under 25 were liable for conscription.[13] By 1917 women were spread throughout industry, on various processes, and the last year of the war saw a levelling off in the demand for them, and the development of their use on some skilled processes not previously open to them.

The real increase in numbers of women employed came in the years 1915 to 1917, and the most striking instances were in munitions. Wool-wich Arsenal, for example, employed 125 women in 1914, and 25,000 in 1917.[14] In July 1914, 3,276,000 women were classed as employed (not including small dressmaking establishments, domestic service, the self-employed, and those employed by husbands), and in April 1917 the figure had increased to 4,507,000. By April 1918, only another 300,000 women were employed, and the total stood at 4,808,000.[15] A.W. Kirkaldy, in his painstaking survey of women's war work, *Industry and Finance*, gave the following reasons for the falling off in the rate of the expansion of women's labour:

(1) the exhaustion of supplies of suitable women;
(2) the return to industry of discharged soldiers;
(3) the high wages enforced by the Ministry of Munitions;
(4) saturation of the industry available to women;
(5) the cessation of certain work employing women.[16]

There was in fact a slackening in demand for certain munitions by 1917-18, and a small number of factories were already closing or changing back to pre-war production. In some industries and areas there was still a demand for more women workers, but in spite of suggestions in 1918 that there should be a 'Womanpower' Bill to conscript women for industry, such measures were never necessary.[17] By early 1918 women war workers were already being dismissed and the peak of their employment was over.

A much debated point throughout the war, and one of some interest now, is 'where the women came from'. Who were the new recruits to industry in general and the munitions industry in particular? Although statistics show that the numbers of women in industry, transport and the professions increased drastically, they do not show the extent of transference between trades. The figures quoted by Kirkaldy for 1914 (3,276,000 women at work) do not include domestic service or small dressmaking establishments, which accounted for many thousands more women. If these unnoted workers then moved into the official trades they were *not* new workers who had previously been unemployed. In fact, it does seem that a large number of women who went into the munitions industry were from other trades or were married women returning to work. I.O. Andrews, in her study of the *Economic Effects of the World War upon Women and Children in Great Britain*, decided that the increase of women in munitions was accounted for by the transference of women from slack to busy trades, the return of married women, the movement of workers from low-paid industries, the entrance of some older women or girls straight from school, and a very few middle- or upper-class women, for, as she said drily, 'Inspite of impressions to the contrary, the proportion of previously unoccupied upper and middle-class women entering "war work" was by no means large.'[18] There was a romantic idea, commonly held, that the classes came together through women's work, or, as Hammond wrote: 'To the popular imagination there have been pictured the figures of duchesses and other ladies of fine breeding running the lathes in munition factories or pouring the deadly TNT into endless rows of shells.'[19] The idea was fuelled by the press, and by such patriotic writers as L.K. Yates, whose book, *A Woman's Part*, is full of breathless descriptions of the wonders of women's work, and who wrote, on the subject of women's background:

> They have come from the office and the shop, from domestic service and the dressmakers's room, from the High Schools and the Colleges, and from the quietude of the stately homes of the leisured rich . . . Even in the early days of the advent of women in the munitions shops, I have seen working together, side by side, the daughter of an earl, a shop keeper's widow, a graduate from Girton, a domestic servant, and a young woman from a lonely farm in Rhodesia, whose husband had joined the colours. Social status, so stiff a barrier in this country in pre-war days, was forgotten in the factory, as in the trenches, and they were all working together as the members of a united family.[20]

Such a picture was far from accurate, both in terms of the social background of the workers in most factories, and the relations between the women when there were middle- or upper-class women present. Hammond estimated that over 200,000 women who went into industry during the war came from domestic service, and that many others had been outworkers, self-employed, or wives who had left work.[21] The *Labour Gazette* concluded from a survey of 444,000 insured women workers that 70 per cent had changed their trade during the war, and that 23 per cent moved from one kind of factory work to another, 22 per cent were previously unemployed (this would have included school-leavers and married women who had retired from work), 16 per cent came from domestic service, and 7 per cent from other non-industrial work.[22] Kirkaldy also noted how many came from domestic service, or the clothing trades, as did the Factory Inspector's report for 1914, and the writers of the draft interim report of the British Association for the Advancement of Science on *Outlets for Labour After the War*,[23] although the latter also revealed that when middle-class women *did* enter industry for patriotic reasons they invariably chose munitions rather than any other trade. Barbara Drake drew attention to another feature: as older women left the standard women's trades like cotton or dressmaking for 'men's work', their places were invariably taken by young girls,[24] which was an ominous sign for women hoping to return to their old jobs after the war. She too believed that about a quarter of the women in munitions came from domestic service. Reports in newspapers often mentioned ex-servants, and in this case they do not seem to have exaggerated the truth, as such women flooded into all kinds of jobs as well as munitions. *Common Cause*, the suffragist newspaper, described the work of several 'street housemaids',[25] one of whom was a former servant who had married, taken in washing, and then moved to this job of road-sweeping – she liked the freedom, the fresh air, and the fact that there was no one to nag her. The *Yorkshire Observer* looked at the social background of those on a course for munitions workers at Bradford technical college, and discovered women from domestic service, dressmaking, other factories, the laundry trade, nursing, and those who were wives of engineers.[26] The *Daily Chronicle*, even in 1915, reported that Nottingham lace-makers were turning to munitions work,[27] and there were appeals at various times in the press for women not to leave the textile mills for the munitions shops.[28] Before the war cotton had been one of the most popular trades for women, and the wages had been comparatively good, but it could not compete with the engineering and explosives industries, which appeared to offer new opportunities and more money. Domestic service, already an unpopular trade, became the last job anyone wanted during the war.[29]

Most women who went into munitions, or other 'men's jobs', therefore, had been workers before. The middle-class women who took up war work were few, and were not necessarily popular with their companions. Monica Cosens, herself a volunteer for the war period only, commented, 'There is no denying immediately a new volunteer comes into a street [the gangway between the machines] there is defiance in the air. She is not gently treated.'[30] There could be a vast gulf between the classes, as will be seen in later chapters of this book.

One group did come into its own during the war: married women. Previously told that they should not work, and that their role was in the home, they were now invited back to industry, and made up a large proportion of workers in many areas, particularly since some firms had a definite preference for soldiers' wives as workers.[31] Married women made up 40 per cent of all working women throughout the country: in Leeds 44 per cent of women in the four main engineering firms were married, although in 1911 only 15 per cent of women workers in the area had been married.[32]

The main effect of the war was, therefore, to bring about the transference of women between the trades, and the return of those previously excluded; there were not really hundreds of thousands of completely new workers in industry as might be assumed at first from the statistics. More detailed information on the work done and the success of working-class women in their new jobs will be found in the next chapter.

The Role of the State

It is all too easy with an outline description of women's expanding employment prospects to give the impression that such expansion was inevitable, consistent within each industry, and smooth-running. In fact, the situation was more complex, and the complexities must be recognised before one can go on to analyse the role of the women themselves and the attitudes of those who employed them, worked with them, or observed them. The question of female labour lay at the heart of the government's efforts to organise war production, and the way the government attempted to control industry had a major effect on women's prospects and popularity.

This was the first time England had fought a war so greedy for men and resources, and to a large extent the machinery for coping with it was experimental — Britain's government during the Second World War certainly learned from the experience of 1914 to 1920, both in terms of organising conscription and the munitions industry (the 'production' of men and weapons) and of coping with the influx of female labour. The structure of control during the First World War was, ironically, at the same time autocratic and inadequate: both the heavy-handedness of the government and the gaps in legislation had a serious effect on the position of women workers. A look at the government's role in the organisation of the munitions industry reveals the dichotomy, and shows why the labour movement felt oppressed by an alliance of state and employers.

The government did take control of the supplies of raw materials and food, but I am largely concerned here with the way it attempted to organise the munitions industry alone, in terms of labour supply and wage regulation. Although discussion of the nature of female substitution in munitions and other trades (which, unlike munitions, made their own agreements between employers and trade unions regarding the use of women, and were not covered by any government orders on wages) is held over until the next chapter, it is important to bear in mind the original strict definition of the term 'dilution of skilled labour', as set out by the Ministry of Munitions and as recognised by the engineering industry. Circular 129, issued by the Ministry in September 1915, stated that:

(1) The employment of skilled men should be confined to work which could not be efficiently performed by less skilled labour or by women.
(2) Women should be employed on all classes of work for which they are suitable.
(3) Semi-skilled and unskilled men should be employed on any work which does not necessitate the employment of skilled men and for which women are unsuitable.[33]

In November 1914 the ASE (the main craft union of the engineers) and the Employers' Federation signed the Crayford Agreement, after trouble about the introduction of women on to some processes at Vickers, Crayford. The fact that Vickers wished to recruit female labour was seen as an early intimation of the labour shortage to come, and immediate union complaints about the threat which female labour posed alerted the government to the idea that munitions production probably depended upon some kind of official policy on wartime substitution and post-war job security. It duly set up the Committee on Production in Engineering and Shipbuilding in February 1915, to act as Court of Arbitration on industrial disputes and to look into the use of less skilled labour. Employers were demanding the abandonment of the usual union regulations regarding the use of female and non-union labour, with guarantees that established conditions would return when peace came. The engineering union suggested the use of colonial labour (white), re-allocation of men around the country, and the re-call of skilled men who had enlisted in the army. The Committee on Production came firmly down on the side of the employers, suggesting the abolition of output restrictions (standard practice amongst engineers, designed to guard against any reduction in piece rates if they produced 'too much'), the use of female labour, and a ban on labour stoppages. It also suggested that appropriate piece rates be fixed, and that the changes should be for the war period only.[34]

On 4 March 1915, the Engineering Employers' Federation and the engineering unions duly signed the *Shells and Fuses Agreement*. Theoretically it was a compromise, designed to prevent the flooding of industry with female substitutes, and to stop the unions holding out against any change in traditional practice. In fact, the unions' retreat from their total opposition to female labour left the way open for further erosion of demarcation and skill in the years to come. The points accepted in the *Shells and Fuses Agreement* were as follows:

(1)   men engaged in the making of tools and gauges should be skilled men, as should those who set up machines;

(2)   such men could be drawn from other branches of the engineering trade, as long as they had the necessary qualifications, and should be paid the standard 'rate for the district' on that job (wages before the war were arranged on a local basis by union branches and firms, not nationally, and could vary from area to area);

(3)   lists of such men should be given to the local unions;

(4)   transferred workers should be the first to be discharged;

(5)   there should be no displacement of skilled men by less skilled, unless alternative skilled work could be found;

(6)   the operations done by skilled men which *could* be done by semi-skilled or female labour should be performed by them during the war: rates would be the usual district rate for the job;

(7)   the removal of restrictions should not harm workpeople, or unions;

(8)   after the war, pre-war conditions should return;

(9)   the proposals offered should not lead to any permanent substitution by semi-skilled or female labour;

(10)   employers should not take advantage of any wartime agreements afterwards;

(11)   employers should agree to distribute government work throughout the country (thus avoiding the situation where some firms demanded overtime while other factories were on short time);

(12)   overtime should be reduced wherever possible;

(13)   semi-skilled or female labour should be the first discharged.[35]

Spring-summer 1915 was the key time for the negotiations between unions and employers and for the emergence of government policy on munitions production and the control of labour. On 9 March Parliament passed a Bill allowing the government to take control of munitions factories,[36] and on 19 March the *Shells and Fuses Agreement* was followed up by a government/union contract, the *Treasury Agreement*. This was designed to deal particularly with the substitution of semi-skilled for skilled workers in engineering, and confirmed that skilled men were to work on skilled processes alone, instead of doing a variety of jobs which *included* skilled work, as before. The unions also agreed that there would be no strikes (arbitration would take place instead), and that processes would be accelerated. In return they were promised that there would be no decrease in skilled men's wage rates, and that women replacing them would receive the fully skilled tradesman's rate.

Problems became evident almost immediately. The government was overseeing the formal relationship between employers and unions, yet the guarantees given to the workmen were inadequate. This had repercussions for women as well. There was never any full analysis of what was meant by the terms 'skilled', 'semi-skilled' and 'unskilled' work. As processes were altered for war production and jobs were subdivided, employers could claim that women who were only doing *part* of a skilled man's job were not entitled to full rates. As Barbara Drake wrote: 'Not one in a thousand of the scores of women introduced into shell and fuse factories proved a claim to take the *whole* place of a fully skilled tradesman.'[37] Thus there was no guarantee that women would not be employed at far cheaper rates on *parts* of skilled work. Nor, at this stage, did the government make any promises at all about the rates for semi-skilled or unskilled work done by women, and within a few days of the *Treasury Agreement* the Employers' Federation issued a note to its members stating that women should be paid the district rate for youths, not adult men, on semi- or unskilled work they were introduced to.[38]

This system of the state's partial control of the munitions industry, which gave power over unions, men and women, without offering full guarantees on wages and prospects, continued to develop throughout 1915. The Ministry of Munitions was set up in June, replacing the earlier ineffective local armament committees, and was designed to organise all aspects of national munitions production. In the same month the first Munitions Act was passed. This embodied the terms of the *Treasury Agreement*, and confirmed the existence of 'controlled establishments' (munitions factories temporarily under government control), set limits on the profits armaments firms could make, limited wage rises, and shelved the engineering unions' standard workshop practices — including union limitation of production and the ban on female labour. It also introduced the Leaving Certificate, one of the most unpopular measures ever tried by the government. Men or women working in munitions could not leave their jobs unless they obtained a Leaving Certificate from their employer; without one, they could not get work with any other employers (even in munitions) for the next six weeks. This ended the 'freedom of the individual' to seek alternative employment if he or she felt underpaid or exploited.[39] Factories in the same area might have widely differing wages and conditions, yet workers could not take up better positions without the permission of their employer in the form of a Leaving Certificate, which was, of course, usually denied.

There remained no guarantees on wages, except on jobs where women were completely replacing fully skilled tradesmen, when the same piece rates were payable (although not the same time rates). The Central Munitions Labour Supply Committee was set up in September 1915 to discuss wages and conditions, and plan a Dilution Scheme. It drew up 5 'L' Circulars on wages and other aspects of substitution in engineering. Women on skilled work 'customarily done by men' were entitled to equal time and piece rates; women replacing other men were supposed to have equal piece rates, and a guaranteed minimum on time rates of £1 a week; women on jobs not previously done by men were to be paid according to the piece rates or premium bonus rates of equivalent jobs in the area. Unfortunately, L2 and L3, the circulars dealing with women's work in men's trades, were not made mandatory at this time, and still there was no investigation into what constituted skilled work. Even when the Munitions Act was amended in November 1915, L2 and L3 were only put into practice in controlled establishments, not in private munitions factories. In addition, as there was no guaranteed *time rate* except for women who were proved to be doing the work of fully skilled tradesmen, the majority of women workers found that they were promptly put on time rate, at whatever their employers chose to pay, in order to avoid equal piece rates. Furthermore, the £1 minimum set for women on unskilled or semi-skilled men's work tended to become the standard, rather than the minimum, wage on time rate.[40]

In March 1916, the government set up Special Arbitration Tribunals to deal with wage disputes concerning women and unskilled men — but they could only *recommend* rates for women, not enforce them. But at last, this same year, Order 49 secured equal time and piece rates for women doing *part* of work customarily done by fully skilled men, and Order 447 consolidated awards made by the Special Arbitration Tribunals for women on work *not* recognised as men's work before the war — but even so these did not apply in every munitions factory. A new Substitution Scheme was introduced in September 1916 to increase further the use of female labour, even on skilled work, which was accepted by the unions, but when in 1917 it was proposed to extend Dilution to private factories (where there were no safeguards on wages and conditions) the labour movement rebelled. The May Strikes followed, the idea was abandoned, and, for good measure, the Leaving Certificate, which had for so long been encouraging discontent, was abolished.

The above, very brief, description of government schemes for organising labour reveals but little of the nature of the relationships between employers, unions and women workers, which will be amplified in Chapter 3. It does, however, show the way in which the government attempted to interfere in industry to an unprecedented extent. The same years which saw the introduction of the Leaving Certificate, and the almost compulsory abandonment of standard union practices in munitions, also saw the use of military conscription and press censorship, both of which were closely linked with what went on in industry. Conscription, introduced in 1916, was after all designed to set up a system which sorted the sheep from the goats: the less skilled, replaceable men were to be taken to fight, while skilled engineers were entitled, until 1918, to exemption, a fact which led to much resentment amongst men in other trades. Not only did this force men to go to war, it divided the unions, and it offered employers a stick to hold over skilled men who protested about wages — a man unemployed was immediately liable to be conscripted. Press censorship, in the meantime, meant that the nation knew neither what was happening in the trenches, nor what was going on in the shipyards or engineering shops: strikes could not be honestly reported, and the government even suppressed the newspapers of the Clyde shop stewards when they became too critical of government policy.[41]

The fact that, in the midst of this fairly autocratic regime, there were gaps in the government's control of wages and conditions of labour is obviously not merely accidental. The government was more concerned about keeping armament firms profitable, and munitions production steady, than with offering permanent guarantees to male workers or ensuring that women (who were vote-less) had equal pay. When factories were threatened with closure the government paid attention to workers' grievances, as during the May Strikes in 1917, but generally the labour movement remained fragmented, and failed to oppose substitution or dilution schemes on a consistent basis. It was divided in its attitude to women, to craft status, to military exemptions and, often, to the war itself, and its stand against government policy was rarely united. The state, meanwhile, had become an employer, and was working with other employers to keep up production: the links between the Ministry of Munitions and private businessmen were strong.

However, it would be untrue to suggest that the government's failure to secure good wages and job security was entirely deliberate. Some efforts *were* made to give skilled workmen in engineering (though not in other trades) safeguards, and promises were made about the return of pre-war conditions. Furthermore, the gaps which existed in state control did not simply adversely affect wages: they extended to other aspects of industry in which the government and employers could well have done with further, efficient organisation. The recruitment of women for munitions or any other trade was never properly organised: labour exchanges were not fully utilised, women were sent to areas where there was no accommodation available, skilled women were sent to unskilled jobs, etc. Nor was there any attempt to standardise training schemes: some firms trained their own workers from the beginning, others took women who had been on government courses at technical colleges and training factories, or to classes set up by private bodies. Recruitment too remained a haphazard matter, as the government relied to a large extent on the press to arouse women's enthusiasm for war work and send them looking for jobs.[42] The disorganised nature of the labour market lasted from the first weeks of the war, when skilled men were allowed to enlist in the army (which would not release them again), right through to 1918-19, when, in spite of the existence of the Ministry of Reconstruction and schemes for the payment of dole, the demobilisation of men and women was chaotic.

Such omissions in state control were partly due to the problems involved in setting up the machinery for war production, machinery which did not exist in 1914 and had to be developed from scratch. There was also the fact that many Ministers and politicians remained extremely reluctant to interfere in industry at all, and were loath to set up any more controls than were absolutely necessary. As E.M.H. Lloyd wrote, a few years after the war:

The idea that industry would have to be deliberately organised for war production encountered subconscious resistance in a government committed to the doctrines of free trade and individualism. It is not surprising that the necessity for state intervention was only gradually admitted by Ministers who had spent the greater part of their political careers in exploding the fallacies of protectionism on one hand and socialism on the other.[43]

The early assumption was that private firms could cope with supplies for war, making their own agreements with workers about overtime and any extra labour required. When it became evident that the government *would* have to play a part, there were two conflicting ideals in the minds of Ministers: first, that 'every private interest must be subordinated to the successful prosecution of the war,' and, secondly, 'there must be as little interference as possible with the normal channels of trade.'[44] The question became, what degree of interference was allowable? There was, as Lloyd pointed out, an almost universal bias against the concept of state control in industry, and the systems introduced were piecemeal or a matter of compromise. Autocratic though certain aspects of government actions were, schemes were nevertheless ill organised. To quote Lloyd again: 'The development of wartime control was thus due almost entirely to the overwhelming force of circumstance, and hardly at all to a deliberate policy of state intervention, consciously thought out and consistently applied.'[45]

So there was an unfortunate and ironic juxtaposition between, on the one hand, new, authoritarian machinery for running a war (which involved extensive co-operation between government and armament firms), together with the curtailment of precious union freedoms and, on the other, the legacy of government non-interference in the recruitment of workers and the bargains struck by employers and unions. Only in the munitions industry was limited control classed as being acceptable. The same uneasy background characterised the work of the Health of· Munition Workers Committee, which noted the over-long hours and made suggestions for improvements, yet did not even do enough to change the munitions industry, let alone the conditions of other factories.

Thus munitions employers did have a trapped, potentially vulnerable work-force, and the nature of government control in munitions, together with the complete lack of government interest in maintaining safeguards on wages and conditions in other industries, mapped out the way in which women were received into industry. It also explained to some extent the way in which they were welcomed or opposed by unions and employers: these feelings were superimposed upon the standard ideas about women's role in industry, as will be seen.

Notes

1. I.O. Andrews, *The Economic Effects of the World War upon Women and Children in Great Britain* (Oxford University Press, 1921), Ch. III.
2. Sylvia Pankhurst, *The Home Front* (Hutchinson, 1932), Ch. VI.
3. Pankhurst, *The Home Front*, Ch. III; Andrews, *The Effects of War*, Ch. III; G.D.H. Cole, *Labour in Wartime* (Bell & Sons, 1915), Ch. VIII.
4. M.B. Hammond, *British Labor Conditions and Legislation during the War*

(Oxford University Press, 1919), Ch. III.

    5. Cole, *Labour in Wartime*, Chs. III and VII; Hammond, *British Labor Conditions*, Ch. IV; Andrews, *Effects of the War*, Ch. IV; Barbara Drake, *Women in the Engineering Trades* (Fabian Research Dept., 1917).

    6. Andrews, *Effects of the War*, Ch. IV; Hammond, *British Labor Conditions*, Ch. VI.

    7. Andrews, *Effects of the War*, p. 33.

    8. Andrews, *Effects of the War*, Ch. IV; Hammond, *British Labor Conditions*, Ch. VI.

    9. Cole, *Labour in Wartime*, Ch. VIII.

    10. Andrews, *Effects of the War*, Ch. IV; Hammond, *British Labor Conditions*, Ch. VI.

    11. Andrews, *Effects of the War*, Ch. IV.

    12. Andrews, *Effects of the War*, Ch. IV.

    13. Cole, *Trade Unionism and Munitions* (Clarendon, 1923), Ch. VIII; Hinton, *The First Shop Stewards* (Allen and Unwin, 1973), Ch. I.

    14. Andrews, *Effects of the War*, Ch. IV.

    15. A.W. Kirkaldy, *Industry and Finance* (Isaac Pitman, 1921), vol. II, section I.

    16. Kirkaldy, *Industry and Finance*, vol. II, section I.

    17. Chapter 5 contains discussions of this aspect; demands for female conscription are indicative of resentment towards women who were not working rather than proof of any labour shortage.

    18. Andrews, *Effects of the War*, Ch. IV, p. 77.

    19. Hammond, *British Labor Conditions*, p. 171.

    20. L.K. Yates, *A Woman's Part* (Hodder & Stoughton, 1918), p. 9.

    21. Hammond, *British Labor Conditions*, Ch. VI.

    22. Andrews, *Effects of the War*, Ch. IV; *Labour Gazette*, December 1917.

    23. Kirkaldy, *Industry and Finance*, vol. II, section I; BAAS, *Outlets for Labour*, p. 7.

    24. Drake, *Women in the Engineering Trades*.

    25. *Common Cause*, 1 Oct. 1915, 'Street Housemaids'.

    26. *Yorkshire Observer*, 31 Aug. 1916, 'War Work in the West Riding'.

    27. *Daily Chronicle*, 3 Dec. 1915, 'Lace Hands Make Grenades'.

    28. E.g. *Yorkshire Observer*, 7 July 1916, 'Keighley's Need of More Women Workers', an appeal from the Mayor; *Manchester Guardian*, 22 Nov. 1915, 'Labour Shortage in the Cotton Trade': an appeal for the Women of Rochdale to go back to cotton.

    29. *The Times*, 18 Oct. 1916, for example, 'Women in the Labour Market'. See also interviews with women at the Imperial War Museum, Dept. of Sound Records. Amongst several munitions workers, an army clothing worker, a crane driver and other substitutes, previous employment had been as weavers, clothing workers or other factory workers, and servants.

    30. Monica Cosens, *Lloyd George's Munition Girls* (Hutchinson, 1917), p. 108.

    31. In soldiers' wives they could guarantee a sense of patriotism, as well as loyalty to the firm, and it was obvious that such women would readily relinquish their jobs to returning men.

    32. Kirkaldy, *Industry and Finance*, vol. II, section I.

    33. Hammond, *British Labor Conditions*, p. 143.

    34. Cole, *Labour in Wartime*, Ch. VII; Cole, *Trade Unionism and Munitions*, Ch. V.

    35. Cole, *Trade Unionism and Munitions*, Ch. V

    36. In Controlled Establishments:

        (a)   4/5 net profits over and above average profits of the two years

        preceding war should be paid to the Exchequer (but certain
        allowances granted);

(b)   no change in wage rates allowed unless changes submitted to
        Ministry of Munitions;

(c)   abandonment of workshop practices which hinder production,
        but safeguards to be restored after the war;

(d)   everyone subject to the control of the Ministry of Munitions —
        hours, conditions, wages.

(Hammond, *British Labor*, Ch. V.) In February 1917, 4,285 Controlled Establishments existed, with approximately 2 million workers (Hammond, Ch. V).

    37. Drake, *Women in the Engineering Trades*, p. 17.

    38. Drake, *Women in the Engineering Trades*.

    39. This 'freedom' may seem illusory, yet it was of significance, particularly when so much work was available for anyone who wished to go into munitions. It should be seen in relative terms.

    40. The minimum rate was raised to 24s for a 48-hour week in 1917.

    41. Hinton, *The First Shop Stewards Movement*; B. Pribicevik, *The Shop Stewards' Movement and Workshop Control* (Blackwell, 1959); Jose Harris, *William Beveridge* (Benn, 1977).

    42. See Chapter 6. The press relayed simple appeals for women to come forward, e.g. *Daily Express*, 2 Oct. 1916, 'Women and their Work': recruiting for the London General Omnibus Co., describing job, pay, conditions, etc.

    43. E.M.H. Lloyd, *Experiments in State Control* (Clarendon, 1924), p. 22.

    44. Lloyd, *Experiments in State Control*, Ch. XXI.

    45. Lloyd, *Experiments in State Control*, p. 260. Lloyd added that further control would have been politically and psychologically impossible.

3 WOMEN IN INDUSTRY: (1) THE ATTITUDES OF EMPLOYERS AND TRADE UNIONS

Women's Work and Efficiency

The new women workers, whether promoted, transferred to different processes or total newcomers, walked straight into the existing and continuing conflict between employers and trade unions. This chapter is about the attitudes towards women expressed by both sides, but the first matter is to clarify women's precise role in industry during the war. So far I have given an outline of the way they moved into new trades, and some intimation of the numbers involved, but in order to understand the reaction of workmen and employers it is important to establish the extent of their capabilities, since debates ostensibly rested on their success or failure as replacements for men, and the likelihood of their continued presence in industry after the war.

There are therefore two matters to clarify: first, the precise nature of women's work as substitutes, and, secondly, the extent to which they were successful in this role. In neither case is it easy to generalise, since the position varied not just from industry to industry but from factory to factory. The extent of substitution was never clearly established even during the war, and information on both this aspect and on the talents of the women concerned often comes from highly biased sources — notably trade unions and employers, whose views will be discussed shortly.

A Board of Trade report in 1917 put the problem succinctly: 'In attempting to estimate the extent of substitution the chief difficulty is one of definition,'[1] while Kirkaldy wrote, in *Industry and Finance*:

> In large munition works it is often impossible to calculate the amount of substitution; it has been proved in such works (a) that it is possible to run them with a large proportion of female employees; (b) that it is possible to employ women on processes which had formerly been undertaken only by the trained engineer; but it cannot be shown that individual women are replacing individual men, because either the work was not done at all or not done on anything like so large a scale before the war.[2]

Difficulties of definition were particularly acute in the munitions industry, where machinery and processes were highly adapted to increase output, but they also existed throughout industry. The only thing certain was that the number of women in industry and transport *had* increased, the number of men in such fields had decreased greatly, and that in some way the nation was surviving through the efforts of women. In this sense, therefore, the majority of women in industry were 'substituting' for the men who were absent, and it may seem pedantic to worry about the extent to which each woman employed was actually doing each man's work, but this in fact mattered greatly — to women, who could be paid less on the grounds that processes had been changed, and to men, who were threatened by the use of women workers as cheap labour. In addition, for us now, looking back at the industrial opportunities offered to women, it is important to know just how capable they were, when given the chance to do skilled or interesting work.

I have said that 'dilution' was strictly a term used in the engineering industry (see Chapter 2), and that it involved the shifting of skilled men on to skilled processes alone, while women performed the easier sections of the work. But this in itself was also a form of 'substitution', and the 'substitution' of women for men occurred in all major industries except those involving very heavy work. It was generally accepted that there were four basic kinds of substitution:

(1) complete, or direct substitution (each woman replaced one man, doing all his work);
(2) indirect substitution (e.g. women replaced unskilled or semi-skilled men while they moved on to more difficult work);
(3) group substitution (several women replaced a smaller number of men);
(4) substitution by rearrangement (the processes were changed, and women replaced men with the aid of improved or new machinery).[3]

The frequency of (1) was overestimated during the first year of the war, and chiefly existed from 1917. Figures showing the number of women who fell into each category are impossible to come by. Apart from the fact that some employers claimed that women were not doing 'men's work' in order to avoid paying women men's wages, many employers in any case had very hazy notions about what the word substitution meant, and the Board of Trade questionnaires designed to establish what kind of work women were doing did not elicit reliable information. The categories of work which seemed to confuse employers were the following:

(1) processes where men and women were previously employed to-
    gether, like weaving;
(2) processes where substitution was incomplete (i.e. women were only
    doing part of the job formerly done by men);
(3) industries where firms now had reduced staff, and where existing
    women had drifted into doing some of the men's work;
(4) processes which had not been done before the war, and were now
    done by women.[4]

But in spite of the confusion, and the lack of figures, generalisations
can be made about many trades, and particular information is available
in some cases.

Munitions: Engineering and Chemicals

Throughout the war, from 1914 onwards, women were extensively used
on so-called repetition work, and unskilled or semi-skilled processes. The
munitions industry was transformed by war, and new machinery introduced very rapidly. Barbara Drake, in her thorough survey of women
engineering workers, describes how machines formerly used by skilled
men could be turned into automatic or semi-automatic machines with
the addition of 'foolproof' appliances like 'blocks', 'formers' or 'cut-
offs'. Jobs were also subdivided for the benefit of women, so that a
process formerly carried out from start to finish by one man could be
done by several women: thus two female workers did the 'roughing' and
'turning' of copperbands for shells which one craftsman would have done
before. Increasingly, skilled work was subdivided in this way. Although
as the war progressed more women did do skilled work, and became
adept at using machines and setting them (to begin with, men always
set, or tuned, the machine), they were confined to work on one or two
processes only, and did not have the range of knowledge possessed by
the pre-war craftsman. Drake described how one complex job could be
split into 22 separate operations, done by 22 women.[5]

Repetition work was supposed to be women's great forte. It could
be boring and monotonous, or it could be light but relatively skilled,
and require dexterity and steadiness. Munitions work could also be unpleasant and dangerous: shell-filling involved the use of TNT, a yellow
powder which dyed the skin and could poison its handlers; explosives
caused several major and minor accidents in shell shops, resulting in
death or injury.

But throughout the munitions industry women were used on different
processes requiring varying amounts of skill, and what was acceptable

as women's work in one workshop was not in another — for example, some firms kept male toolsetters throughout the war, while others allowed women to look after their machines themselves. In some factories 95 per cent of the workers were female, and they included not only all kinds of semi-skilled mechanics, gaugers, examiners and tracers, but also some fully skilled tradeswomen; in others, women were confined to strictly limited processes throughout the war.[6]

Women were doing men's work, but there were of course also increases in the number of women doing work which had been done by them before the war in the smaller munitions industry, and women were taken on to completely new work as well. A factory which took on hundreds of new female workers was not necessarily replacing many men, and, as Hinton pointed out, the effects might be far more striking for the prospects of both men and women in, for example, general machine-shop work, where relatively fewer women were introduced, but where they were working on skilled or semi-skilled work formerly done by men.[7] General engineering could not be simplified for the use of extensive female labour, but women did dominate light munitions work, and did much heavy work with the aid of trolleys, cranes and male labourers.[8] But it is impossible to make any other generalisations about how many women were 'replacing' men, or how many women had taken over skilled work.[9]

Women also worked in shipyards and foundries, where the work was very heavy and their potential limited, in the new aircraft industry, where many became skilled carpenters, and as optical instrument makers, a field which expanded because German goods were no longer available, and which required both skill and dexterity.

Clothing and Boot and Shoe

Uniforms were needed for the army, and both the clothing trade and boot and shoe industry required extra labour. Many of the new women taken on were doing traditional women's work, and could not be classed as replacing men. However, women were newly employed on cutting out material (a skilled and heavy job) on both army and civilian work, and also graduated to some processes previously classed as just above their capabilities in both trades, which included heavier work, like pressing. As a result lighter machinery was introduced in factories where women were employed on such work, and processes were subdivided.[10]

Textiles: Cotton and Wool

In the cotton trade additional women were employed to replace men, but they were largely doing weaving, which was traditionally open to both sexes. Interestingly enough, Kirkaldy's figures show that in the textile industry as a whole, the numbers of women increased drastically until 1917, when they began to drop. By April 1918 there were actually 19,000 *fewer* women in textiles than there had been in July 1914, yet 65,000 women were said at this time to be replacing men. In cotton, women were to a limited extent allowed in the spinning room as piecers, replacing boys, but there was much opposition to this from mule spinners' unions. The woollen industry required extra workers to weave khaki, but although many women went into weaving, combing and spinning, men still did the night work and set the machines.[11]

Other Industrial Work

Leather: women were employed in place of men only when the latter were unavailable; in leather goods making, however, an increasing number of women were employed, but on standard women's work. They were tried on some substitution work, like riveting. China, pottery and earthenware: women were introduced on to men's work, but obviously this trade was not very important during the war. Printing and paper: some women were used on men's work, including compositing. Cakes, bread and biscuits: women were already extensively employed in the food industry, and now they were introduced on to men's work in cakes and biscuits. However, bread was said to be too heavy for them and the night work required also meant that they were seldom employed.[12]

Transport, Retail and Other

Women were employed as bus and tram conductors (i.e. they were directly replacing men) and eventually as drivers. On the railways they worked as carriage cleaners, porters, ticket collectors and guards, but were confined to easier, lighter jobs. They were mostly kept out of industrial work in the docks (in spite of the fact that they were employed on shipbuilding), as the male dockers disapproved of them.

In shops they replaced men, and in fact the public came into contact with women in all the service industries — as road sweepers, lift attendants, window cleaners, etc. Here there was direct substitution, or a larger number of women replaced fewer men. Women also went into clerical work and agriculture, but their position is outside the scope of this book, partly because of the nature of the work (non-industrial), and partly because middle-class women filled most of these places.[13]

Women were, therefore, spread throughout industry, but the extent to which they were replacing men on a one-to-one basis varied considerably, and this leads to problems when one tries to evaluate their 'success'. Obviously industry did continue to produce goods, munitions were forthcoming, and civilians continued to have their shops, their lifts and their trams in working order. But were women as good as men at the jobs they did? Was their work good training for similar work in peacetime? Could they work side by side with men or replace them? Did they actually prove to the nation that instead of being inefficient, casual, cheap labour they could be skilled or semi-skilled workers, involved with their work?

Unfortunately, the very nature of wartime substitution makes it very difficult to compare men's and women's capabilities, particularly in industries requiring skilled workers. Subdivided processes meant women learned only sections of the work their male predecessors had done, and machinery transformed skilled into semi-skilled work. Much anger was aroused amongst working men by the exaggerated comments about women's capabilities which appeared in the press: increased output in munitions was often due to new machinery or the wartime abandonment of workshop practices by which men limited their output in order to guarantee fair piece rates.[14]

In addition, there are difficulties with source materials for the historian. An enormous amount was written about women workers during the war, but much of it was written by observers with an axe to grind; the government and Ministry of Munitions wished to convince employers that women were worth employing, and intended to keep up public morale; trade unions saw women primarily as competitors with men; employers made excuses for *not* employing women, or for paying them lower rates; feminists wanted to prove women's capabilities and show they were worthy of the vote; the press wanted good stories. All these different approaches explain the variety of opinions on women's work, but do not give concrete information about women's success or failure in industry. There were, however, a few surveys which stand out amongst the others: their authors approached the situation in industry with a genuine desire to examine facts and opinions rather than propagandise. One of the most perceptive and complete is *Industry and Finance* by A.W. Kirkaldy, a two-volume work written from reports submitted by investigators all over the country. It was not written to be a best-seller, it was not written for the bodies with vested interests, government, employers and trade unions, and it remains of prime importance to anyone trying to evaluate the success of women workers; it is a good touchstone by which the opinions of employers and trade unions may be tested.

There is little doubt that some work was made 'easier' for women than it had been for men; they had to learn less, use less skill or less strength; they were sometimes on the easier sections of processes while men were on the difficult parts. But some of the adjustments simply brought jobs into line with women's strength: as when trolleys, lifts or lighter machinery were designed for them. Then, workshops were altered, but women could not have been expected to lift or carry the same weights as men, and although such alterations involved additional capital expenditure for employers, they were not symbolic of lower female efficiency.

There was general agreement that women were very good at 'repetition' or automatic work, some of which was highly adapted and was obviously for the war period only. A large proportion of munitions work fell into this category. Women were praised for being quick, deft and tolerant of boredom — far more tolerant than either boys or men were. Their output was high and their efficiency beyond dispute.

As far as skilled work was concerned, opinions were divided about women's capabilities. Some employers did not allow women the chance to try it at all; others claimed that they were less accurate, less efficient or less adaptable. Others still found that there were women who compared favourably with men on a number of processes. As Kirkaldy wrote:

> The opinions expressed on women who were replacing men vary so greatly that it is a temptation to state that women's success depends on the skill with which suitable women are selected and the type of management under which they are placed.[15]

He considered that women's output was likely to be less than men's on heavy work; on skilled work, where performance depended upon the length of time a woman had been employed, and on jobs with long hours, the position would be similar. Women's output exceeded men's where there had previously been trade union restrictions on output, where the work was repetitive, and where special deftness was required.

In industries other than munitions it is difficult to generalise even this far, as processes varied from workshop to workshop, and employers held their opinions accordingly. Similarly, there were differing views about women's timekeeping and initiative throughout industry, and one can only come back to Kirkaldy's comment that women did as well as their conditions allowed. Where they had very long hours, and had difficult journeys to work, they were bound to be more tired, and this would affect absenteeism, the rate of sickness, timekeeping, and even enthusiasm. In areas where many married women were employed domestic duties had an effect and, particularly if husbands were away at the Front, sick children meant extra days off work. In the matter of initiative, this too was affected by circumstances: in some factories training was given, and knowledge enabled women to cope confidently with the different situations they found themselves in, while in others they picked up the work as best they could and initiative was discouraged.

Miss O.E. Monkhouse wrote a paper on 'The Employment of Women in Munition Factories', which she presented before the Institute of Mechanical Engineers in 1918. She listed the problems connected with employing women: many were unaccustomed to factory life and discipline; many men were not used to managing women workers; workshop conditions were usually organised with men, rather than women, in mind; women were not used to machinery; men had difficulties in maintaining discipline; women did not like long hours; women lacked physical strength. She too decided that lack of success could often be traced back to poor workshop conditions and organisation.[16]

So women were capable of much, and excelled at delicate operations: they were exceptionally good on aircraft work, oxyacetylene welding, scientific instrument making. Where they did not do well, it could often be put down to poor conditions, lack of training and lack of organisation. Their only inherent disadvantage was their inferior strength, which could not always be compensated for. Otherwise, when given the chance, they proved to be willing, and often skilful, workers.[17] Unfortunately, this potential was not necessarily admitted by the other interested parties in industry; the writers of the BAAS report on labour stated, 'They have carried out arduous operations such as forging, hitherto only done by men, and have shown a mechanical ability and initiative which few employers or trade unions will admit.'[18] Kirkaldy put it more bluntly when he wrote, 'Considering the strength of the prejudices against women's employment, it is astonishing that it became so widespread.'[19]

The Unions' View

Hall Caine, in his wartime tribute to women munitions workers, wrote of relations between male and female workers:

As far as one can see the sexes get on well together. Common interests and common labour seems to have brought them into friendly relations. Constant intercourse and work appears to have given the men a high opinion of women, of their steadiness and power to endure.[20]

But in 1916, a journalist with the *Daily Mail* reported that women faced, at work 'a barrier of distrust, disparagement, and probably amused contempt'.[21] The truth lies somewhere between these two views, but unfortunately the latter reaction seems to have been more common.

It is not possible to describe the views of the labour movement *en masse* to the influx of women workers. Unions had varying policies on the matter of women, and in addition the rank and file did not always approve of their leaders' decisions. The fact that a union accepted women's presence for the war period did not mean that the men in the factories no longer distrusted them; and, conversely, the fact that a union opposed women workers and did not allow them to join its ranks did not mean that individual workmen were not kind and helpful to those women who worked with them. Nevertheless, although some writers at the time condemned unions as a whole for their response to women,[22] a division can be made between the reactions of the general labour unions, or those which included a large number of less skilled men, and of craft unions, such as the ASE. Many unions which had not accepted women before the war, either because there were no women in the industries they covered, or because women worked on different processes from men, did take them in during 1914-18; for example, the National Silk Workers' Association (1915), the National Union of Bookbinders and Machine Rulers (1915), the NUR (1915), the National Union of Operative Bakers (1915), the Electrical Trades Union (1916) and the National Union of Brushmakers (1918).[23] The Workers' Union (WU), the General Union of Municipal Workers (GUMW) and the National Federation of Women Workers (NFWW) continued to recruit women, as they had done before the war, and gained many skilled and semi-skilled female workers who were not allowed into other unions. The Workers' Union had only 3,000 women members in 1914, but 10,000 in 1915 and 80,000 in 1918.[24] General unions like the WU took up the cause of those neglected by the craft unions, which remained most concerned with maintaining their members' industrial status; as the writer of an editorial in the *Trade Union Worker* (WU) stated in 1916: 'Our special object, in a humble way, is to champion the cause of the woman worker, the labourer, and the semi-skilled worker.'[25]

The attitude of the shop stewards and the Industrial Unionist workers towards women was more ambiguous. These groups of socialists, found mostly in engineering and shipbuilding, often objected to the elitism and status-seeking of the old craft unions, and were inclined to welcome dilution if it could be used to the workers' advantage.[26] Industrial Unionists claimed to support the idea of equality of men and women in industry,[27] yet few women were involved in the new socialist groups like the shop stewards, the amalgamation movement, the syndicalists or the Guild Socialists, all of which blossomed during the war,[28] and some middle-class spokesmen for these were vitriolic indeed about the rights of women to work at all.[29] But all these groups, and the general unions, were bitter about the role of the craft unions during the war, which, said *Solidarity* (paper of the Industrial Unionists), 'sectionalised' the workers, and most anger was directed at the ASE. As Dallas wrote in the *Trade Union Worker*:

> These people don't care how long the war goes on. They don't care who has to go in the Army. They have no conscientious objection to manufacturing the munitions of war for someone else to use. They are determined to push anyone in the Army; all may go, but not them. Nothing has been more discreditable to the labour movement than the attitude of this section of the alleged skilled men.[30]

And it was from the skilled unions that women encountered most opposition, particularly in the munitions industry but also in other trades. The Amalgamated Society of Carpenters and Joiners never allowed women to join,[31] nor did the ASE. Women were working side by side with skilled men, often on skilled work, in both the aircraft and engineering industries covered by the above unions, and their prospects were severely limited by the men's refusal to accept them as members: as a correspondent pointed out in a letter to the *Nation* in 1917, the way was thus neatly left open to push women out of all skilled work after the war.[32] As far as the behaviour of individual men is concerned, there is evidence of both kindness and overt hostility in the workshops; while one woman recalled that her foreman never showed any jealousy, though she had heard of other men who did, and added that since she set her own tools she was spared the caprices of a male setter-up,[33] others referred to jealousy and even sabotage.[34] There remained some unions, like the Preston Operative Spinners Association (cotton mule spinners) which, with the full support of their members, would not allow women on to men's work, let alone into the unions.

It is easy to assume that such hostility towards women was a result of the standard suspicion of the skilled towards the unskilled, and indeed women were generally classed with the unskilled by craft unions, no matter what their actual or potential skills.[35] Skilled men did feel under attack during the war, and their fears were not groundless. Even before 1914 status and security were being eroded. By the early 1900s

Birmingham and Coventry, centres of the motor and cycle industries, had many workshops where women were doing the work of 'semi-skilled mechanics', or even 'skilled' work (on trades classed as women's), without apprenticeships, and for less than trade union rates. They were also working, even then, on fuse and cartridge making, small ammunition, gun engraving and gun belt making; they were regarded as a cheap and docile labour force and were a threat as such.[36] During the war, as I have shown, women were brought on to many processes formerly done by men and were not necessarily paid good rates. Barbara Drake described how employers were free to classify work as they chose fit:

> Thus, with a tool-making firm, introducing female labour on 'centre' and 'turret' lathes, the women were confined to comparatively light and straightforward operations, and require additional skilled supervision and assistance in setting the tools until they gain experience. But no other readjustment is made in the process; the brains are put in by the operator and not by the machine; and the job remains in a category reserved to fully-qualified or skilled tradesmen. Nevertheless, the employer classes the women without more compunction than before as semi-skilled labour, reducing the men's rate by about one-half, or from 10¾d and 11½d to 5¼d an hour.[37]

The use of such cheap labour on similar work undermined men's status and was potentially dangerous, even though skilled men faced no wage reductions themselves during the war. Women were being introduced at a time when 'scientific management' — the speeding up of processes and the further use of automatic machinery — was much discussed: the war gave employers the chance to experiment while unions were unable to fight effectively. In addition, there was no doubt about the fact that women *were* often a more docile labour force, particularly those who remained completely unorganised. Employers were prepared to exploit this fact, and sometimes attempted to keep the sexes separate in order to avoid women's unionisation. A London manager reported to Kirkaldy:

> At first the men and women worked together and the women came too much under the men's influence; they refused to work for the wage offered them and were continually limiting output. All these girls were discharged; another shop was opened into which girls were put separately under male toolsetters etc.; ever since then they have been perfectly contented and the arrangements have been of great advantage to the firm.[38]

Dilution was therefore a real threat to the skilled engineers, and to a lesser extent substitution in other trades could also have led to a reduction in men's wages or complete displacement, theoretically.[39] Even the writers of the Majority Report on Women in Industry recognised that men's fears were justified,[40] and such fears were further increased by rumours that employers were planning to dismiss, then re-employ, women at lower rates once the war ended,[41] and by the extent of control the government already had over workers thanks to the Munitions Act and other legislation; it must be remembered that the Ministry of Munitions included a number of employers.[42]

Solidarity saw ominous signs for the future; and one writer was disturbed at the armbands and coloured overalls worn by women munitions workers for the first time:

> Dilution of labour was only supposed to increase production. But undoubtedly it has been used to regiment the workers, and to cheapen labour. To what degree the employers will proceed with the regimentation of the women workers it will be interesting to see. Already many of them are arrayed in uniforms characteristic of comic opera.[43]

Caps and overalls did look strange to all those who were used to seeing women working in their own clothes, and could be seen as dehumanising the work-force.

There are two obvious reasons why the women substitutes should have been more unpopular with skilled men than the temporary male workers who were also introduced before conscription.[44] First, there were increasing numbers of them while male substitutes became less common; secondly, they were traditionally associated with low wages. But there was more to women's unpopularity than this. G.D.H. Cole discussed men's instinctive distrust of female workers. Many women, he said, were determined to stay in their new jobs if they were offered the opportunity, and he continued:

> It is clear that this opens up difficult problems for the male wage-earner, who may well find his job taken or his standard of life threatened, by the competition of female labour. He is apt to regard women much as the Australian regards Chinamen, or as the American regards East European immigrants, as interlopers, whose different standard of life renders them not only dangerous, but also unfair, competitors in the labour market. And the history of women in industry has given some warrant for this attitude.[45]

At this point the complexities of the situation become more obvious. Women were not simply resented because they were unskilled or semi-skilled workers, but because they were *women*, a class apart, who were encroaching upon men's work. It emerged during the war that even if women were receiving equal pay (so could not be used to undercut men), were unionised, and guaranteed, through their union, that returning soldiers could have their jobs back, much resentment towards them still existed. Many male workers apparently did not trust women to keep their promises, and *they did not approve of them working at 'men's work'*. Thus there were significant differences between the way skilled men and unions treated the male substitutes and the females. For example, the ASE ultimately decided to admit men on engineering work who had not been apprenticed but who had learnt the skills during the war to a special section. They resolutely refused to admit women: instead they made an alliance with the National Federation of Women Workers, which obligingly promised that its members would withdraw from men's jobs at the end of the war. Any idea that women should be admitted to the fraternity of the skilled was unacceptable: when employers of women in scientific instrument making suggested a three-year apprenticeship for girls, men in the workshops objected.[46] Even when women were graciously allowed into a male-dominated union they ran the risk of constantly being classed as workers of less value; thus the Power Loom Carpet Weavers and Textile Workers of Kidderminster accepted women, but said that one man's vote was worth 25 women's.[47] This summed up the attitude of many men and many unions.

Ironically, although all working men accepted the idea that women were a threat, they also found it difficult to believe that women were really capable of doing men's work; when women were obviously successful they were resented none the less for encroaching upon male preserves. Barbara Drake described how skilled men shown fine gauges at first refused to believe that women had made them. Some men were indeed converted to the idea that women could do skilled work, although quite probably they accepted the prejudice shown even by Barbara Drake, who wrote that 'The supreme mechanic belongs, perhaps, to the masculine sex, as the supreme artist, chef or valet. Supremacy is a masculine quality, whether in art or industry.'[48] Other men continued to treat women as though they were children. As Naomi Loughnan, a middle-class volunteer, reported: 'As long as we do exactly what we are told and do not attempt to use our brains, we give entire satisfaction and are treated as nice, good children.'[49]

It was even less easy to change the prejudice of men who were against the whole idea of women working on jobs which might be classed as careers: women might be *capable* of doing skilled work, but should they be allowed to do it? They were classed as a category on their own because of their sex. Whereas unskilled or semi-skilled men could aspire to status through rising within their trades, even though they did not have the pride of the skilled man in his work, women were not supposed to be interested in an industrial role. They were not 'breadwinners', so they should not be interested in the development of skills or high wages.

Ideally, many men wished to keep women out altogether – not just out of the union but out of the trade – and some unions succeeded in doing this. Rowland Kenney, writing in the *New Age*, a Guild Socialist journal, spoke for the most extreme of those who disliked the idea of women being in industry at all:

> When women organisers of women ask what about the women going into industry, should they not be organised, what should be done with them? the reply is that that is their funeral, not ours. They should be kept out. If the men in industry have not the sense to keep them out then let us organise the men more strongly and show them that their duty is to clear them out as soon as possible.[50]

Rowland Kenney was peculiarly anti-feminist, and the *New Age* was a paper for middle-class intellectual socialists, not ordinary working men, but similar emotions often lay behind certain union policies, together with the frequently stated belief that women had more important duties than industrial work. The Lancashire mule-spinning unions were bitterly opposed to the idea of women working in the spinning rooms, and the Preston Operative Spinners' Association held out against women even when other areas of the county had accepted them as piecers. James Billington, the Secretary of the Association, made a succession of statements to the press, and his basic objection was that spinning was not women's work (ironic, considering which sex had been responsible for spinning before the factory system was introduced). Early in 1915 he stated: 'We are not by any means suggesting there is anything of a "degrading" character about this work, as you well know, but it is not a suitable occupation for young girls and women.'[51] By the end of the year he was claiming that conditions made employment 'unsuitable', if not 'harmful', and that conditions in Preston and Oldham were quite unlike those in Bolton and south Lancashire, where women were allowed.[52] The year 1916 saw him becoming increasingly dogmatic about the ill effects of the spinning rooms: 'it cannot possibly improve their [women's] sense of refinement or delicacy; and there are people still living who do not desire to see that sense deadened or killed outright, even amongst girls of the "common people".[53] By 1917, when the need for female labour in the cotton industry was most acute, he was fighting a losing battle, but hit new heights of emotive prose:

> If the spinners of Preston think fit at any time to work with females that is their business, and if any parent thinks so little about his daughter as to send her into a spinning room that is his business.
>
> For my own part, I stick to what I have said before, that I would sooner see my daughter dead than do such work.[54]

Such views raised the question of whether the work was really 'suitable' for men, who had to strip off in the heat, and change their clothes frequently. Changing rooms and washing facilities would have improved matters, but James Billington did not take up such causes as these, although others discussed them: women were supposed to leave both the work and the bad conditions to men.[55]

Other unions excluded women from work with similar excuses. 'We think a woman's place is at home, looking after the home, husband and family; and if she is a young woman, unmarried, she ought to be learning something better than pit bank work,'[56] said John Wadsworth, General Secretary of the Yorkshire Miners' Association when faced with the proposal for women to work on the surface, while the Amalgamated Society of Tramway and Vehicle Workers opposed women's employment as drivers 'on the grounds that the work was highly injurious to women and threatened the welfare of the future generation, while in many districts driving by women was a danger to the public'.[57] Its sister union, the Licensed Vehicle Workers, proposed a resolution at the TUC in 1916 calling for the removal of women from the transport industry after the war 'so that the men can resume their work and the women can find better work elsewhere, under conditions that will not be harmful to their moral welfare'.[58] One can see here (and in the outbursts by the cotton spinners) apparent concern with the health and welfare of mothers and wives, which although entirely economically convenient was probably at least partly genuine, since it was shared by women's sympathisers, as will be seen later in this book.

There was, amongst these unions which opposed women's right to work in 'men's jobs', great glee when union power pushed out those women stubborn enough to take such work. In the ASE *Monthly Journal and Report* for 1917 there is an account of one such triumph:

The Leeds City Tramways, who had introduced two women in their depot to do work formerly done by our men, were approached forthwith to pay the district rate, which Mr. Hamilton, the Manager, declined to do, contending, as usual, that the women were not doing identical work. After several letters had passed between us, I referred the matter for arbitration, and Mr. Hamilton now informs me that the women are no longer on the work. This is far more satisfactory than any award would have been.[59]

Men seemed sometimes to forget altogether women's need for work, and ignored the fact that they too were often perfectly willing to press for equal pay. Women simply did not count, except as pawns in the battle between capital and labour. The *Trade Unionist*, which claimed to be a paper sympathetic to women, in 1916 carried a hymn of praise to the dockers of Liverpool for keeping out women, even though they had been receiving equal pay and were not undercutting men. The tone can be gathered from the opening paragraph:

It is quite inspiring in these days to be able to record a really complete and bloodless victory for Trade-unionism against the insolent incursions of capitalism. But the firm stand taken by the dockers of Liverpool against the employment of female labour in their industry has resulted in such a victory, and we are not likely to hear of any attempt to introduce women onto work at the docks again for a long time to come.

From here, the author seems to turn more and more against women rather than capitalism, and he continues:

we should have thought that even those women who clamoured for a chance of undercutting the normal price in this sphere would have revolted at the ghastly lack of provision made for common cleanliness. But we got something better than the revolt of women, we got the revolt of men.

He finishes with a final flourish of pseudo-chivalry towards the hapless female dockers:

[Men are] determined that women shall not be allowed to encroach upon this particular industry. If the general sense and humanity of the people at large is not strong enough to rebel against such an outrage as the employment of women to load and unload vessels at the docks, then the dockers themselves will rebel.[60]

Other men were not quite so biting in their attacks, and refused to accept the idea of excluding women altogether,[61] although they too talked about what work was 'suitable' for women, and talked of the dangers of undercutting — but there is no doubt about the fact that in many circles the new female workers were regarded with a mixture of contempt and distrust. Even *Solidarity*, otherwise radical and often sympathetic to women's cause, could not resist pouncing on a notice circulating at William Beardmore's factory, showcase for women's labour, and reporting triumphantly: 'from this we learn that an average of 20% of the shells is scrapped each week on account of careless and inaccurate machining; the workers being earnestly enjoined not to throw difficult jobs under the machine.'[62] Relief was evident when it was proved that women were not really as skilful as the press made out; it soothed male pride and bolstered up the idea that men were superior workers — though to be fair to *Solidarity* in this case, the writer was evidently just as pleased to undermine the publicity handed out by the government and big engineering employers.

Nowhere do the ambiguities of unions' and workmen's approach to women workers become more evident than in the debates over wages. When women were kept out of a trade altogether, or were confined entirely to jobs they had done before the war, they were not a problem to men's unions: those who worked in the latter trades were usually in the National Federation of Women Workers, Workers' Union, or National Union of General Workers, all of which expanded rapidly during the war.[63] In economic terms the problem arose when women were employed on work similar to men's, and theoretically the answer lay in equal or equivalent pay for women and men, which would have removed the danger of undercutting, and made the prospect of keeping women on after the war less attractive to employers. There were three things which hampered the fight for equal pay: (1) the inadequate and partial government control over industry, which ignored all trades but munitions, and even here did not enforce the terms drawn up for dilution, or check employers' claims about the nature of the work done by women; (2) the attitude of employers (to be discussed shortly), who instinctively assumed women were worth less money, and who were, in any case, willing to use women to undercut men if they could, (3) the attitude of trade unions themselves, which was riddled with contradictions because of their view of men's and women's roles in industry and the home.

Throughout industry women were still paid lower wages than men. They were still working in trades which were classed as 'women's work' in large numbers, like tin box making, uniform making, etc., which, although part of war production, were not classified as munitions, did not have strong trade unions, and were often let down by Trade Boards (which were supposed to set respectable minimum wages).[64] Wages were sometimes staggeringly low. For example, the Southampton Trades and Labour Council reported that Pirelli's were paying women 1¾d an hour, plus 1s a week war bonus: even the Trade Board rates, the minimum acceptable in sweated industries, were around 3d an hour at this time. It is incredible that the Dartford Poor Law Guardians protested to the Ministry of Munitions about the low wages paid to widows in their area, which necessitated extra allowances from the Guardians.[65] Government bodies themselves, in the form of local tribunals, upheld low wages by refusing to grant Leaving Certificates to women receiving poor rates of pay: thus they could not leave jobs to find better-paid ones. The general labour unions did their best to negotiate for women, but their bargaining power was not strong, and they were sometimes heavily criticised for the low wages they accepted on women's behalf.[66] Women replacing men in many non-munitions trades, like shopkeeping, post office work and other factory work, also received lower rates of pay than men unless unions held out for better pay,[67] and this applied both to working-class women and middle-class women in clerical trades. Looking across the board, the Standing Joint Committee of Industrial Women's Organisations concluded that 'the bulk of the depressed women's industries have not obtained a rise in wages anything like equivalent to the increased cost of living, nor is there any evidence to lead us to believe that women engaged in substitution for men have, unless in exceptional cases, obtained the men's full rate.'[68] After the war, M.A. Hamilton summed up the position as follows:

> By the time of the armistice, the general women's standard had been raised to 5½d and the 'substituted' standard to 6d per hour, plus cost of living bonus of 11s. Allowing for the 150% increase in the cost of living, this meant a real advance of 50% . . . equal pay, of course, was not secured. Outside munitions the advance secured by women workers seldom did more than keep their real wages up to the level of the cost of living — and not always that.[69]

It was, of course, standard to pay women on 'women's work' low wages, but on men's work it was another matter: it was a threat to the labour movement, and caused far more anxiety amongst male trade unionists than women's pre-war wages had ever done.

I have described, in this chapter and in Chapter 2, how the government, through legislation, attempted to gain something akin to equal pay in certain branches of the munitions industry, and how their degree of control was inadequate, even by the end of the war. Lloyd George made certain promises to skilled men in 1915, and to women, that 'the government will see there is no sweated labour,'[70] but employers still evaded the limitations which existed with utmost simplicity, as Barbara Drake described:

> With one firm, the men are paid full-time during a Zeppelin raid, while the women are subject to a deduction from wages, although paid a lower rate. With a second firm, the men secure time-and-a-quarter during a breakdown, and the women no more than bare time, although both are employed on piece work, and the loss of earnings is the same for each. With a third firm, the women are refused the men's overtime allowances and paid a lower scale instead, or nothing at all. The women explain another time how they are employed part on shell and part on fuse-making, the terms of L2 being avoided because the latter is only a 'women's trade'.[71]

Employers also paid women in munitions according to the ubiquitous premium bonus system, a hybrid between piece and time rates. Under this, the worker was guaranteed a certain rate per hour, and then given a bonus for output. A 'basis time' was allowed for the job and a worker doing the job in that time or longer received only the basic rate. The worker who 'saved time' by producing things faster than the basis time allowed received in addition a bonus on output (a 'premium bonus'), equivalent to a fixed proportion of the basic rate (perhaps ½ or ⅔), for each hour of time 'saved'. So workers were paid for only a proportion of the extra goods produced, unlike those who worked on piece rate. As Drake said, 'the employer extracts, in fact, from the worker a piece work effort at a time work wage.'[72] Many female munitions workers were paid in this manner, and in any case the £1 minimum for time workers was not enforced and was thought to be too low.[73]

The answer was for men's unions in the munitions trades and others to fight for equal pay if they felt threatened. Equal pay was a loaded issue: it was supported for the best of reasons by feminists, who believed women deserved good wages, or who did not want to blackleg men, and by various other people throughout society who felt that the current system of unequal rates was prejudicial to both men and women. Equal pay was supported by some officials of general labour unions for similar reasons. But when it was taken up by craft unions it was with the aim of making women's labour unpopular and expensive for employers, thus safeguarding certain trades for men. This motive was recognised by many, and the Industrial Unionist paper, the *Socialist*, was right when it warned of those unions which used equal pay as a weapon 'under the cover of an alleged magnanimity for womankind'.[74]

But the unions which fought for equal pay for the benefit of men, rather than women, faced something of a dilemma. By virtue of their own status as craftsmen they classed women as inferior workers, yet they were obliged to admit that women could do certain jobs as well as they could, in order to justify demands for equal pay. And, in spite of all the evidence of women's skill on certain processes, they did not like to admit that women could be successful on such work. In addition, the idea of equal pay was directly contrary to the traditional acceptance of higher wages for male 'breadwinners' and lower wages for female 'dependants' — notions which had been upheld by the trade union movement as well as anyone else, and which were interconnected with the ideas concerning the nature of married women's duties as home-loving wives and mothers. This is why it was seen as such a triumph by many male trade unionists when women were removed from 'men's work' rather than given equal pay: the latter went against custom and against the feelings of the workmen, even though it made good economic sense. These feelings were recognised by many of the women who worked with them: Joan Williams, munitions worker, wrote:

> I could quite see it was hard on the men to have women coming into all their pet jobs and in some cases doing them a good deal better and I sympathised with the way they were torn between not wanting the women to undercut them, and yet hating them to earn as much.[75]

One woman, interviewed by the Imperial War Museum, was asked whether the men were rude to her when she went to Woolwich for training, and replied, 'Yes, they didn't want to show us their livelihood. You see they knew it was their livelihood. Women were coming in, you see. They were going to cut the wages.'[76] They resented women, distrusted their skills, and yet, for economic reasons had to demand equal pay, which in addition was seen as symbolic of the government's promise that the status of skilled men would not suffer, and pre-war practices would return.[77]

Not only did such a policy hurt the pride of men, who still instinctively believed women were less capable, it went against custom, and it
was hard for many men to accept that women 'needed' higher wages.
Some of those who pressed for equal pay felt obliged to explain that
this need not upset the concept of women's traditional role: one woman
writer in the *Trade Union Worker* assured readers that:

> We, as women, too, love the old tradition that the wife's place is in
> the home, and if we are going to be content with a woman's wage
> for a man's job, then we shall be serving not only our dear ones be-
> hind the guns and trenches, but their old enemies, the master classes,
> who will be seeking for cheap labour.[78]

If high wages led to the exclusion of women after the war, this would, of
course, guarantee that women remained primarily in the domestic role.

One of the other arguments often used was that women's health,
and therefore the health of the race, was dependent upon good wages[79]
– the 'health of the race' was often a useful catch-phrase for all kinds
of campaigners, as will be seen in Chapter 5. All these issues are interconnected. Some of the women's sympathisers in the labour and socialist
movements pointed out that discussions on equal pay were closely linked
with those on women's position in society, and that in fact society
would have to be revolutionised to make sense of equal pay.[80] This
matter was taken up for public debate, but most of the craft unions
were not interested in such complexities: they wanted to safeguard
men's industrial position, not revolutionise women's.[81] Although they
were prepared to strike for equal pay when men were working with
women, they sometimes refused to take such action when women on
'women's work' put in pay claims. In January 1918, for example, the
women filers at Wells Aviation Works, Chelsea, struck for an extra 1d
an hour. The women welders (skilled workers, with their own union)
would not support them – they were 'ladies', said *Solidarity* bitterly
– and neither would the male workers, who were craft unionists.[82]
Similarly, the grocery union refused to interest itself in the wages of
female grocery assistants – the men preferred to work out how the
'spare' wages saved by employers could be shared out amongst them.[83]

Sometimes these mixed priorities put unions in a dilemma. In August
1918 the women on buses and trams struck for completely equal pay,
including equal war bonuses, the money added on to keep wages in line
with the cost of living. In this strike they were supported by the London and Provincial Union of Licensed Vehicle Workers and opposed by

the Amalgamated Association of Tramway and Vehicle Workers. The *National News* reported that 'Male employees who are opposed to the women's claim base their opposition on the fact that many of the conductresses are the wives of soldiers and receiving separation allowances, while the men had families to support.'[84] Those who supported the strike felt that this fact was outweighed by the danger of cheaper female workers. Unfortunately, both unions had opposed the use of women as drivers, and also, as described earlier in this chapter, spoke out strongly against their continued presence in the transport industry.

Alliances for the sake of equal pay were strictly temporary expedients, and often the products of fear. The hostility to women simply revealed itself in different ways. In some factories they were taken off piece work because men objected to them earning so much;[85] in others, when they took less than men they were bitterly criticised. Thus one man wrote to the *Aberdeen Journal* complaining that women were preferred by employers because they only wanted pocket money: 'She has only to look for additional pocket money — an additional flash dress-out, and so be considered to be patriotically "doing her bit".'[86] It was also pointed out at the time that many male trade unionists actually resented wives, daughters or girlfriends becoming trade union members, necessary though they knew the organisation of women to be: perhaps it appeared that women were trespassing on the serious world of male employment when they did so.[87] Union membership was symbolic of a commitment to work.

It would be neither true nor fair to claim that the trade union front was unitedly 'against' women, and pursued policies which were entirely self-seeking, even when incidentally useful to women. Many men and women worked hard for both sexes, and saw the struggle for pay as a means by which all workers could be brought together — although even amongst these people there were differing views about women's future prospects and the jobs they ought to do after the war when the men 'came home' — aspects which will be discussed later in this book as they were concerns shared by all classes. Much of the above evidence about the general unpopularity of women workers comes from craft unions, it is true, but two points should be made. First, in spite of all the differences in method, and approach to the problems of war, some of the feelings expressed by these particularly organised and voluble groups of men were certainly held by men in other, less elevated unions: women were distrusted because they could undercut at any level in industry; they were seen as stepping outside their true sphere if they showed interest in the idea of their work being more than temporary; they were held to be inherently less skilled at 'men's jobs'; there was concern about what work was 'suitable' for them. Secondly, the influence of the craft unions should not be underestimated, even in 1914. They did hold the keys to the skilled occupations, and they could keep women out of many jobs. Although their members were outnumbered by those in the general unions and less skilled workers, they had a determination and status which many other working men lacked. It remained of great significance to men and women, both economically and psychologically, that the ASE was prepared to allow men without the full apprentice- ship into the union in special sections, but would not countenance the idea of recruiting the newly skilled women. Women were always classed as second-class workers in industry, in spite of the evidence of their skill and commitment. This is the one generalisation one can make about the views of the majority of trade unionists, in spite of all their differences.

The Employers' Views

Certain views of women workers and their merits were held throughout industry, from boy apprentices to the Ministry of Munitions officials. Ray Strachey reported the views of one of the latter:

> 'Dilution and all that,' he began, 'very necessary no doubt, but en- gineering's not suitable work for women.'
>   His tone was infinitely patronising, so I said a few things as gently as I could.
>   'Oh yes, of course, of course,' he answered, 'very clever with their fingers, no doubt. But it's not women's work, you know, their place is in the home . . .' '. . . and then these wages,' he went on, 'what do women want with such preposterous wages? Three pounds and five pounds a week they get sometimes: it's perfectly out of the ques- tion.'[88]

'Unsuitable work', 'their place is in the home', 'preposterous wages' — the phrases are all too familiar. If anything more is needed to show the extra dimension in the standard conflict of employers versus workers lent by the presence of women, it is the distinct lack of enthusiasm with which the former greeted the idea of recruiting women for the war period. In spite of the notion, widely held at the time, that unions alone held up the expansion of female labour throughout industry,[89] and in spite of the fact that some employers did indeed employ women voluntarily from 1914 onwards, many other employers remained suspicious of them, and doubted whether they could do anything but the simplest work. The newspapers might have described women's talents in glowing terms, but it took more than this to convince most employers and managers. Cole pointed out the ironic similarity in the view of women held by employers and workmen:

> women had to contend with the strong feeling, largely shared by the employer and the male workers, that they had no business to be in the factories at all. Their failures therefore produced a far greater psychological impression than their successes; and failures which were the fault of management or of the skilled supervision were readily attributed to them.[90]

A surveyor from the Board of Trade came to a similar conclusion[91] and a writer in the Ministry of Munitions drily compared their propaganda efforts with those of a religious crusade:

> It was the business of dilution officers to 'convert' recalcitrant managers and shop foremen to the Gospel of Employment of Women. Officers were assisted in this task by output records from firms already employing women, photographs of women already engaged on various machine operations and testimonials of other 'converted' works managers.[92]

Non-munitions firms found themselves obliged to recruit more women as their male workers volunteered, or were conscripted, and ordinary industry was not given much attention by the government; munitions firms were another matter, and the Ministry of Munitions worked both to expand production by increasing the use of labour-saving machinery and the number of people employed, and to persuade employers to 'release' more men for the trenches by replacing them with women. The Ministry's officials produced extensive propaganda, as noted above, and they were aided in their efforts by such journals as the *Engineer*, which was taken far more seriously by employers than was the daily press.

From the beginning the *Engineer*, through its editorial columns, worked hard at converting munitions employers. It started by self-righteously blaming the unions for the labour shortage,[93] but as time went on it seems to have become increasingly evident to the magazine that many employers too were reluctant to use women as replacements, and the *Engineer* attempted to demonstrate how well women were doing. It was the duty of employers to use them, an editorial late in 1915 insisted,[94] and the journal printed quite excessively rosy pictures of Beardmore's successes[95] — which of course partly accounts for *Solidarity*'s triumph in revealing that all was not running quite so smoothly at the firm in question.[96] In 1916 the journal continued to insist that 'the dilution of labour has been an unqualified success', but complained that there were still employers who would not take women.[97]

The praise heaped upon women's adaptability, hard work and increasing skill in engineering might have been very gratifying to the women themselves (though better wages would have been preferred) and it probably had its roots in reality, as many less prejudiced observers pointed out. Unfortunately, it can only have irritated the unions, sensitive as they were to the idea of replacement; in addition, it failed to convince many employers. Two articles written for the *Engineer* deserve particular attention. They were not propaganda pieces: they are examples of some men's unshakeable belief that women were by nature less skilled and should be paid less than the pre-war male engineer. They also show how convenient such a philosophy could be, economically, to the employer. The first one appeared in October 1915, and made a deep impression upon the ASE, which saw it as being representative of employers' future approach to female labour. It expresses perfectly the connection between assumptions about women's social role and their economic position. The author described how women did not take their work seriously because they looked forward to marriage, and added that if they were sensible they would defy the unions and stay in industry — on the usual casual basis at lower rates. He went on to demolish the idea that women could be serious workers:

> The prospect to which a man looks forward is to earn enough money to keep a wife; the prospect to which a woman looks forward is that *he* may succeed . . .
>
> But, it is urged, there is always a number of women who desire to make a vocation of workshop life; why should they not be treated equally with men? The answer is so obvious as to be scarcely worth making. Marriage being regarded as a bar to continuation in a factory, as for the best reason it usually is, what value can be placed on the wish of a girl of 14 or 16 years of age to devote herself to the workshop? Unless she is abnormal she will certainly desire before many years have passed to marry, and her training as an apprentice will be thrown away.[98]

Women were not a good investment, he insisted, if they were to be paid high wages; however, they were useful if they were paid *less* than the old skilled rates. The work was now easier than it used to be, not only because of technological change, but by definition, because women were doing it, so 'The fact of the matter is really, not that women are paid too little – or much too little – but that men are paid too much for work which can be done without previous training.'[99] These were the ideas that the ASE dreaded, and the article as a whole shows how entirely the existence of cheap female labour depended on the concept of short-term, unmarried non-unionised women workers. The ASE took account of the danger, but could not countenance the logical solution: that women should be allowed to be part of the 'serious' work-force, and should no longer be encouraged to be temporary workers, excluded from skilled jobs. This article in the *Engineer* in fact drew an irate letter in reply from one man: men and women were human beings, he wrote, and why should women be obliged to sacrifice themselves industrially just because they were wives and mothers? Such matters did not appear to trouble the writer of the article: in his scheme of things it was necessary for women to go on sacrificing themselves and earning low wages. Craft unions accepted this tradition without question in a similar fashion, and worried themselves about the results, not the cause.[100]

The second noteworthy article appeared in the *Engineer* in 1917. It was astute about the dangers of exaggerating women's skills, but patronising about the whole concept of women as skilled workers:

The public appears to have been considerably misled over this matter. It commonly attributes the success of women 'engineers' – we have heard them frequently so called – either to some hitherto unsuspected trait of feminine nature whereby they take kindly or by instinct to things mechanical, or to the comparative failure of the pre-war male worker to achieve the output of which he should have been capable. The first view is merely amusing; the second, containing as it does a half-truth, is to a certain extent dangerous, for it is apt to lead to friction between male and female workers if not now, then after the war, when the whole question of women in engineering works will have to be reconsidered.[101]

Whenever women were employed, employers wished to pay them less. This was undoubtedly because it made economic sense; it was also because, it was claimed, women 'cost more', as new machinery, extra supervision, cloakrooms, etc., had to be provided; in addition, it was

the custom. It must not be forgotten that the men who complained bitterly about women 'doing their jobs' in munitions, and in other trades,
had long accepted that in normal times women ought to be paid lower
wages, and indeed men of the artisan or skilled class were amongst the
most dogmatic upholders of the idea that women should be supported
by their husbands after marriage. The Women's Service Bureau (of the
National Union of Women's Suffrage Societies) wrote a letter to the
Ministry of Munitions about one case of low pay:

> Miss Long, teacher at the School of Elementary Engineering, 1 Elm
> Park Road, Chelsea, went to Messrs Gwynne and saw Mr Meyer about
> a week ago to ask him why the women she had sent him were only
> receiving £1 a week [on time rate], and were not on piece work. He
> said, 'If I paid these women on piece work they would earn £3 a
> week and the men would not like it. Some of them have incomes
> and £1 should suit them nicely.'[102]

He was probably right when he said that the men would not like it, and
when they did not, they played into the employers' hands. No man liked
the idea of women earning high wages; as one foreman said to Barbara
Drake, 'What can one do when a girl is earning as much as 15s a week
but lower the piece rate?'[103]

In general, employers of women narrated a series of complaints
about their workers. Those who appeared before the Ministry of Reconstruction's Committee on Women in Industry reported variously
that women's value was only two-thirds of men's (munitions); that their
time-keeping was worse than men's (chemicals); that they lacked initiative (chemicals); that they were incapable of overseeing, had inferior
output (china and earthenware); were less reliable, less strong and caused
more public complaints (transport).[104] Similarly, Mr Charles Wicksteed,
at the Institute of Mechanical Engineers, expressed his belief that engineering was a man's job, and that women were less honest, truthful
and reliable than men, and less good at time-keeping or staying at the
job.[105] One employer at the 1918 Conference on Women's Wages neatly
mixed together the issues of women's capabilities, and what they deserved simply by virtue of their sex: 'in his opinion, women were not
as capable as men. He believed in the old-fashioned idea that wages
should be based on the cost of living of a man, his wife, and the average
family.'[106] This was the most common approach; women's capabilities
were connected with their biological destiny, and their pay rates
stemmed from their social role; as one employer interviewed by the

Westminster Gazette just after the war said grandly:

> Man is, and always will be, regarded as the breadwinner and woman
> as the mother. She is, speaking generally, only in industry until she
> is married; and her object whilst in industry is — again speaking
> generally — to support herself.[107]

He used the same excuse for not giving equal pay.

Skill and interest in work certainly existed, but many employers
found it hard to accept. I have already mentioned that Kirkaldy and
other observers blamed the comparative lack of success of women in
some factories on the structure of their employment and the inefficiency
of individual workshops. Their failure could also be attributed to the
attitudes of the employers themselves. Kirkaldy reported:

> In one [factory] it was frankly said that the women's work was very
> expensive, that they were not nearly as good as men, and were quite
> unskilled; in this case a small number of women were employed
> among a considerable number of men, no special supervision arrange-
> ments were made, and the firm seemed to accept the idea that women
> could not be expected to be as good as men as an established fact
> and to consider their employment as a temporary expedient to be
> treated with good natured tolerance; no attempt was made to train
> them or give them an interest in their work.[108]

In munitions and other industries employers were reluctant to allow
women good opportunities, not expecting them to stay after the war;
they also assumed, as a bakery employer in Fife pointed out, that
women could pick up in a week what men had taken years to learn.[109]
Women who were not *allowed* to supervise or set tools, or who were
not given formal training, could not reasonably be condemned for their
lack of initiative or skill, yet blamed they were.

Unfortunately, many of those who did accept women and praise them
also confined them to repetition work, and kept alive the old ideas about
women's natural patience, dexterity and lack of ambition. The differences between men and women were emphasised; reported the *Scotsman*:

> The superintendent of a well-known armament firm declares that
> girls are much more satisfactory than boys at repetition work. A boy
> usually wants to become a fully-trained mechanic, and grows dis-
> contented if kept at one job indefinitely, whereas girls, who do not

actually enter the factory with the idea of staying in it more than a few years, are willing to concentrate their attention on attaining dexterity at a particular task.[110]

At the end of 1915 a group of journalists was taken on a tour of Birmingham's munitions factories (another publicity exercise); they were told how women were punctual, good-tempered and willing to stay on one job:

> one works manager put the difference between male and female labour in this way. 'If you put a man on the same job for 10 days he comes to you and wants to strike. If you put a woman on another job to that which she is used to she weeps.' Herein lies the value of the woman worker. She prefers to remain at one machine and does not tire of the work.[111]

Both the above passages were written quite early in the war, but praise for women's performance on repetition work remained constant, and obviously this affected the prospects of women in engineering rather than any other trade. Only in engineering were so many processes fully adapted for women and major technological progress made: here women were employed on light, fairly monotonous work, and it was possible that they would be retained after the war on similar work. As long as the really skilled jobs remained men's it was unlikely that the male unions would object too much to the use of women on repetition work. Employers welcomed the idea of keeping women on such processes. It was all the better that this kind of work, which need not (could not) be taken too seriously by women — since it led to nothing with more skill or responsibility — would not disturb the existing and accepted patterns of work and marriage, and would not merit higher wages; as a writer for *Machinery Market* said smugly, near the end of the war:

> The feeling of the working man has always been the honorable one of desiring to support his wife without requiring her to earn; and marriage has always been, and, we trust, will always be, a reason for discontinuance of factory life by women.[112]

Much was made of the importance of the family by many employers who gave interviews to the press, trade journals and investigators, even while women were criticised for their lack of ambition and poor time-keeping, both of which were acknowledged to be due to domestic commitments in many cases. One employer, a representative of the Yorkshire and Lancashire Manufacturers, who gave evidence to the Committee on Women in Industry, said:

> There is one experience we have about the employment of women, and this particularly relates to piece-work as distinct from time-work. They stay away more for what are from the point of view of the employer trivial reasons. A day's washing may be a very serious thing for a woman, but to stay away and leave her machine idle for a day's wash does not appear to be anything but trivial to her employer.[113]

No woman on piece work would lightly have missed a day's work and wages: if it were possible to have had washing done any other way women would gladly have given up the pleasure of hours over a wash tub and ironing board and concentrated on paid factory work rather than unpaid domestic duties.[114] The degree of women's overwork as they attempted to cope with housework and factory work is revealed by the above quotation – but the employer did not realise it. Nor did he wonder what would happen if women did *not* do the washing; clean clothes were a symbol of good motherhood to many, and there were plenty of people ready to accuse women of going out to work instead of looking after their families properly. The romantic idea of full-time wives and mothers, upheld by employers as well as the rest of society, did not fit in well with the practical realities of combining outside work and housework. At the same time employers claimed that they were paid lower wages at least partly because of their lack of commitment to industrial work.

The prospects for women workers after the war were not bright, given the lack of enthusiasm amongst many employers and the opposition of some of the most powerful sections of the trade union movement. Most employers were prepared to welcome back men to 'men's jobs' with open arms; women were seen as being entirely acceptable as longer-term replacements only in some light industrial work, offices and shops. In all these they could continue to be low-paid, unskilled or semi-skilled workers, who required little training and could leave on marriage.

The skilled unions were leaving nothing to chance, and were determined to ensure that women in their trades were strictly temporary, although only the ASE had a government promise in writing. The general labour unions talked bravely of helping women, but how many of their male members really thought that women's prospects were of top priority? – unless they adversely affected men, of course. Men in such unions had their own problems, and their own prejudices about married women working. Even the NFWW, which fought for better wages and conditions for women workers, had made a pact with the ASE guaranteeing women's departure from men's work after the war: in addition, it had leaders who retained romantic ideals of woman's role and the importance of motherhood, as will be seen in Chapter 5.

Thus the majority of employers and unions continued to believe that unmarried women were less skilled, efficient, ambitious and trainable than men, and that married women did not really belong in industry in peacetime; they were all classed as being cheap and docile labour. Most working men were completely blind to the fact that women would cease to be potential blacklegs, and might learn to be skilled and interested workers, if they were accepted on equal terms and were liberated from their role as men's unpaid houseservants and industry's blacklegs.

In spite of all the conflicts between capital and labour, and the role women played as pawns between the two sides, it should be recognised that men of all classes *shared* prejudices about women's role and capabilities. Men showed contempt for women workers, as the women themselves often noticed, and Barbara Drake noted the words of one man which summed up prevailing feelings: '"I have to bear with a woman for 12 hours a day and I will not bear with women for 24," an aggrieved tradesman declares, and his view forms one point of sympathy between himself and his employer.'[115] Women workers were on the other side of that sexual barrier, and male workers largely failed to realise how they were playing into employers' hands by accepting the sexual division of labour.

Notes

1. Beveridge Papers, III, 48, 'Report on the State of Employment in all Occupations in the U.K. in October 1917', Board of Trade typescript.
2. A.W. Kirkaldy, *Industry and Finance*, vol. II (Isaac Pitman, 1920), p. 33.
3. I.O. Andrews, *The Economic Effects of the World War upon Women and Children in Great Britain* (Oxford University Press, 1921), Ch. IV; Report of the Standing Joint Committee of Industrial Women's Organisations on *The Position of Women after the War*.
4. Beveridge Papers, III, 48.
5. Barbara Drake, *Women in the Engineering Trades* (Fabian Research Department, 1917); Branco Pribicevik, *The Shop Stewards' Movement and Workers' Control* (Blackwell, 1959) esp. p. 48.
6. Drake, *Women in the Engineering Trades*; BAAS, *Outlets for Labour after the War* (1915); G.D.H. Cole, *Trade Unionism and Munitions* (Clarendon Press, 1923), Ch. III; J. Hinton, *The First Shop Stewards' Movement* (Allen & Unwin,

1973), Ch. II; Kirkaldy, *Industry and Finance*, vol. I; The *Engineer*, 30 Mar. 1917, 'Women Mechanics'; The *Engineer*, 20 Aug. 1915, 'The Employment of Women in Engineering Workshops'.

7. Hinton, *First Shop Stewards' Movement*, Ch. II.

8. Kirkaldy, *Industry and Finance*, vol. II, section III.

9. The *Engineer*, 11 Dec. 1916, 'Women in Workshops'. See also the discussion of this matter in Marion Kozak's thesis, 'Women Munition Workers during the First World War, With Special Reference to Engineering', PhD thesis, University of Hull.

10. Kirkaldy, *Industry and Finance*, vol. II, section III; Ministry of Reconstruction, Majority Report on *Women in Industry*, section on clothing and boot and shoe trades.

11. BAAS, *Outlets for Labour*, Ch. V; Majority Report on *Women in Industry*, section on textiles.

12. BAAS, *Outlets for Labour*; Majority Report on *Women in Industry*; Kirkaldy, *Industry and Finance*; Andrews, *Effects of the War*; Pribicevic, *The Shop Stewards' Movement*.

13. See note 12.

14. The attitude of the press will be discussed in Chapter 6, but, to give one example, the *Women's Dreadnought*, 20 Nov. 1915, drew attention to an article in *The Times* which stated that women on the lathe, in engineering, were turning out 150 per shift from their machines instead of the 30 previously produced by men. The whole matter of the nature of 'skill' is one which I cannot discuss here, but it is worthy of consideration. What is 'skilled work'? Why have women doing complex and difficult work in, say, millinery, or knitting, not been classed as 'skilled workers'? It has always been up to powerful unions to make sure that certain work remains defined as skilled, and that higher rates are paid accordingly. In this book, when I refer to 'skilled' or 'unskilled' work I am using conventional contemporary terminology, not making value judgements.

15. Kirkaldy, *Industry and Finance*, vol. II, p. 13.

16. The *Engineer*, 22 Mar. 1918, Report on the Institute of Mechanical Engineers' meeting.

17. Chief descriptions of women's work and performance appear in the following: BAAS, *Outlets for Labour*; Hammond, *British Labor Conditions and Legislation During the War* (Oxford University Press, 1919) – which specifically states that women were held back by lack of training and by prejudices; Kirkaldy, *Industry and Finance*, volumes I & II; Drake, *Women in the Engineering Trades*; Ministry of Reconstruction, *Women in Industry*.

18. BAAS, *Outlets for Labour*, p. 12.

19. A.W. Kirkaldy, *British Labour 1914-1921* (Isaac Pitman, 1921).

20. Hall Caine, *Our Girls* (Hutchinson, 1917), p. 46.

21. *Daily Mail*, 23 June 1916, 'Will Woman lose her Balance?'

22. For example, see Mrs Fawcett, in W.A. Dawson, *After War Problems* (Allen & Unwin, 1919), Ch. XII; 'With every disposition to recognise – nay, warmly to appreciate – the absolutely indispensible service of Trade Unions, their admirers must face the fact that in the matter of their attitude to women's labour they have taken the wrong turnings and have been responsible for a great deal of the misery and degradation of the sweated woman' (p. 198).

23. Sheila Lewenhak, *Women and Trade Unions* (Benn, 1977), Ch. X. See also article on the NUR in the *Liverpool Post*, 24 June 1917, 'The Nation and its Labour'.

24. Richard Hyman, *The Workers Union* (Clarendon, 1971).

25. *Trade Union Worker*, January 1916, editorial notes.

26. See the *Socialist*, February 1916, 'Round the Yards', for the views of

David Kirkwood of the Clyde shop stewards at Parkhead; also John Muir in the *Worker*, 15 Jan. 1916, on Dilution: 'Its progressive character is lost to the community unless it is accompanied by a corresponding step in social evolution.'

27. *Socialist*, February 1916, front page article, which stated that industrial unionism was for all workers, black, white, male and female. See also *Socialist*, August 1916, 'To our Women Comrades'.

28. For descriptions, see Pribicevik, *The Shop Stewards' Movement*; Hinton, *The First Shop Stewards*; Cole, *Trade Unionism and Munitions*.

29. See page 73.

30. *Solidarity*, February 1917, p. 1, and *Trade Union Worker*, April 1918, editorial.

31. S. Higenbottom, *Our Society's History* (Amalgamated Society of Woodworkers, 1939); also article in *Evening News*, 15 Jan. 1917, 'Carpentry, a Man's Trade'.

32. The *Nation*, 3 Feb. 1917, letters.

33. Joan Williams, 'A Munition Worker's Career' (typescript); interviews made by the Imperial War Museum, London.

34. Naomi Loughnan in Gilbert Stone (ed.), *Women War Workers* (Harrap, 1917).

35. See *Trade Unionist*, November 1915, 'Engineers and the War': 'The unskilled, the semi-skilled and women will continue to be employed unless we, the organised workers, have the requisite power to demand that this shall not be the case.'

36. Drake, *Women in the Engineering Trades*.

37. Ibid., p. 61.

38. Kirkaldy, *Industry and Finance*, vol. II, p. 65.

39. See G.D.H. Cole, *Labour in Wartime* (Bell & Sons, 1915), p. 227: 'In every direction the coming of the war has had the effect of speeding up the process of industrial change; it has caused tendencies to become far more marked, and has turned into actualities what seemed only distant possibilities. This is the case more especially with regard to women's labour.'

40. Majority Report on *Women in Industry*, p. 27.

41. See, for example, a letter to the *Nation*, 19 May 1917: 'I have, for instance, heard of an employer who stated cynically that he would, of course, dismiss all the girls in his controlled establishment on the day peace was declared, but added that this would not prevent him from re-engaging them the next day at lower rates.'

42. Hinton, *The First Shop Stewards*, Ch. I.

43. *Solidarity*, April 1917, 'The Gathering Storm'.

44. After conscription was introduced, men who were exempt on the grounds of age or health, and invalided soldiers, were used as substitutes.

45. Cole, *Labour in Wartime*, p. 228.

46. Drake, *Women in the Engineering Trades*, p. 117.

47. Lewenhak, *Women and Trade Unions*, Ch. X.

48. Drake, *Women in the Engineering Trades*, p. 92.

49. Loughnan in Stone, *Women War Workers*, p. 36.

50. *New Age*, 5 Aug. 1915, 'Women in Industry'. See also, by the same author, 'Women in Industry Again', 25 Nov. 1915, and a letter from Gladys Biss, 26 Aug. 1915.

51. *Manchester Evening Chronicle*, 26 Mar. 1915, 'Not for Women'.

52. *Preston Herald*, 18 Dec. 1915, 'Female Labour'.

53. *Lancashire Post*, 25 July 1916.

54. *Manchester Dispatch*, 12 May 1917, 'Women in the Mule Rooms'.

55. Other articles on the subject were: *Northern Daily Telegraph*, 7 Mar. 1916,

'Blackburn Spinners Refuse Employers' Request'; *Manchester Guardian*, 7 Feb. 1917, 'Cotton Trade'; *Textile Mercury*, 23 Dec. 1916, 'Rochdale Spinners and Women Workers'; *Textile Mercury*, 19 May 1917, 'Women Cotton Piecers'; *Cotton Factory Times*, 29 Oct. 1915, 'Females in the Mule Room'; *Manchester Evening News*, 27 Nov. 1915, 'Female Labour'; *Manchester Daily Dispatch*, 22 May 1916, 'To Keep the Looms Going'. Obviously there was an underlying fear that women might be used in peacetime, as they were in ring spinning.

56. *Yorkshire Evening Post*, 15 Jan. 1916, 'Employment of Women at the Collieries'.

57. *Common Cause*, 30 June 1916, 'Women as Tramway Workers'.

58. Ben Smith at the TUC, 1916, p. 302 in bound copy of the conference report.

59. ASE *Monthly Journal*, report of Division 6, Halifax.

60. *Trade Unionist*, April 1916, 'Exit Women Dockers'; *Everyman*, 24 Mar. 1916, 'Women as Transport Workers'. All women were dismissed from Liverpool Docks by 20 Mar. 1916. It has been pointed out by Noelle Whiteside that the dockers had only just won their battle to decasualise the industry, and thus were sensitive about any attempts by employers to alter the system of employment they had won. But the fact remains that women were *automatically* classed as being undesirable working companions. They had no chance to prove their class loyalty. In addition, the language of the dockers' protest is important: economic considerations were mixed with arguments about women's health and the suitability of labouring jobs, with seeming disregard for the differences between these approaches. This is typical of the response to women in many trades.

61. See, for example, *Manchester Guardian*, 21 July 1915, 'Women and Railway Work'. Mr J.H. Thomas of the NUR, in what seems to be a reply to the kind of sentiments expressed in *New Age*, said: 'if there are any people who assert – as has already been suggested in a very limited quarter – that we ought to refuse to work with women labour, let me beg them not to follow any such course of action.'

62. *Solidarity*, March 1917.

63. In 1918, the figures for women were as follows: WU, 80,000; NUGW, 60,000; NFWW, 76,000 (Norbert C. Solden, *Women in British Trade Unions* (Gill & Macmillan, 1978), p. 85).

64. *Woman's Dreadnought*, 10 Apr. 1915, 'The Tin Box Trade': the appropriate trade board set a minimum of 14s 1d for a 52-hour week for women over 18; *Woman's Dreadnought*, 24 Apr. 1915, 'Sweating in Khaki Work still Continues'; *Woman's Dreadnought*, 19 June 1915, 'Legalised Sweating': trade boards fixed the minimum for workers in sugar, confectionery and food preserving at 13s a week for women and 26s for men; *Woman's Dreadnought*, 13 Nov. 1915: at Bryant and May's the highest earnable wage was admitted by the firm to be 19s 11d; *Northern Whig*, 14 Dec. 1915, 'Women Workers in Springfield Mill': wages at this Belfast cotton mill were 10s 6d for a 55½ hour week; Sylvia Pankhurst, *The Home Front* (Hutchinson, 1932), p. 91: women making kitbags and military uniforms were paid 25% less than the minimum of 3½d an hour set by the clothing trade board; discussion of the low rates in aircraft trades, p. 340; *Common Cause*, 24 Sept. 1915, 'Girls' Work on Khaki'; *Common Cause*, 17 Mar. 1916, 'More Girls' Work on Khaki'; *Woman Worker*, March 1917, editorial.

65. War emergency: Workers' National Committee Papers, letter from James Laing to J.S. Middleton; *Woman Worker*, April 1916: 'the Guardians also strongly object to supplementing inadequate wages by grants from the rates', p. 5.

66. The Workers' Union, for example, made an agreement with the Midland Employers' Federation in November 1915, guaranteeing 18s a week (for 54 hours) for women in the area over 21. This was condemned by many as being too low.

67. *Woman's Dreadnought*, 17 July 1915, 'Sweating of Women in War Service': in the GPO women were receiving less than men, and only half their war bonus; *Woman's Dreadnought*, 7 Aug. 1915, carries a list of firms paying women less than men; *Woman's Dreadnought*, 8 Jan. 1916, 'Sweating by Order': the case of one particular woman was quoted by the secretary of the Railway Clerks' Association; she was doing her husband's job while he was away fighting; he had received £90 a year, she received £26. Postwomen were giving up their jobs because they were getting 25s a week while men had 35s; TUC 1916: the government introduced women to its offices on 18-21s a week, instead of the 35s it paid to men. Mrs Williams of the NFWW claimed that on some jobs men and women were working beside each other for respectively 7d and 2¾d an hour. The Standing Joint Committee of Industrial Women's Organisations noted the correlation of strong unions and better rates of pay.

68. *Common Cause*, 16 Feb. 1917, quoting the committee.

69. M.A. Hamilton, *Mary Macarthur* (Parsons, 1924), p. 161.

70. Sylvia Pankhurst, *The Home Front*, p. 346. See also *Woman's Dreadnought*, 3 Apr. 1915, 'We Demand Equal Pay for Equal Work'.

71. Drake, *Women in the Engineering Trades*, p. 56.

72. Ibid., p. 20.

73. Material on women munition workers' wages: *Woman's Dreadnought*, 12 Feb. 1916, 'The Growth of the Slave State'; *Daily Chronicle*, 16 Mar. 1916, 'Sweated Women': Margaret Bondfield reported one factory where women were making hand grenades at 2¼d an hour; *Common Cause*, 1 Sept. 1916, 'Wages of Women Munition Workers': Mary Macarthur reported that there was no sign of women earning over £2 a week in Manchester and Salford; *Daily News*, 5 Jan. 1917, 'Munition Girls' Pay'; *Daily News*, 12 Sept. 1918, 'Munition Girls' Pay'; *Woman Worker*, March 1917, editorial; *Woman Worker*, March 1918, 'Who shall be Master?'; S.J. Chapman (ed.), *Labour and Capital after the War* (Murray, 1918), chapter by Susan Lawrence; Monica Cosens, *Lloyd George's Munition Girls* (Hutchinson, 1916), Ch. IV on the Premium Bonus System.

74. The *Socialist*, August 1916, 'To Our Women Comrades'.

75. Williams, 'A Munition Worker's Career'.

76. Thomas, Elsa: oral history interview 676/08; Imperial War Museum, London.

77. ASE *Monthly Journal and Report*, August 1915, report from Division 7.

78. *Trade Union Worker*, June 1916, 'The Least of These'.

79. E.g. *Trade Union Worker*, June 1916, 'The Least of These'.

80. E.g. *Socialist Review*, January-March 1918, 'Equal Pay for Equal Work', although the writer ultimately comes to the conclusion that it would be easier if women stayed at home.

81. Revolutionising women's industrial position would have necessitated changes in men's domestic and work role as well: this was too much for many men to consider.

82. *Solidarity*, January 1918, 'Women Workers Make a Stand'. See also the comments of the men interviewed by the Imperial War Museum, including those of one man who described how he supported the strikes by skilled men, but not those of the 'cartridge girls'. The divisions amongst the women themselves complicated things further. The welders were from a different class, and had little in common with working-class women.

83. *Woman's Dreadnought*, 19 June 1915, 'Women and the Grocers'.

84. *National News*, 18 Aug. 1918, 'Women's Strike Begins'; *Solidarity*, September 1918, 'Equal Pay for Equal Work'.

85. *Women's Industrial News*, April 1917, 'A Promise and its Fulfilment'.

86. *Aberdeen Journal*, 12 Sept. 1916, letter from 'Considerate'.

87. *Trade Union Worker*, April 1916, 'Pin Money'; *Trade Union Worker*, January 1917, letter from F. Palmer, who could not explain the reason for this resentment himself.

88. *Women's Industrial News*, April 1917, 'A Promise and its Fulfilment'.

89. E.g. *Times Engineering Supplement*, June 1915, 'The Production of Munitions'.

90. Cole, *Trade Unionism and Munitions*, p. 217.

91. Typescript of Miss Clapham, of the Board of Trade, 2 Dec. 1916, *Note on Substituting Woman and its future Extension in Connection with the Utilising of Manpower*, Bev., IV, 9.

92. Anonymous typescript, 'Dilution', written post-war, undated. Bev., IV, 9.

93. The *Engineer*, 26 Feb. 1915, 'The Government and the Dearth of Labour'.

94. The *Engineer*, 20 Aug. 1915, 'The Employment of Women in Engineering Workshops'.

95. The *Engineer*, 3 Sept. 1915, 'The Employment of Women as Machinists'.

96. See page 76.

97. The *Engineer*, 11 Feb. 1916, 'The Employment of Women on Munitions of War'; and the editorial 'Women in Workshops'; *Engineer*, 5 Jan. 1917, 'The Engineering Industry in 1916'; *Engineer*, 30 Mar. 1917, 'Women Mechanics'.

98. The *Engineer*, 1 Oct. 1915, 'Women's Wages and Apprenticeship'.

99. This article was recalled by the ASE *Monthly Journal and Report* in January 1917, 'The Coming Slavery'.

100. The *Engineer*, 8 Oct. 1915, letters.

101. The *Engineer*, 30 Mar. 1917, 'Skilled Women Mechanics'.

102. Fawcett Library Collection: Letter from Women's Service Bureau to John Murray, Ministry of Munitions, 26 May 1917.

103. Drake, *Women in the Engineering Trades*, p. 19.

104. Majority Report on *Women in Industry*, Ch. III.

105. The *Engineer*, 22 Mar. 1918, report on the Institute of Mechanical Engineers.

106. *Labour Woman*, November 1918, 'Women's Wages'.

107. *Westminster Gazette*, 28 Jan. 1919, 'Women and Wages'.

108. Kirkaldy, *Industry and Finance*, vol. II, p. 54; see also pp. 17 and 38; Cole, *Trade Unionism and Munitions*, BAAS, *Outlets for Labour*, Chs. III, IV.

109. *Dundee Advertiser*, 21 Nov. 1916, 'Women Bakers a Success in Fife'.

110. The *Scotsman*, 12 Nov. 1915, 'The Development of Munitionmaking'.

111. *Liverpool Daily Post and Mercury*, 11 Nov. 1915, 'Women War Workers'.

112. *Machinery Market*, July 1918, 'Trade after the War'.

113. Majority Report on *Women in Industry*, Mr G.H. Wood, p. 90.

114. This is shown by the fact that many women were prepared to pay money for childminding, laundry and prepared food when they went out to work, even though their earnings after such deductions were considerably lower.

115. Drake, *Women in the Engineering Trades*.

Women can be seen, and were seen, as pawns in the battle between capital and labour; they were important to the arguments of each in the fields of scientific management, efficiency of workers, craft status and wages. However, those people who actually worked in industry were not the only ones interested in women's wartime role in the labour market. There had existed extensive interest in women workers, both married and single, and their relation to their jobs and fellow workmen before the war; this interest could only increase once women flooded into wartime industries and began to exhibit skills and enthusiasm few had suspected.

While observers outside industry, whether individuals (socialists, feminists, social surveyors, eugenicists) or representatives of official bodies (e.g. the Factory Inspectorate, the War Cabinet Committee on Women in Industry), did not wield such direct power over the wartime position and prospects of women workers as the Ministry of Munitions, factory owners and trade unionists, their views still need to be considered. They are interesting in their own right, and in addition they encouraged public debate about the issues raised by women's labour, through books, reports and articles in the press. The range of the arguments and the nature of the approach towards 'the problems of women's labour' both reveal much about society's concern with women workers during the war, and also show how widely certain views were held. It becomes clear that the dominant concern was not simply with women's industrial skills, but first with men's and women's wages, and the significance of equal pay, and secondly with women's post-war industrial prospects and social role (which will be discussed later in this book).

It was frequently in the interest of either employers or unions to denigrate women's industrial capabilities — the previous chapter has shown how many men from both sides remained prejudiced against the idea of women doing 'men's work', resented them performing any but the most simple operations, and refused to believe that they might become interested in their work. The majority of women's observers outside industry did not find it so difficult to accept that women could, if given the chance, perform more difficult work, and develop enthusiasm

96

and ambition. Such observers were not threatened with the potential dangers of women's labour as workmen were, nor confronted with the problems of the employers, including the dilemma of whether or not to train women and how much to spend on extra facilities. For the most part, therefore, the extent of women's wartime skill was not a matter with which the various surveyors and reporters concerned themselves: it was readily accepted that women were doing much of the work well, and that they could probably do even better if given full training and better working conditions.[1] The only problem in this field was that the press and government would exaggerate the extent of women's new-found talents, a fact that the suffragist paper *Common Cause* recognised, in spite of its unrestrained glee that at last press and politicians were taking women more seriously: 'To underestimate women's work would be an injustice; to overestimate it would do almost more harm in fighting the other interested parties, the employers and the men.'[2] The feminists were understandably interested in women's success and their developing capabilities. Women were entering areas of work which only the war could have opened for them and both suffragettes and suffragists were only too pleased to report their achievements, and repeat the praise of those who had hitherto been anti-feminist; they also castigated the government for not using women more efficiently.[3]

The majority of individuals and government bodies investigating women's work, however, did not spend much time dwelling on the extent of women's success (with the exception of the Ministry of Munitions, which had propaganda to produce); they described the work which was being done, praised women's efforts, and then moved on to the important matter of the problems posed by women's extensive entry into industry, the major one being the effect women were already having on wages, and might have in the future.

The reasons for the unions' distrust of women have already been described, and the issues discussed in the context of industrial relations. However, such concern was shared not only by trade unionists but by many other sections of society. There was a strong feeling that women should not be allowed to pull down men's wages, a feeling shared by many men (and many women) of all classes, as it must be remembered that middle-class women were entering professional and clerical spheres of work as well, and theoretically men in many occupations were threatened by displacement. But the ambiguities which expressed themselves in the arguments of male trade unionists ran throughout society, and women's wages were recognised to be a complex issue, and perhaps the root of the 'problem of women's labour'. The state set up the machinery for the promotion of equal pay in some fields in order to protect the position of skilled men, but it ignored the matter in other areas of employment; the Special Arbitration Tribunals preferred to evade the issue, although they dealt with many women replacing men;[4] war bonuses were always higher for men; and trade boards, the arbiters of wages for the low-paid, staunchly upheld the idea that no matter how low wages were, women should have less than men.

Generally, the demand for equal pay was designed to safeguard men's jobs and wages, not to offer justice to women. But when one examines the widespread debates about equal pay one finds a number of different approaches and motives amongst its proponents and enemies; in addition, ambiguities were evident in the arguments, ambiguities of the kind already noted in the words of trade unionists, their origins lying in current ideas about women's role. Equal pay was supported and opposed by both feminists and anti-feminists; it could be put forward as a progressive demand, or one which was designed to maintain the *status quo* in industry; it was seen by some as benefiting women, and others as hindering them; it was also a matter which would affect the future as well as the present, for both sexes. The arguments surrounding it reveal clearly the way different people and groups saw women's part in industry, and those for and against it cannot neatly be divided into those who were for and against women's rights.

The problem of women's wages was all too easy to establish, and has been described already; before the war and from 1914 women were invariably paid less than men, even on similar work. This fact had long been recognised and analysed, and during the war there was further discussion of the reasons for this discrimination. Many of the writers of the time reiterated the reasons for women's low industrial and financial status: they were generally poorly trained, uninterested in careers, wanted temporary work which could be left on marriage. But from these recognised and accepted facts different writers took up different points, and disagreed about solutions. Eleanor Rathbone, of the Labour Party, assumed that women were intrinsically worth less to employers, and this was one of the major barriers to equal pay — Mrs Fawcett of the NUWSS strongly disagreed.[5] *Labour Woman* brought up the matter of the position of dependent wives of working men, and *their* feelings about equal pay and the existence of women in men's trades: '[they] will have to consider how far the presence of female labour, with all its traditions of low wages and weak organisation, will mean the lowering of the whole standard of life for the working people.'[6] H. Stanley Redgrove, of the *Socialist Review*, decided that equal pay was an impossibility unless society was changed, men's and women's responsibilities were brought into line, and such responsibilities were shared; this would, he added, make women reluctant to leave work on marriage, and so lead to a falling birth rate.[7] *The Observer* discussed the 'dilemma of the work-man', who could not deny the right of *unmarried* women to share in the labour market, yet feared for his job. Theoretically the answer lay in equal pay, but what was equal work?[8] This problem was taken up by many others, including the writers of the British Association's Interim Report on 'Outlets for Labour After the War', who pointed out that employers always made excuses about women's work being different from men's, and considered that defining equal work would be a major difficulty.[9] The TUC and the War Emergency Workers' National Committee, which accepted the principle of equal pay, also recognised the problem of definition,[10] and Beatrice Webb went so far as to condemn the slogan 'equal pay for equal work' as a meaningless catch-phrase.[11] She was not the only one to have doubts about the bandying of such words, and few feminists believed that women's position would be transformed by the acceptance of this principle alone — some thought it would make matters worse, and lead to women's exclusion from further trades, and even those who did support the concept pointed out that pay was simply a part of the problem women faced as workers. More was needed, as the Family Endowment Committee (an offshoot of the Labour Party) stated:

> To tell a woman that she shall have equal pay, whenever she is allowed to do a man's work, is a mockery if at the same time the doors of all the upper rooms in the house of industry are closed against her. Her battle is only beginning, as long as all the more exclusive crafts, from barristers to compositors, refuse to admit her to their privileges.[12]

Nor did feminist writers forget to point out that the existing wages structure was *not* based upon economics alone — women were paid less because most of them were classed as dependants and subsidiary workers,[13] regardless of their personal financial hardship; they were paid less because, in fact, they were women,[14] and there were psychological and social reasons behind this, as well as economic ones.

Yet equal pay was a much discussed subject during the war, judging by the space papers, books and reports devoted to it, and one which was seen as a vital part of discussions of the future. The government itself recognised the widespread concern with wage rates when it set up the War Cabinet Committee on Women in Industry, which was appointed

to investigate and report on the relation which should be maintained
between the wages of women and men having regard to the interests
of both as well as to the value of their work. The recommendations
should have in view the necessity of output during the war, and the
progress and well-being of industry in the future.[15]

It is also significant that the Committee tied itself in knots with the
problem posed, as will be seen later, and that eventually Majority and
Minority Reports were produced, the latter being the work of Beatrice
Webb alone.

But to many, the achievement of equal pay, at least in theory, would
have been symbolic: it would have necessitated changes in society, and
could have gone hand in hand with greater economic independence for
women, particularly if connected with schemes for 'family endowment'
or 'mothers' pensions'. Pay, after all, affected women's own view of
themselves in a society where earning capacity was linked with status.
This aspect was raised by writers of *Equal Pay and the Family*:

> Few of us realise how constantly and subtly this half-conscious, but
> ever present sense of the economic dependence of the woman upon
> the man corrodes her personality, checks her development, and
> stunts her mind, even while she is still a girl, with marriage as yet in
> prospect.[16]

The psychology of dependence is clearly important, and many questions
asked by feminists then can be asked now: does women's low pay lie at
the heart of their oppression, or does it simply reflect their low status?
Could women's status be improved by the implementation of equal pay
for equal work? Does equal pay mean anything at all without increased
opportunities for employment? How much does pay matter, compared
with the problems of work in general, childbearing, housework and
looking after husbands?

Unfortunately, as we have seen, the demand for equal pay was not
necessarily progressive in itself, and even amongst those who spoke up
for it on the grounds that it would aid *women* there was not necessarily
a desire to radicalise women's overall position in society. The only way
to appreciate the range of opinions on this subject is to work through
the views of some of those who discussed the matter at the time. This
method is unavoidably piecemeal and sketchy, but it does give some
idea of the variety of approach, and point to certain underlying assumptions about women's role.

Few outside the male trade union movement pressed for equal pay solely for the benefit of men, or admitted frankly that they supported the idea because employers would favour men if women workers were not cheaper.[17] Generally, the matter was rather discussed as one of 'justice' for both men and women: equal pay would safeguard the jobs of those men who had joined the army,[18] keep secure the position of the skilled workman, and ensure that women doing equivalent work obtained suitable reward, also eliminating the financial advantage unmarried men had over women with dependants.[19] When it was seen in such terms it was frequently linked with suggestions for improving the financial position of parents, since justice did not allow that married men should find themselves worse off than single women. The ideal, therefore, in the short term, was that women doing men's work should be guaranteed equal pay, and men should be able to return to their jobs without fear, while in future, if women stayed on in such work, the sexes could work together without blacklegging by women. At the same time there were plans for fathers to get extra tax allowances or other cash benefits, or for women to be paid special pensions to enable them to stay at home and look after the children without financial worries. Both these schemes were for the long term and were designed to remove the classic excuse for paying men more money than women, as they would no longer be classed as the sole family breadwinners.[20]

This may sound quite straightforward, but in fact there were considerable differences of opinion and motivation behind various schemes. To begin with, 'equal pay for equal work' as demanded would only help women in so-called men's work, not those in the classic female trades, hence Margaret Bondfield's call for £1 a week minimum for women to start off with, and the implementation of equal pay when it was possible.[21] In addition, equal pay would certainly safeguard men's jobs, but it would not help the women who were displaced after the war as a result: what of 'justice' for them? Many people who joined in the call for equal pay ignored this aspect, but as the War Emergency Workers' National Committee pointed out, there had to be unionisation, training and state maintenance of women undergoing training, if they were to have some chance of improving their position permanently and making use of pay legislation.[22]

Equally, there was a world of difference between suggesting, as some did, that married men should have tax allowances or other benefits,[23] and the idea of married women receiving pensions or child allowances. The former, in conjunction with equal pay, would obviously have been an improvement over the usual idea that all men needed more money than all women, but it still maintained the concept of women and children being the dependants of men. The latter, however, encompassed the idea that mothers should be able to achieve some independence from their husbands, and that the state should share part of the financial burden of child-rearing. Such allowances could, of course, increase women's self-respect — as the Family Endowment Committee suggested — and eliminate the idea of mothers being inferior, dependent creatures because of their childbearing capacity and their subsequent withdrawal from the labour market. On the other hand, they might bolster up the idea that women were automatically responsible for children, and that fathers need have little to do with them. In this context it is important to note that the Family Endowment Committee stated quite frankly that it believed that mothers' pensions would mean the withdrawal of women with children under five from the labour market.

The connection between demands for equal pay, family endowment and the ideal of non-working mothers should not be ignored. Those who entered *Labour Woman*'s essay competition on 'What is your opinion as to the Proposal to Prohibit Married Women's Work' automatically recognised the association. Although one winner, M.P. Cudworth, suggested that men's wages be raised to enable them to support wives and children better, another, Miss S.R. Perkins, pressed for the endowment of motherhood:

> so that mothers can devote themselves to their children. No creches, etc., can make up to children for the mother's love. Whatever a childless woman may do for the community is nothing to the service rendered by her who gives it healthy and good children.[24]

Miss Ida Smith too claimed that if the state supported mothers they would withdraw themselves from work. Family endowment could therefore be used to persuade married women to stay in the home, and although theoretically it could have been campaigned for in isolation, in fact such demands usually went hand in hand with those for equal pay.

Eleanor Rathbone's position on this subject is particularly interesting, as she falls between the pro- and anti-equal pay factions. The leading light of the Family Endowment Committee, she did support the Labour Party's views on the principle of equal pay for equal work (she wrote a letter on this subject to *The Times* in August 1918), nevertheless she also stated her belief that since it was so difficult to bring men and women into line in industry, given their differing backgrounds and duties, it might be better to allow women to continue in their existing poor position at work, and improve their status through family endowment *after they were married and had left work*. She wrote, in 1917:

> The one thing that might conceivably reconcile the woman worker to a continuance of the present limitation upon her industrial opportunities, to meagre earnings and to monotonous work, would be the belief that her sacrifice was a necessary part of a social system upon which the maintenance of family life, the welfare of future generations, depended. For, after all, the majority of women workers are only birds of passage in their trades. Marriage and rearing of children are their permanent occupations.[25]

Eleanor Rathbone was supposedly a feminist, yet she still found it possible to accept the economic and social *status quo*, while pressing for financial help for mothers. Similar views were put forward by H. Stanley Redgrove, in an article already cited;[26] the idea was that equal pay should be the norm where women were doing 'men's work', and the state should recompense women for staying at home to look after children — thus men's jobs would be safeguarded, and women would be encouraged to devote themselves to the bearing and rearing of children.

But, at the same time, equal pay and family endowment were being pressed for by groups and individuals who were convinced that women's overall position would be improved by such reforms. *Common Cause* believed the two would safeguard both men and women,[27] while others decided that equal pay would lead to a revolution in the labour world, giving the women the right to work,[28] and that equal pay was the only thing which would allow men and women to work peacefully, side by side, without the usual antagonism.[29] Yet all these ideas were mingled in the minds of many with feelings about ideal motherhood and family life. H. Brailsford wrote in the *Daily Herald* in 1918 about the way in which schemes for extra money for married men with dependants ignored the status of the woman: 'Her service to society in making a home and rearing children remains unrecognised. She is still the unchartered servant of the future, who receives from her husband at his discretion, a share in his wages.'[30]

This was true, but Brailsford was reluctant to consider whether it was desirable for women to be confined to the home after marriage, however appreciated their work might be in an ideal society; he, like so many others, assumed that women were the natural servicers and nurturers of society. They were the mothers of the race, and equal pay plus family endowment could simply be seen as making them healthier happier mothers, who had gained good wages before marriage, *if they happened to be working on men's jobs*, and who retired to live on state pensions quite contentedly once children arrived. The words of Eleanor Rathbone in her letter to *The Times* should be born in mind.[31] Family endowment would remove excuses for unequal pay, she wrote, and

> it would put an end to the increasing practice among all the more thrifty and farsighted parents of deliberately limiting the number of children, while the slum dwellers and mentally unfit continue to breed like rabbits, so that the national stock is recruited in increasing proportions from its least fit elements.

The concern for the health of the race emerged in many arguments, equal pay amongst them, and was linked with the idea that 'fit' women should be happy to bring more children into the world if there were no financial disadvantages. It did not appear to occur to Rathbone at this time that contraception might be practised for reasons other than those of economy. Nor, twenty years after Charles Booth's survey of London had shown that poverty was not the result of idleness, viciousness or stupidity, did she see 'slum dwellers' in any but these terms, when it came to the matter of childbearing.

Amongst those who opposed the concept of equal pay there were some who believed it would be harmful to women economically — although such an attitude was hardly conducive to women's best interests either. The Committee of Economists which wrote a report on the 'Probable State of Industry After the War' decided that it was not really fair that women in men's industries should earn so much more than those in the female dominated industries, and also that women's advantage in industry would be taken away if equal pay were enforced:

> If they are not allowed to work cheaper in industries in which they can do it cheaper and yet make higher earnings than are open to them elsewhere, the most powerful lever for increasing the industrial opportunities of women will be taken away.[32]

This may have been a depressing view, but it was a realistic one, and the writers at least showed some interest in women's position in industry. For the most part, the opponents of equal pay showed no regard for women, and based their views on the idea that men deserved more money. The reasons given were all the traditional ones, well known before the war, and were frequently used to oppose family endowment as well. Typically, women's 'needs' and their 'worth' were dealt with together: it was said that women did not 'need' so much money, since their 'standard of living' was lower (this was never actually confirmed and seemed to be based solely on the fact that some kind of average woman ate less than an average man), and at the same time they were 'worth' less, as workers, in industry. Such claims were given the support of pseudo-science; thus a reporter for the *Spectator* wrote that at first sight demands for equal pay seemed reasonable — 'But it is notorious that in all classes the necessary minimum for a woman differs on average from the necessary minimum for a man.'[33] The social-scientific terms were there, but not the facts.

The idea that female workers were less useful to employers could not be eliminated, and it was inescapably bound up in the minds of many with the idea that they could always live on less money,[34] even though strictly speaking the two had no connection. Equal pay would not be *fair*, ran the argument. 'Are the wives and children of working men to be maintained, or rather starved, on wages which provide a luxurious plenty for the single woman?'[35] demanded an indignant correspondent to the *Manchester Dispatch*, immediately assuming that men's wages would go down rather than women's up, that all women workers were single, and that in some way the whole equal pay debate was women's fault. In the meantime a writer to *The Times* insisted that there were natural inequalities in the wages system and that women were demanding something exceptional if they wanted equal pay. In any case, he continued, women did not *need* so much money as they had fewer dependants.[36]

Such claims were not altogether logical, as many of those in favour of equal pay pointed out; unmarried men were not paid less than married men, in spite of the difference in their financial responsibilities. However, they were given credence by Seebohm Rowntree's book, the *Human Needs of Labour*. In Chapter IV he analysed women's wages with the idea of finding out what women actually needed as subsistence wages, and whether they needed extra allowances for dependants, as men implicitly did. He looked at the following aspects: (1) the wages earned; (2) whether the women were married; (3) whether they lived at home or in lodgings; (4) whether both parents were living; (5) the father's trade or wage; (6) the mother's earnings if any; (7) wages and ages of other members of the family; (8) the house rent; (9) the money needed for board, lodging and laundry; (10) any other payments to parents or dependants. Rowntree came to the conclusion that the majority of women workers did not have dependants, and that those who did had them through accidents such as the death or illness of the main breadwinner. The answer, he claimed, was to provide for such circumstances through pensions, insurance and higher male wages; women's minimum wages should be fixed according to the needs of the single woman.[37] He considered that it was more important to set such a minimum wage than to gain equal pay.[38]

There are many criticisms one can make of Rowntree's survey. *Labour Woman* picked up one false assumption: his conviction that wages could be looked at in isolation from their social and economic effect upon both men and women.[39] But in addition, his findings can be criticised on the grounds that the survey itself was totally inadequate. A total of 516 women were investigated, and it was found that 83.3 per cent supported no dependants, and only 16.7 per cent partially or completely maintained others. But of these women 455 were single, 55 married and 6 widowed. Obviously, the majority of the single women were likely to be living with parents and did not have dependants, and thus the figures for the total number of women were heavily weighted from the start. Rowntree did not investigate how many women would have helped with finances had they earned higher wages, nor did he consider that York, being a non-industrial town, was likely to have a far lower proportion of married women working than many other areas.

But his survey said what many people wanted to hear, and gave a scientific veneer to the usual prejudices about women, work and wages; it fitted in with the strong feelings amongst all classes that men should support women, and that higher male wages were more important than equal pay or a form of family endowment.[40]

So far I have not discussed the views expressed by the government committees which looked into women's work and wages. They deserve a section on their own: partly because they are such wide-ranging documents, and partly because they encapsulate so neatly the dilemmas faced by those who attempted to solve the 'problem of women's employment' without appreciating the fact that women's industrial position would never be changed unless there was an alteration in their social role.

The War Cabinet Committee produced its majority report on *Women in Industry* in 1919, and in some ways its recommendations were far more radical than the government could or would consider. Its members suggested, amongst other things, that women should receive equal pay for equal work on similar jobs to men's where output was equivalent, and that this should include time rates; where jobs were subdivided, wages should be such that their cost to the employer did not drop, and if employers maintained that women's work was less efficient than men's, it was up to them to prove it. The government was urged to set an example with equal pay in its own departments as soon as possible. However, at the same time the Committee recommended that in *women's work* wages should be appropriate to the area, and to the food, clothes and transport needs of a *single woman of 18*. Thus the ideas that equal pay was for men's protection, and that women's wages were inherently less important, were maintained.

The report itself showed much sensitivity to the reasons for women's poor position in industry and their low wages, and members expressed their belief that although low pay had been tolerated in the past because women had not been independent, this state of affairs would now change.[41] They also noted that the single man did not need as much as the married man, nor did he need more than the average single woman (although, they added, the former might be saving up for marriage while the latter anticipated being supported), but in spite of this, there was no suggestion that single men should also be penalised for their lack of dependants, as women were, and they assumed that the wages for women's subsistence should be lower than those for men's. Brave words were spoken in favour of change, thus: 'Once it is admitted that an adult woman ought to receive an independent living wage in respect of her work, whether she is domestically independent or not, the old system becomes indefensible,'[42] but the Committee ultimately came back to the idea of patching up the existing system, and preserving the *status quo*, guaranteeing men's wages and helping women become good mothers. This may not seem surprising in view of the fact that this was a government Committee, not a group of feminists, but the members themselves felt that they were proposing radical changes:

> Allowances to widows and to women without husbands capable of supporting their children, payment in full of the cost of lying-in and the fixing of a subsistence wage to ensure adequate maintenance of all individual women in industry, should bring about that revolution in the position of these women which appears to be essential.[43]

Conditions for many women might have been improved by such measures, but little could have been 'revolutionised'. It is clear that the majority of the Committee members shared the beliefs of the Women's Employment Committee, which reported the same year, and which decided that the primary function of women in the State must be regarded: it is not enough not to interfere with her service in bearing children, and the care of infant life and health, but she must also be safeguarded as the home-maker for the nation.[44]

Similarly, this idea lay behind the views of many of those who campaigned for or against equal pay and family endowment. In the above words the Women's Employment Committee summed up the stated concern of the nation. The writers of this report, like those of *Women in Industry*, expressed sympathy for women workers, and were sensitive to the reasons for women's poor position in the labour market. They pressed for equal pay in order to preserve the standard of living of the working class; they also believed that since industrial work preceded marriage, women should be appropriately trained for it:

> The fact that a woman is trained to be a skilled worker is not only a gain to herself, but to the community, in that through the fuller development of her powers she attains a more complete sense of citizenship, and is a more valuable member of society, while, if she does not marry and has to return to work, she has the means to do so within her power.[45]

The adverse effects of the tradition of women giving up work on marriage were noted — limiting training opportunities and the possibility of good wages — *but* the Committee still stated that it hoped that every inducement would be made to keep married women at home with their children.

Thus we return to the convictions so apparent before the war — the idea of women's labour as a problem (to men and to the state), the idea that women's work outside the home was temporary, the idea that all women ought to be wives and mothers. These views ran through the equal pay debates. They lay alike behind Eleanor Rathbone's schemes for family endowment, and Rowntree's opposition to equal pay. They were a strong force within the labour movement as well as more conservative sections of the population, and were by no means rooted simply in the fear of cheap female labour so apparent in the words of trade unionists. *Labour Woman* reminded its readers:

> What has to be considered amongst other things is the question whether it is advisable in the interests of the whole community that women shall do work as a regular and permanent rule in many of the

industries and occupations, having regard to the one great function they, and they only, can fulfil.[46]

Adelaide Anderson (who was against equal pay) solemnly wrote of 'the social risks inherent in a widely extended and intensified employment of women in all great industries'.[47] Women, their work and wages were therefore seen as a social problem, even in the midst of the successful war effort, and as such were a suitable subject for discussion and criticism at all levels of society.[48] Although theoretically much of this discussion revolved around women's wartime work and wages, in fact nearly everyone was looking nervously forward as well, and the same arguments were to continue after the war — although by that time far more hostility was shown to women who worked after marriage.

Ultimately, it hardly mattered to women themselves whether the pro- or anti-equal pay factions succeeded in catching the ear of the government (and of course those in favour of equal pay were at an acute disadvantage since the unequal wages already existed and sweeping legislation would have been required to change matters), since both sides showed, to a greater or lesser extent, the same preoccupations with women's wages in relation to men's, and women's lives in relation to their actual or potential husbands and children. Some feminists, it is true, stood apart from this obsession when they demanded equal pay, but others did not. Even Sylvia Pankhurst could be found wondering whether the driving of trams was 'suitable for women',[49] and Beatrice Webb, who severely castigated the writers of the majority report on *Women in Industry* (she wrote her own minority report) for their preoccupation with keeping women's financial status lower than men's, nevertheless decided that, in the event of high unemployment, women should be laid off first. Domestic economy classes were, she said, cheaper to provide than public works, and in addition, women were less likely to be 'demoralised' because they had their domestic duties to perform.[50] Such views hardly challenged the basis of women's position in society, and are disappointing coming from socialists. Most of those who discussed the issues of women's work were even less likely to consider radical change.

Notes

1. As described in Chapter 3.
2. *Common Cause*, 17 Nov. 1916, review of *Labour, Capital and the War*, by

M.V.C. Ashley. But *Common Cause* itself could fall into the trap of exaggerating women's success.

3. *Common Cause*, 24 Sept. 1915, editorial, and *Common Cause*, 10 Dec. 1915, 'Notes and News'.

4. I.O. Andrews, *The Economic Effects of the World War upon Women and Children in Great Britain*, 2nd edn (Oxford University Press, 1921), Ch. X.

5. *Economic Journal*, March 1917, 'The Remuneration of Women's Services', Eleanor Rathbone; *Economic Journal*, March 1918, 'Equal Pay for Equal Work', M.G. Fawcett.

6. *Labour Woman*, February 1916, 'Working Women and the Problems of the War'.

7. *Socialist Review*, January-March 1918, 'Equal Pay for Equal Work'.

8. *Observer*, 6 Oct. 1918, 'Labour Notes'.

9. BAAS, *Draft Interim Report on Outlets for Labour after the War*, Ch. V.

10. *Labour Year Book*, 1916, 'The Future of Women in Industry', Margaret Bondfield.

11. Beatrice Webb, Minority Report on *Women in Industry*.

12. Family Endowment Committee, *Equal Pay and the Family* (Headley Bros., 1918), p. 7.

13. *Fortnightly Review*, January 1919, 'Equal Pay for Equal Work', Gertrude Tuckwell.

14. *Common Cause*, 6 Oct. 1916, 'Women and the War Bonus'.

15. Majority Report, *Women in Industry*, p. 2.

16. *Equal Pay and the Family*, p. 10.

17. Some did admit to this, however; see *Sussex Daily News*, 25 Apr. 1916.

18. For example, *Manchester Dispatch*, 31 Aug. 1918, 'Equal Pay for Women'.

19. *Manchester Guardian*, 24 Aug. 1918, letter from Ida Cawley.

20. General articles on this: *Reynolds Newspaper*, 25 Aug. 1918, 'Lessons of the Strike'; The *Star*, 26 Aug. 1918; 'Equal Pay for Equal Work'.

21. *Labour Year Book*, 1916, 'The Future of Women in Industry'.

22. War Emergency: Workers' National Committee records, Report on the National Conference on War Service for Women, 16 Apr. 1915.

23. As put forward by the *Observer*, for example. See note 8.

24. *Labour Woman*, September 1916.

25. *Economic Journal*, March 1917, 'The Remuneration of Women's Services'.

26. See note 7.

27. *Common Cause*, 20 Aug. 1915, editorial; *Common Cause*, 19 May 1916, 'Standing by the Men'; *Common Cause*, 9 June 1919, 'Need for Co-operation'; *Common Cause*, 15 Sept. 1916, 'Because she is a Woman'.

28. *Daily News*, 6 Sept. 1918, 'Equal Pay; the Woman's View'.

29. *Labour Woman*, November 1918, 'Women's Wages'. Marion Phillips, in October 1918, said that 'it was quite impossible to hope for economic independence of women unless the principle of equal pay for equal work were established. Men and women would never work harmoniously together while women felt they were being treated unjustly.'

30. *Daily Herald*, 31 Aug. 1918, 'Equal Pay and the Family Wage'.

31. *The Times*, 26 Aug. 1918.

32. Beveridge Papers, III, 48 (4).

33. *Spectator*, 24 Aug. 1918, 'Women's Work and Wages'.

34. For example, one letter on this subject to the *Manchester Guardian*, 20 Aug. 1918.

35. *Manchester Dispatch*, 2 Sept. 1918, Letters.

36. *The Times*, 23 Aug. 1918. See also the *Globe*, 6 Sept. 1918, 'Women in Industry'.

37. Seebohm Rowntree, *The Human Needs of Labour* (Thomas Nelson, 1918).

38. *Daily News*, 5 Sept. 1918, 'Equal Pay for Equal Work'.

39. *Labour Woman*, October 1918, 'Women's Wages'. The reviewer added: 'he cannot thus treat the subject as quite separate. In practice he is either encouraging the women as blacklegs, or he is proposing the relegation of women to illpaid and less attractive employments. The question is social as well as economic.'

40. See Adelaide Anderson, *Women Workers and the Health of the Nation* (pamphlet, 1918); The *Standard*, 12 July 1915, 'On Organising Women's Work'; the Majority Report on *Women in Industry*; the comments of the Lancashire Card and Blowing Room Operatives on the necessity of higher wages for husbands; the *Labour Woman*'s competition, mentioned above, and M.P. Cudworth's belief that if men's wages were better women would withdraw from work.

41. Majority Report on *Women In Industry*, Ch. V.

42. Ibid., p. 174.

43. Ibid., p. 180.

44. Report of the *Women's Employment Committee*, p. 60.

45. Ibid., p. 45.

46. *Labour Woman*, June 1916, 'Women's Work after the War'.

47. In S.J. Chapman (ed.), *Labour and Capital after the War* (Murray, 1918), p. 85. See also Anderson, *Women Workers and the Health of the Nation*.

48. See *Kentish Independent*, 23 Jan. 1915, 'Women and Employment', report on discussions of the Woolwich Tutorial Class on (1) Women and Employment and (2) the Position of Married Women as Workers.

49. *Woman's Dreadnought*, 1 Apr. 1916, 'Economic Equality of Men and Women'.

50. Minority Report on *Women in Industry*, Ch. III.

5 BIOLOGY AS DESTINY: WOMEN, MOTHERHOOD AND WELFARE

It has been established that ideas regarding women's duties as wives and mothers played a large part in the discussions about their role in industry and their wages. When one turns to the arguments surrounding women workers' welfare during the war, it becomes clear that such concerns were a national obsession. Before 1914 there had been debates about the 'health of the race', and whether or not it was desirable for married women to work in industry: the effect of the war was to intensify existing fears about infant mortality and the health of England's mothers. This may seem ironic. In the trenches men were dying, or were suffering dreadful physical and emotional injuries — yet the common soldier did not merit a campaign for the saving of England's fathers. Attention was focused instead upon the women left behind, whether they were the mothers of existing children or the mothers of the future. Fears for the very survival of the race were pinned upon the health of working-class mothers, and the irony of the state's, and the public's, apparent concern for women and babies to the exclusion of men was not always recognised. The *Woman's Dreadnought*, a pacifist socialist feminist paper, printed an article expressive of popular sentiment in 1915: 'The present time is a period of awakening national needs and national welfare, and with the flower of our youth perishing and worse than perishing on the battlefields, we must save every saveable child.'[1] Such feelings were expressed over and over again during these years, by people from all sections of society. In a curious way, the war was almost welcomed for the attention it brought to the standard problems of health; Adelaide Anderson noted that it had brought about improvements in preventive medicine, and hoped that it would lead to new ways of 'making industrial work enhance the health of the nation, and of safeguarding maternity and infant welfare'.[2] This was a fairly typical comment from those interested in women's health in industry, which now merited more concern than ever before.

There was a very real need for the further reform of working conditions for *both* sexes in industry and, theoretically, any extra attention was to be welcomed. It is also clear that pregnant women, whether workers or not, badly needed reforms in their favour, particularly the provision of medical care. The conditions of these two groups of people, workers and mothers, were adversely affected by the existing state of society; thus workers were exploited by their employers through long hours, poor working conditions and inadequate safety regulations, while mothers were handicapped by poor diet, bad housing and the demands of husbands, children and employers. However, during the war, the majority of those who discussed women's health and the 'health of the race' did not concern themselves with the exploitative nature of the system which governed working men's and women's lives; instead they brought together the two undeniable facts that women were doing industrial work and that they produced children, and concentrated largely upon the possible adverse effects of the former upon the latter. It is the nature of this approach which I will discuss here, since it had repercussions for women; all the wartime discussions about their health and welfare became entangled with questions regarding their right to work and their role as wives and mothers.

Working Conditions during the War

The influence of the war upon women's working conditions varied from trade to trade, factory to factory, and even woman to woman. In some industries there was very little change; production of many items was not directly associated with the war effort, and women continued to do the jobs they had always done, with similar hours and unchanged facilities (or lack of them). In others, where women took the place of men on work which was new to them, but which was not part of war production — for example, in the service trades, transport and many factories — they found new, different, and perhaps cramped, dirty or harsh conditions, but they were not required to work abnormally long hours, or make long journeys to work. The most pressure was undoubtedly upon women in the war industries. In many munitions factories, hours were long (often 12 hours, plus overtime) and conditions poor; women lacked seats, eating facilities and proper toilets, particularly in the early years of the war, when the female labour force increased drastically in factories and workshops designed for smaller numbers of men. In addition, the Factory Acts were effectively put to one side,[3] and women were employed on night work once more; this in turn meant that the journeys to work (often long) were made more hazardous by the lack of public transport and the inadequacy of the roads laid down for the newly built munitions factories. Sylvia Pankhurst put such aspects of work to the fore:

Sometimes a woman wrote to me, broken down in health by over-work, complaining of long walks over sodden, impromptu tracks, ankledeep in mud, to newly-erected factories; of night shifts spent without even the possibility of getting a drink of water; of workers obliged to take their meals amidst the dust and fumes of the work-shop.[4]

Periodically the press took up the matter of the long hours and poor conditions women worked under, and there is no reason to suppose that such reports were exaggerated, given the evidence from govern-ment reports and other commentators. Was a twelve-hour day too long? inquired many people;[5] Lilian Barker, the Superintendent of Woolwich Arsenal, declared that it was not, but also admitted that only the pres-sures of war necessitated such abnormally long hours.[6] The press also reported the complaints of the Women's Trade Union League regarding long hours, low pay and poor conditions,[7] and space was often given to the discussion of possible cases of exploitation, particularly where women were working with such dangerous substances as aircraft dope or TNT.[8]

Both these substances could kill, and women who worked with them were in immediate danger. The *Lancet* reported its findings on TNT in 1916. First irritative symptoms were nasal discomfort, nose bleeds, smarting eyes, headaches, sore throat, tight chest, coughs, pains in the stomach, nausea, constipation alternating with diarrhoea, and skin rashes. These were followed by toxic symptoms: nausea, anorexia, gid-diness, the swelling of hands and feet, drowsiness and finally death.[9] Even when the effects were not fatal they were unpleasant, and other industries had less widely reported ill effects on their workers; amongst the complaints listed by women interviewed recently for the Imperial War Museum archives were boils from pin pricks whilst making khaki uniforms and nausea from furnace fumes; Joan Williams, in her memoirs, complained of the constant grit in the eyes, and minor inflammations or burns which affected her in munitions work;[10] copperband turning, also in munitions, resulted in the inhalation of copper dust, which pro-duced nausea, digestive disturbances and bad teeth, while many fine jobs led to eye strain.[11] There was also the constant risk of explosion in ammunition factories.

All these aspects of industrial work could adversely affect both men and women, but the extensive use of women during the war for abnorm-ally long hours in place of conscripted men meant that more attention was paid to them. They were working for longer than the recommended hours for women (although of course there were plenty of women who had worked for far longer than the Factory Acts laid down before the war in trades which lay outside their jurisdiction); they were also working with dangerous substances in specifically wartime industries, which employed far more women than men (particularly ammunition factories and aircraft workshops), and they were working under conditions of nervous strain which could exacerbate fatigue. In addition, employers often took advantage of women's patriotism to make them work harder and longer than they would have done in peacetime. The idea that the war effort was more important than individual women's health was sometimes accepted even by those authorities which were supposed to be protecting their interests. Greenwood and Batley, a Leeds munitions firm, was prosecuted in 1915 for working women for continuous periods of 25 and 30 hours. The magistrate refused to convict, saying, 'The most important thing in the world today is that ammunition shall be made.'[12]

Many of these dangers were of course those of *workers*, who could be exploited by employers, and who increasingly looked to the state to improve or regulate conditions. But women worked under additional strain because of their sex; a proportion of them had to cope with pregnancy, childbirth, child-rearing and housework, none of which was strictly speaking an 'industrial problem' (nor were any of them new), but all of which clearly influenced their health and their ability to cope with the conditions of work. The health problems endemic amongst working-class mothers were intensified amongst those who also did paid work, simply because they had less time and energy to deal with industrial and domestic work together, and there were certainly jobs which exacerbated the minor illnesses to which hard-worked women were prone, namely varicose veins, menstrual irregularities and poor digestion.

On the other hand, in spite of the above disadvantages, both immediate and long-term, it would not be true to say that working women's health declined during the war. Opinions varied as to the effects of war work amongst those who took the trouble to examine the evidence systematically. B.L. Hutchins, investigating the effect of industrial work upon young girls, decided that the evidence varied not only from trade to trade, but according to whether one was speaking to doctors, welfare supervisors or trade union officials,[13] and it is certainly true that observers with differing political perspectives chose to emphasise certain statistics and reports accordingly. In any case, the fact that conditions varied so much around the country meant that industrial women really were affected in different ways. Although Sylvia Pankhurst chose to describe the *bad* conditions experienced by women workers, there is ample evidence from other quarters[14] to show that women's health often improved. There were two reasons given for this; first, although their wages were usually lower than men's, they were still often higher than women could earn before the war, and the extra earnings, plus separation allowances for the wives of soldiers, led to a better diet. Women who were now the breadwinners felt justified in eating more than they had before the war, when wives were notorious for the way in which they sacrificed their own need for food to those of their husbands and children. Secondly, it is possible, though not proven, that the provision of canteens, seats, rest periods, ventilation, etc. in some (though not by any means all) munitions factories as the war progressed had a beneficial effect on the workers. Such improvements were recommended by the government, as I shall show, but were not put into practice everywhere, and left non-munitions industries untouched. But many women did work in the munitions trades, and it was here that the strain and danger of fatigue were probably greatest. As I have said, fatigue left women open to other illnesses, and munitions workers badly needed the rests, shorter hours and good food suggested by the Health of Munition Workers Committee. These recommendations were certainly not without effect in particular factories, as some of the female volunteers from the early part of the war testified; conditions often changed as more women were employed.[15] Unfortunately, it took a long time to convince employers that longer hours did not necessarily mean increased production, and even by 1916 some factories were actually introducing twelve-hour shifts in place of eight-hour ones, a fact which caused one woman to write despairingly to the *Woman Worker*:

Dear Mr Editor,
   Kindly allow a small space in your valuable paper to voice my opinion as regards the hours worked at Messrs Vickers Ltd., Barrow, which is at present three 8 hour shifts. They are making an attempt to alter it to two long shifts, which I think would be very injurious to the health of the majority of girls, as the 8 hours is quite long enough to be kept standing at the machine without a rest, and I am quite sure that it could not increase the output. The girls would be too tired to put the same energy into their work, and I don't think the Minister of Munitions could be justified in giving his sanction to such a scheme.[16]

The long shift became less common after 1916, but for women who did have long hours, difficult journeys to work and additional housework,

it is difficult to say whether improved conditions and better diet outweighed the adverse effects of such a life-style. The balance obviously
varied from woman to woman.

The Mother of the Race

Some of these industrial and social influences upon women's health
were long-term, others were exacerbated by the war; in all fields there
were ways in which the state could have aided women – the nature of
the government's intervention will be discussed later in this chapter.
But first I want to examine the way in which the matter of women's
health was taken up in general by people during the war, particularly
the form this concern took, and the implications for women workers. I
have already said that those who expressed anxiety about the 'health of
the race' also worried about the effect of industrial work upon women's
physical capacity to bear and raise children, and upon their moral fitness
to be wives and mothers. Some, it is true, used the current fears to press
for much needed reforms, and an organisation made up of members from
the Women's Labour League, the Women's Co-operative Guild, the Railway Women's Guild, the War Emergency Workers National Committee
and the National Association for the Prevention of Infant Mortality early
approached the Local Government Board on the subject of 'The National
Care of Maternity in Time of War' in the belief, as the *Co-operative News*
put it, that 'the desolating waste of life inseparable from the operations
of war makes it increasingly incumbent upon the nation to assist mothers
and to render the conditions of childbirth as favourable as possible.'[17]
Their demands were for medical advice, extra nourishment for mothers
and the provision of midwives, all of which would have aided pregnant
women during peace or war. The careful exploitation of public fears in
this way was something that B.L. Hutchins had suggested might happen
in 1915: she hoped much might be won for women in this way.[18]

But far more people used the climate of opinion to voice their distrust and dislike of industrial work for wives, and of 'men's work' for all
women. Even people who recognised the harmful influence of capitalism upon the health of the working class were drawn into using the prevailing language of the time, and gave serious consideration to arguments
about whether women with children should be allowed to work. The
implications for women of every class were serious, but above all attention was directed at the working-class mother and, to a slightly lesser
extent, the 'potential' mother. As Sir George Newman, Chairman of

that unique body, the Health of Munition Workers Committee, told his listeners in 1918: 'Woman labour involved a physiological and a social problem. Woman was a peculiar and particular physiological instrument, and the woman labour question raised the great problems of maternity, infant welfare, and home building.'[19]

'This war is bringing home to many of us the value of the mother as a national asset', wrote a *Daily News* reporter in 1917,[20] making women sound rather like cattle or gold reserves, resources to be utilised for the good of the nation. Others used more emotive language, and had high expectations of the extent to which women would sacrifice themselves to the home. The romantic hyperbole about motherhood, which resulted in such extraordinary and confusing statements as this, by Adelaide Anderson — 'In the greatest convulsions of human society, such as that in which we stand, those people and nations will no doubt endure who possess the most intelligent, true-hearted mothers'[21] — was accompanied by near hysteria about infant mortality in some quarters. A common misconception existed that infant deaths and cases of child neglect were increasing during the war, although there was no evidence for this. As an NSPCC member wrote: 'since the war commenced the pessimists have not lost an opportunity of spreading statements likely to lead to despondency.'[22] He went on to say that in fact cases of child abuse and the rate of infant mortality had both dropped between 1914 and 1916; there were also fewer cases of malnutrition and lack of adequate clothing. But such evidence, and reports that women themselves were better fed than before the war, had little effect on those whose concern for the Race bordered on the obsessive. Thus Margaret Hamilton began her article for the *New Witness* in July 1915 with claims which were blatantly ridiculous when she said, 'if the incursion of married women into industry continues, the very existence of the next generation is jeopardised to a considerable extent.'[23] According to her, mothers were leaving their babies to go into the factories, and the babies died. It was useless to suggest crèches, she continued, as children belonged with their mothers, and to her eyes the figure of Belgium in Mrs Pankhurst's procession to the Prime Minister (which was designed to show women's willingness to do war work) appeared more like 'a symbol of dispossessed motherhood — the woman who, driven from her home, is forced to work in the factories and the workshops while her baby lies dead'. She finished the article in fine style, blaming all social evils on married women's work:

Meanwhile, inspired propagandists triumphantly announce the further enlistment of 5,000 women in the munition factories and prophesy an immense increase in the output of shells, and the number of dead infants increases also and the rate of wages steadily falls.

This was journalistic excess, but ideas about the harmfulness of women's work were even given a scientific gloss by such people as Dr C.W. Saleeby, a eugenicist, who pompously informed the public that if a woman worked while pregnant, 'the mother puts into the products of her external work the energy which should have gone into the internal work which she alone could do, of creating and saving the future,'[24] to which Clementina Black promptly replied that home work was far more harmful to women than factory work.[25] But Saleeby was resolutely anti-married women's work, and referring on one occasion to the high rate of infant mortality in Bradford, he explained it simply by saying, 'practically all the mothers in Bradford go out to work . . . That is a fundamental sin against the laws of life.'[26]

Of course such ideas had existed before the war, but they were given a boost by the appalling death toll in the trenches. The language of racial health was suddenly everywhere, for, as the *North Mail* said, it was up to the women to repair the ravages of war.[27] (In the meantime, the Countess of Warwick was urging women to bear more children because it was their 'duty to the white race', significantly implying the existence of a new enemy in the future.[28]) From the beginning, therefore, praise for women's wonderful war work was often tempered by concern for its long-term effects — thus the *Ladies' Pictorial* carried the following warning:

as we have said on more than one previous occasion, the strain now being imposed on women and girls who are working in munition factories and replacing men in offices and elsewhere, is likely to have a deleterious effect on the nation's health in the coming by and by. It is recognised that it is of the utmost importance to our Empire that we should maintain a healthy race.[29]

The writer of the above also pointed to the degree of strain which resulted from women's double burden of work at home and in the factory, but it was *outside work*, not housework, which was supposed to threaten women's strength and vitality. In a similar fashion, the *Daily Express* warned that women's work must not be allowed to interfere with their major duty, 'guarding the welfare of posterity'.[30]

An article in *The Times* brought in another factor — the fear that even though women's health might be adequately preserved, good factory conditions might have their own special dangers:

> It would be deplorable if the measures taken to preserve the health of
> girls and mothers in the war factories led married women definitely
> to abandon their homes for industrial work. If their incursion into
> skilled labour is to be permanent, then we have paid infinitely too
> high for any immediate advantage to our arms. But one must feel
> that public opinion, if not the instinct of the women, will restore
> them, after the war, to their traditional place.[31]

A new dimension can be seen here; for many it was almost irrelevant if
women remained *physically* healthy while they worked; the issue was
rather, were women being lured away from their true role by their war
work? This fear was evident in the discussions of many social reformers
and observers. For example, the British Association for Industrial Reconstruction, which was made up of trade unionists and employers,
decided that it was 'the duty of the State to ensure that women are only
employed as factors of industrial efficiency in so far as the interests of
family life and the development of the race are not prejudiced'.[32] Similarly, Adelaide Anderson, a factory inspector, stated, 'in my belief we
must never lose sight of the fundamental need of the nation from its
women, the power to make and keep its homelife sound and to guard
the nurture of the race.'[33] She also decided that the health of individuals and the nation depended upon attention being paid to '*the primary
occupation of women as housewives and mothers*'.[34] Basil Worsfold
came to much the same conclusions in *War and Social Reform*, when
he wrote, 'it cannot be emphasised too strongly that the service which
the State most requires from the generality of women is motherhood
and the maintenance of the family in purity and happiness.'[35] Like *The
Times* and others he did not like the idea of women seeing outside work
as a desirable alternative to full-time domestic work, classing clinics and
crèches as 'intermediate institutions' which would not be needed once
women retreated to the home after the war.[36]

With biology as destiny women could not win, for even if their work
was physically harmless it could be seen as dangerous to family life.
Although one aspect or the other could be emphasised by those who
claimed to be concerned about racial health, in general a combination
of the two was used by the critics of women's work. Such views were
not entirely without opponents. The writers of the British Association
for the Advancement of Science report on *Outlets for Labour After the
War* noted drily, 'It may be suspected that in many cases conditions

which are stated to be morally or intellectually bad for women are not altogether beneficial for men!'[37] This comment could suitably have been aimed at the Mule Spinners' Union, which, as described in Chapter 3, made much of the harmfulness of the spinning rooms. In addition, as a writer for the *Sunday Chronicle* pointed out, it was strange that so much fuss should be made about the health of women doing men's work while those doing traditional female jobs remained neglected:

A great deal of weary nonsense has been talked and written recently about the suitability, or unsuitability, of certain forms of manual labour for the supposedly fragile female form.

The sight of a muscular spinster of 39 selling tram tickets or inspecting the gas meter arouses the most chivalrous concern for the future generation in the breasts of many worthy persons, who remain quite unmoved by the more familiar spectacle of their own obviously pregnant charwoman scrubbing the stairs or carrying up the coals.[38]

The writer had considerable doubts about whether the attention paid to racial health would lead to anything constructive, as

in practice chivalry is apt to wear rather thin when an employer is confronted with a mass of unorganised, ignorant and docile female labour. Quite apart from her sex or her capacity for childbearing, it is not good for a woman — it would not be good for a man — to work excessively long hours in an ill-ventilated building for a wage which only allows her to support herself upon a diet of bread and tea.

This was really the most important question — the extent to which long hours and low wages wore out men *and* women, but the language of racial health threw a smoke-screen around such debates, and put responsibility firmly upon the state, to restrict female labour, and upon women themselves. The call remained for something to be done about 'the conditions of employment which reacted injuriously upon them as actual or potential mothers',[39] and women were urged to prepare themselves to bear more children. Even those who accepted the fact that married women were doing, and would continue to do, more industrial work called for studies to investigate the effects of such labour, and expressed fears about the 'undue strain' experienced by women working.[40]

The interesting thing is that such feelings existed amongst nearly all political groups and all classes. It might be supposed that the spokespeople for the labour movement would have paid less attention to emotive words about noble motherhood and the health of the race, and more to the exploitation of all workers' health by capitalism. In fact, however, the same kind of language was used, and the same fears expressed, amongst members of the Labour Party and trade unionists.

Marion Phillips, Labour Party activist, wrote in the *Trade Union Worker* that women's wartime sacrifice was misplaced, and that they must keep up their health for the sake of the race — 'for the woman worker has a double duty. First there is the duty of wifehood and motherhood. Let her starve and work out her strength to-day, and what will be the fate of her children in the future?'[41] Mary Macarthur of the NFWW spoke to the TUC in the same vein:

It has been said that we are financing this war by borrowing from future generations. In nothing is this more true than in the case of women workers. We are, in fact, borrowing the health and efficiency of generations unborn.[42]

These statements were typical. I have already shown that an assumed concern with women's health was useful on occasion for men in skilled or male-dominated trades who wished to exclude women, and certainly this aspect cannot be neglected. But fears about the effect of women's work upon the health of the race were more deep-rooted than the statements from the spinners' unions or the dockers (see Chapter 3) might suggest. Where economic fears were uppermost, it was usually transparently obvious; an example of this is the following letter to the *Woman Worker* from the Secretary of the Marylebone branch of the enginemen's union:

Dear Madam,

I am instructed by the members of this Branch to inform you that it has come to our knowledge that a Bill is being drafted for the Conscription of Women; and to instruct you of this Branch's disapproval of it on the general grounds that if the government require women other than the single or leisured classes to go to work, we have very grave doubts as to the health and number of the future generation. For this Branch contends that women cannot be expected to become mothers if they are compelled to leave their homes to go to rack and ruin by having to work; and as much danger is to be experienced (we contend) in the future through lack of population as there is today through the same cause. We also beg to inform you that women are taking over men's jobs at less money.[43]

The threat mentioned in the last paragraph must inevitably have influenced the way the men viewed women workers in general, and the concern voiced earlier was not entirely altruistic. But there were other speakers and writers who were not directly threatened by an influx of female labour, and who expressed grave fears about the future – and who concerned themselves with a mixture of worries about women's health, maternal and infant mortality, and standards of home-keeping. As *Labour Woman*, in a paragraph already quoted once, phrased it:

> What has to be considered amongst other things is the question whether it is advisable in the interests of the whole community that women shall do work as a regular and permanent rule in many industries and occupations, having regard to the one great function they, and only they, can fulfil.[44]

War conditions were the immediate problem, but everyone looked forward as well, partly because adverse physical effects might only show themselves in years to come, but also because there were many who feared the likely outcome if women *continued* to work in a broader field.

Although women's circumstances could have been used to press the state to take further responsibility for factory conditions and medical care (and some people did try this approach), in practice the labour movement did not concentrate on these matters. Instead there was a strong campaign to curtail married women's work in certain circumstances, racial health being given as the reason. There was no questioning of the fact that women alone had the task of running the home, cooking and bringing up children – this, rather, was seen as their most noble duty and one they should be pleased to fulfil, in spite of the fact that it took a toll on women's health itself.

Women trade unionists and Labour Party leaders usually accepted such a destiny for women as willingly as the men; Marion Phillips' statement of moderate aims was this: 'I am quite clear what our aim should be: to secure as wide a sphere as possible consistent with the health and welfare of the race, and without in any way lowering existing standards.'[45] These people too believed that babies were being sacrificed to women's work,[46] that full-time motherhood was women's destiny,[47] and that if necessary married women should be withdrawn from certain jobs. Sometimes it was simply suggested that women not be allowed to do 'unsuitable work' (the definition of unsuitable varied) which might damage them physically,[48] and Marion Phillips considered that there might be a Departmental Committee to decide which jobs might fall inside this category.[49] On these lines, the Workers' Union magnanimously decided that women should not be excluded from work for economic reasons, and agreed that 'the community had no right to interfere with the occupations of women *except on the grounds of motherhood*'[50] (my emphasis).

This harping on the destiny of women as mothers alone was not only constricting for wives, but insulting to single and childless women, as the following quotation shows. Miss Perkins, in the *Labour Woman* essay competition on 'What is your opinion as to the proposal to prohibit married women's work?' wrote, 'No crèches etc. can ever make up to children for the mother's love. Whatever a childless woman may do for the community is nothing to the service rendered by her who gives it healthy and good children.'[51] Those who were not mothers were thus classed as almost useless.

The labour movement was also, through the Standing Joint Committee of Industrial Women's Organisations, associated with the National Baby Week campaigns, the aim of which was to promote the health and care of babies. Some of the lectures given under the auspices of the Baby Week Council were distinctly disturbing. To begin with, there were undertones of racialism, exemplified by the words of Dr Saleeby, who informed his audience that the white population of the British Empire was outnumbered, and that there was a danger of England having nothing but an 'empty empire' — the indigenous population did not, apparently, count.[52] In addition, the responsibility for the race and the blame for child death and illness were put fairly and squarely on women, almost to the exclusion of other factors. Saleeby was fearful for the future of the British race because of women's indulgence in alcohol and industrial work,[53] while another speaker stated, 'efficient housewives are more important than bricks and mortar to the making of healthy homes.'[54] One imagines families living in slums or substandard housing might not have taken kindly to such a comment, since no amount of hard work from a woman could have counteracted damp conditions, poor ventilation or overcrowding. Still they were supposed to try, and education for this destiny ideally started early, as 'a thorough training in cooking, housework, laundry work and needlework leads up naturally to mothercraft,'[55] while sex roles were carefully established in a children's essay competition run by the Council; for boys, the title was 'Why I Should Kill that Fly', and for girls, 'How I mind the Baby'.[56] The 1917

Report which carried the winning essays also contained Dr R.M. Wilson's classic summing up of the joys of womanhood: 'what greater right could any woman have than to be the wife, mother or sister of a British soldier?'[57] Thus were women defined in their relation to men, and the demands put on them were severe. They had to be taught that their 'particular and peculiar duty' was childbearing, and that 'they owe it as a duty to the State to care for the babies that belong to the State as well as to themselves.'[58]

These words were not directly from representatives of the labour movement, but there was strong support for the Baby Week Campaigns from a number of trade unionists and Labour Party members, and the connection cannot simply be dismissed. The most vitriolic prose, however, came from a socialist paper, the *New Age*; the sentiments were purely anti-feminist (and anti-woman), and the excuse for them was an assumed concern for the health of the race. A wealth of prejudice emerges from the articles the paper carried on women in industry in 1915, some of them already discussed in Chapter 3. The message hammered home was that woman's only role was motherhood, and that her responsibility was for 'race preservation and perfection'.[59] Consequently, she should not be allowed to damage herself through doing industrial work, and in addition, the possible moral dangers of outside work should be taken in account. The dangers lurked not only in industry; Frances Low decided that night work for girls in offices which also contained men was unsuitable, because 'the work is not of a kind that offers safe and healthful conditions to young women, the future mothers of the working-classes', and also that agricultural work for local women (as opposed to imported middle-class Land Army girls) meant that careful attention was required to ensure that mothers and babies were not separated for too long: 'You don't want these young wives to lose their interest and sentiment for their homes and babies, but if you take them away all the week there is immense danger of this.'[60] In the meantime, Rowland Kenney concluded that exploited women (i.e. those who worked) were flung into 'the fanged maw of Lancashire Cotton Lords', and that the influx of women into new jobs should be regarded as 'one of the blackest tragedies in Labour's Modern Records'.[61] The *New Age* no more spoke for the labour movement than did the Baby Week Council, but its speakers were supposedly from the left, and they indicate the depth of feeling which existed on the subject.

These beliefs resulted not only in the glorification of motherhood but of the role of housewife, since the bearing of children then, as now, was seen as being inextricably bound up with cooking, cleaning, mending, etc.[62] One of the proposals put forward for helping working-class women was 'co-operative housekeeping', which some people hoped would liberate women from isolating duties in the home; as one writer in the *Trade Union Worker* expressed it:

> Each woman, then, set free from the incubus of home slavery, would be able to follow the work for which she is best fitted by temperament and training. Under the present primitive conditions of home-life, the great majority of women are forced to engage in housework — whatever their capacity may be. This is just as wasteful and illogical as forcing all men to engage in one particular trade.[63]

She went on to say enthusiastically, 'I should like to make women rebellious against such conditions — I want them to be world workers, not houseslaves.' But it is a mark of the extent to which the ideal of woman as the home worker and man as the breadwinner had penetrated labour circles that Marion Phillips went out of her way to deny that she or the *Labour Woman* wanted co-operative housekeeping to get women out of the home:

> It is being openly advocated as an advantage because it would allow women to go out to work. A certain school of thought believes that if mothers of families were set free from their household tasks they would be able to gain economic freedom by continuing to work for wages, and they advocate the extension of co-operative housekeeping for that reason. They could not well suggest one with which the average working woman is less likely to agree. So far as we are concerned we do not advocate co-operative housekeeping in order that women may work for wages, but because we believe that it might help them to live far healthier and more interesting lives. Mothers as munition workers, as millhands, as shirtmakers, do not seem to us any better than mothers as houseworkers, but we do believe that mothers who have time to be thinking citizens would make infinitely better homes for their children than those whose hours are filled with the drudgery of working in overcrowded, inconvenient and ugly homes.[64]

The Labour Party did push the image of woman as home-maker very hard, even when it demanded shorter working hours for women in the home, and assistance with laundry and child care.[65] Their discussion of their housing campaign in *Labour Woman* was headed:

The Working Woman's House.
Woman's Chief Task
is to make a home[66]

even though it is clear that a number of women did want to do less housework, as the response to the article on co-operative housekeeping showed; *Labour Woman* received a strongly worded letter from one woman who wished that husbands would realise the need for joint responsibility in the home.[67] It is worth recalling at this point the words of one of the miners' leaders, already quoted in Chapter 3: 'We think a woman's place is at home.'[68] This fits in all too well with the ideals expressed in *Women and the Labour Party*: 'the woman of our country will prove her right to the name of housewife, and be given at last throughout the land the opportunity of becoming the perfect home keeper of the race.'[69] The very evening classes proposed for women's education by the Labour Party were on such subjects as citizenship and home life, housing, food problems, maternity, education and child welfare. Such classes kept women in the same sphere as usual, and maintained the idea that there were special 'women's interests' in politics; there was no widening of opportunity.

It may seem that I have travelled a long way from the original issue of the health of women workers, but these are the discussions which were bound up with the matter of health at the time. Similar sentiments existed amongst employers of female labour as well. Many were prepared to over-work women, just as they had done before the war, but lip-service was paid to the ideals of motherhood: 'It is the sacred duty of the State to ensure that women are only used as wealth producers in so far as it does not affect the healthy development of the race,' to repeat the words of O.E. Monkhouse.[70] A number of employers backed up their words with actions. The government demanded that certain standards be met in munitions, and suggested some other provisions; these were sometimes accompanied by classes in domestic subjects arranged by the employers on their own initiative. Dorothea Proud, the writer of a book on welfare work (which will be discussed shortly), was a firm believer in the importance of marriage and motherhood, but was nevertheless disgusted that employers should insist that women concentrate on these subjects in classes which were theoretically educational: 'Evidently, employers who establish domestic economy classes for their girl workers consider them as housewives of the future, not as factory workers,' she wrote, and said of a factory school which offered only gymnastics, needlework, cookery and housewifery:

'The curriculum is framed with the view of training the girls to become proficient housewives.' The tragedy of a factory girl's life could scarcely be expressed more eloquently! She toils in the factory to earn her daily bread; she often drudges at home because it is expected of her; and when education is granted her, it is merely that it may fit her to become a 'proficient housewife'. As a thinking, sentient being she is given little or nothing; she is trained to work and not to live. Moreover, she is trained for two entirely different types of work, in neither of which can she hope to attain the ideal. She is hardly likely to rise to an important post in the factory, nor dare she hope for such a home as she may learn to picture.[71]

Needless to say, there was logic in encouraging women's domestic role — it kept the bulk of the female labour force single and temporary, thus 'cheap and docile'; but almost certainly, as I have discussed in Chapter 3, employers were also influenced by the prevailing propaganda and many stated quite sincerely that married women should be at home looking after their husbands.

The *Worker's Dreadnought* was scathing about this much vaunted concern for women and babies:

Our capitalists realise that 'deep down in every woman's soul there lies the vision of the dreamchild which will be reality one day'. And they have placed Woman upon a pedestal simply because they desire a great increase in the birthrate . . . And so the cry goes up: 'We want more babies in order to save the Empire and the race.'[72]

But in fact what is more surprising is the extent to which such sentiments penetrated the feminist movement as well, even though here there were certainly no underlying economic fears about women's participation in outside work. The majority of feminists did welcome the opportunities given to women by the war, and hoped that the demonstration of their physical fitness for all kinds of jobs would have a lasting effect. As Lady Churchill wrote hopefully: 'We shall be able to clear our minds of any cant that may survive about women's physical limitations. No one was ever much concerned with these limitations in the case of charwomen or sick nurses.'[73] A cynical eye was cast over much of the material written about women's industrial welfare; Margaret Roper, in *Common Cause*, demanded to know why it was that 'sedentary gauging operations should evidently be confined to women': 'Nature, I suppose, built women to sit everlastingly on seats and men to improve their muscular power by movement.'[74] Many welcomed the shelving of the Factory Acts as well, having seen them as unfairly restrictive,[75] and from the beginning there were warnings that the current concern with welfare might lead to a 'crusade . . . for indiscriminate raising of the birthrate',[76] together with further restrictions on working women.[77] None of this meant that attention was not also paid to the possible ill effects of over-work on women's health and to the exploitation by employers of women's eagerness to do well. But in addition, *Common Cause* warned that the pressure on workers in munitions factories might be harmful to the future of the race, and in 1916 carried an extraordinary article by Carol Ring, entitled 'For the Sake of the Race', which is worth looking at in some detail. Her immediate assumption was that in normal times wives would not work:

> For the sake of the race it is an admitted principle that married women should not go to work; provided, that is, that married men earn enough to keep the children from want, or that earning it they bring it home. But for 'the sake of the country' — which, somehow, in time of war, gets separated in people's minds from the race — it is essential now that married women take their places in munition factories. This they are told; and with splendid response they go.[78]

She described how the Birmingham Women's Suffrage Society had investigated the homes and babies of munitions workers (which must have been popular!) and found them not as bad as they had expected. However, there appeared to be a decline in 'home discipline', which, she claimed, would lead to juvenile delinquency and neglected and dirty homes. Babies obviously needed crèches but, she added:

> Many experts on this subject in the city of Birmingham are not altogether in agreement with the principle of unlimited crèches in ordinary times. There is no doubt that it is necessary to be careful not to in any way encourage married women to go out to work.

She proceeded to express her distrust of working women's motives, and doubts about their ties to their children:

> Where they can get their children really well cared for at a cost to themselves which is altogether out of proportion to what the children receive, the temptation is strong to go out and earn extra money; which involves temptation to the husband to make no effort to meet

the increasing needs of a growing family, and in addition is an inducement to the woman to accept inadequate wages because she is not
wholly dependent upon them.[79]

If women did leave their children to go out to work then a weakening in
the bond between mother and child was 'bound to result, whether the
mother leaves her child for the sake of pleasure and excitement, or because she is driven by bitter necessity to take the place of breadwinner,
or is serving the country in shell factories'. These ideas follow on from
one of the strands of the pre-war feminist movement, which glorified
motherhood, and praised the virtue and self-sacrifice of those who
became mothers.[80] But at the same time they reveal a contempt for
working-class women, and doubts about their intelligence and motivation. Carol Ring's approach has distinct similarities with that of the
National Baby Week Council, whose members started with the premiss
that infant mortality was due to the women's stupidity or laziness, and
believed that all could be solved with education in 'mothercraft' and a
liberal amount of middle-class patronage. This contempt is not simply
a symptom of class differences, however, for it is evident in the words
of speakers within the labour and socialist movements as well. The
Labour League suggested that women should be taught to lead the way
in thriftiness during the war (and was roundly criticised for this by one
woman letter-writer, who pointed out that the League could know very
little about the difficulties of a working-class housewife in making ends
meet[81]), while a journalist for *Labour Woman* despaired of the way men
in general condemned nursery schools because they might encourage
women to work, and allowed women to struggle on in poor conditions
with children underfoot because of 'the mother being the proper person
to look after the child in every way'.[82] Within labour and socialist groups
there were signs of misogyny; how else can one explain the following
remark made by a writer in the *Daily Chronicle* in 1918? Having decided
that it was better for men to earn good money and support their wives
in 'sheltered comfort' than for women to work, he concluded, 'The best
they [women] can have is not too good for the race. Many women would
prefer to be men; but no man in this world wishes himself a woman.'[83]
This last statement has absolutely nothing to do with the rest of the
article. It reveals an appalling amount about the author's own attitude
to women — they were blacklegs in industry and nothing more than
childbearers at home, and these two facts were clearly enough to make
the writer find them faintly disgusting. In spite of all he had just written
about the good of the race, and the necessity of giving women ideal

living conditions, he nevertheless came to the conclusion that women must wish they had been born male — which assumes that women dislike themselves. That there might be anything good about being female obviously never occurred to him, and he did not consider that those women who envied men might want their power and freedom more than their gender.

The war period brought out and intensified the ambiguities which already existed in attitudes to women, and they were revealed as clearly in discussions about the health of the race as they were in those concerning employment and industrial aptitude. On the one hand, women were put on a pedestal in literature about motherhood: they were the guardians of the race, the homekeepers, those who nurtured children and kept their husbands on the straight and narrow path — if only by their very dependence, making sure that men worked hard enough to support wives and children. On the other hand, women were distrusted when they appeared to be moving out of their true sphere (and welcoming the chance to do so!), and seen as being inferior in intellect, health and strength by many men. Working-class women were in a particularly difficult position. They were patronised alike by men of their own class, and by middle-class do-gooders of both sexes, who saw them as being ignorant and in need of education in how to be good wives and mothers. They were also suspected of threatening to abandon their homes (plus husbands and children) if they were relieved of domestic chores, and were supposed to need constant reminders about their true vocation. The words of Benjamin Broadbent, one of the speakers for the National Baby Week Council, sum up this attitude. We must not try to tell mothers things they know better, he informed his audience, but it must be remembered that they are ignorant: 'For myself, I must refer back to what I have already said as to the duty of the educated and leisured classes towards the uninstructed, the toil-driven multitude of mothers.'[84]

The Government and Welfare

Much of the book so far has been concerned with the interaction of sexist ideology and capitalism. Many employers stated that they would not employ married women, yet they accepted that wives who were laid off would find less well paid work with other employers, and that this system kept women's wages down, with all the adverse effects on women's health and family life such wages had. Trade unionists said that they did not want their wives to work, and accepted that their daughters would be paid less than their sons, yet blamed women in general for accepting low wages and remaining a danger to men. The situation becomes even more complex when one considers the role of the government in the field of welfare during the war. For although the government was certainly no ally to labour, and had indeed become an employer in its own right, its motives and aims were not the same as those of other employers. The government had to consider its own image with voters, take account of pressure from labour politicians, consider national efficiency and racial health (widespread ill health is expensive once the state is paying sickness benefit), none of which were issues which concerned capitalists, and, in addition, many of those experts who advised government, or sat on its committees, by no means approved of the standard capitalist approach to labour.

The government was fighting a war, and it was essential that labour be used efficiently in the munitions industry at least. But there were differences in the concept of efficiency. Some employers wanted the right to work their employees for as long as they thought necessary, clearly assuming that this was efficient use of labour. It was up to the government to show them that it was not, and that shorter hours and better working conditions led to higher output. Yet the research which dealt with the beneficial effects of factory welfare schemes was also concerned with the techniques of 'scientific management', which included reorganisation of factory layout, the accurate timing of jobs and the subdivision of processes for the purpose of mass production, all of which were anathema to trade unionists, and also, importantly, still viewed with cynicism by many employers at this time. Was it 'better' for workers to work in a clean modern factory, with good ventilation, subsidised canteens and welfare officers, for shorter hours, or in a cramped dirty factory, with few safety regulations, and nowhere to eat meals, for a day which was far too long, but involved more skilled or interesting work? This, basically, was the choice as many saw it. In fact, both involve the exploitation of the worker; the former means monotonous work and close supervision; the latter means scant regard for safety or comfort. There are discussions still about whether 'welfare' in all its forms (state benefits, employment protection, factory legislation) is necessary as protection for the workers instigated by the state, or whether it involves unacceptable interference with individuals and represents an alliance between government and employers, and is designed to control the work-force and soothe discontent. These questions were also discussed during the war, in debates about government intervention and factory welfare, but other factors made the issues even more complex.

The state was, as we have seen, an employer itself during the war, and its interests were assumed by many to be closely allied with those of industrialists, particularly after the passing of the Munitions Acts, and the establishment of the Ministry of Munitions, with its complement of businessmen. The government also introduced press censorship and conscription, both of which were seen as attacks on freedom. Furthermore, the field in which the government was encouraging experimentation with industrial welfare was one where unions and workmen were acutely worried about the long-term effects of de-skilling and alterations in workshop practice. Unions were all too conscious of the fact that factory welfare schemes could not be judged on their own; they were associated with state intervention in general, changes in the labour process and increased profits for employers.

In addition, there was the fact that the welfare of women was seen as a particularly important question by society at large. The views of capital and labour were not the government's only consideration, nor were they of primary importance to many of those committee members and civil servants who discussed the issues raised by women's role in industry. The efficiency of the existing work-force had to be raised *and* women had to survive the war in a condition fit to bear children. Women's health was regarded as an important matter for discussion by all those who looked at their expanding role in industry. But this raises an important question; to what extent did the government actually take any notice of those who expressed concern about women's health and welfare? The answer to this will emerge as I discuss the findings of the various committees. The other matter to be considered is the effect this stated concern with women's health had on their industrial prospects in general.

It is with all these factors in mind that one must approach the various committees which discussed women's work and health. These committees were set up for different reasons. The Women's Employment Committee and the writers of the War Cabinet Committee report on Women in Industry were considering women's work and pay in general terms, while the Health of Munitions Workers Committee was concerned with munitions workers and war production, but there are nevertheless similarities in their views of women workers, since all were strongly influenced by the current ideology concerning women's reproductive and social roles.[85]

The report of the Women's Employment Committee included a section on 'Women and the Race', and on 'Women and Men as Workers: How they Differ'. In the latter, the Committee decided that the data for accurate comparison did not exist, yet members still went on to say that mothers should be induced to stay at home, and wondered whether further official restrictions should be put upon married women workers. Significantly, when the Committee came to examine 'Suitability of Employment', members considered that physiological *and* social ill effects should be looked at: the former might arise from jobs which involved bodily injury, strain, accidents or poison; the latter from jobs which were dirty, wet, hot, required exposure to the weather, and necessitated lonely work or night work. The Committee hammered home the fact that the preservation of physical health was not enough:

> In applying these standards [of suitability of work] again the primary function of women in the State must be regarded: it is not enough not to interfere with her service in bearing children, and the care of infant life and health, but she must also be safeguarded as the home-maker for the nation.[86]

The members of the War Cabinet Committee report on Women in Industry also considered the effect of work upon women's health. The members noted the evidence of women's poor health before the war (as shown by the workings of the National Health Insurance Scheme) and decided that women's health had actually improved during the war, in spite of night work and long hours, thanks to more interesting work and better nutrition.[87] They called for further improvements in conditions of work, such as the provision of canteens, regular medical inspections and the use of more factory inspectors, but decided that work *per se* did not have an adverse effect on infant mortality rates, which had actually fallen since more women went out to work,[88] and that it would be unfair to force married women out of employment.[89]

The report also contained a Memorandum by Dr Janet Campbell on the health of women in industry, which, together with the material produced by the Health of Munitions Workers Committee, is the most important evidence of opinions held by the government's advisers. In her Memorandum, Janet Campbell immediately stated that she was looking at the effect of war and pre-war conditions upon women's 'health and the function of maternity', and added:

> In considering maternity, questions inevitably arise as to the personal capacity and inclination for motherhood, the influence of employment, if any, on the birthrate and on infant mortality, the effect of the married woman's labour on the care of her home and children.[90]

Thus the social effects are assumed to be on a par with the physical effects even here. Although Dr Campbell mentioned the differences in physical development between men and women (women were smaller and lighter, and this affected their strength), there is no doubt about the fact that she viewed women's capacity to bear children as being the most important consideration, and this dominated her view of *all* women workers, whether they were young or old, married or single:

> The second fundamental physiological difference between a man and a woman is the fact of actual or potential motherhood. This necessarily governs to some extent her industrial power, efficiency and value. It wholly prevents absolutely equal competition in industry, and though undue weight should not be given to possible impairment of the maternal function which may arise from circumstances connected with the nature of the employment, it cannot be disregarded if women are to be employed under the conditions most appropriate to them not only as individuals, but also with a view to the well-being of the race as a whole.[91]

Ironically, Janet Campbell's careful investigation, motivated as it was by fears that industrial work might cause injury, in fact revealed the importance of the conditions women *lived* in, as well as worked in, a matter so often neglected by the campaigners against women's work. Janet Campbell noted that before the war married women had often been forced into the roughest kinds of work,[92] and decided that when looking at the effects of employment upon health it was difficult to differentiate between the influence of *work* and all other factors which could weaken women. Sedentary occupation, low wages and poor diet had led to anaemia, over-strain and a variety of minor and major illnesses, particularly before the war. She quoted Mary Macarthur's words on this matter from the report of the Departmental Committee on Sickness Benefit Claims:

> The Committee has recorded its convictions that women are more liable to incapacity by sickness than men and it is my contention that (apart from normal physical reasons) this extra sickness in women is due to their greater poverty and to the character of their employment. Long hours, long standing, lack of fresh air, long intervals without food, are undeniably, especially in the case of young anaemic girls, detrimental to health and the low wages which attach to most women's employment involve insufficient and often improper food.[93]

Janet Campbell went on to describe how infant mortality varied acutely
from area to area, and how poverty, sanitation and the occupations of
both parents seemed to have an effect, while mortality could not be
directly associated with the fact that married women worked. The highest infant mortality rates were in mining, pottery and textile districts;
the former area contained women whose energies were concentrated on
heavy domestic work in their own homes, the latter contained wives who
commonly worked outside the home. Employment itself was classed by
Dr Campbell as being important for the effect it had on the health of
working wives, and upon the well-being of homes and children; the dual
role could lead to women being over-strained, which could, she decided,
have adverse effects upon their home lives. On the other hand, she
added, the light pleasant work of a factory worker might be far better
for women than the heavy domestic tasks of their own houses, and
'Such [evidence] as there is suggests that suitable employment under
reasonably good conditions is beneficial rather than harmful. In whatever class of society, a sedentary, unoccupied life is not healthy for the
expectant mother.'[94] Janet Campbell's own attitude to the evidence she
produced was ambiguous. She sympathised with women workers, and
urged that conditions of work be improved; she also deplored the ill
effects of bad housing and drudgery. But although she decided that
outside work might even be desirable for health reasons, she remained
worried about the effect it would have on homes and children. If one
accepts, as Campbell did, the idea that a mother's absence from the
home was automatically morally harmful, in simple terms, the question
which arises from her evidence is this: were the physical and intellectual
or emotional advantages gained by women from outside work of an
interesting and active nature outweighed by the moral disadvantages of
wives working away from their homes and neglecting their husbands
and housework? Most of those worried by the state of health of the
race denied that there might be anything beneficial about women working outside the home, and so did not encounter this problem. Similarly,
those who realised that the physical ill effects of well organised work
were in fact minimal, concentrated instead on the moral disadvantages.
But Janet Campbell admitted that women might be healthier and happier
working away from home, and therein lay her dilemma, as she found it
impossible to admit that women need not be the pivot around which
the home revolved. Since she could not solve this problem, she could
only suggest that conditions both at work and in the home should be
improved; such improvements were supposed to help women cope better
with the strain of maternity.

Very little happened as a result of these reports, both of which were published in 1918, too late to affect wartime policy. The government did not try to tackle the problem of women's low status in industry, in spite of the implications this had for health. Similarly, the idea of a minimum wage was never acceptable, and trade boards (themselves under attack from the government in the early 1920s) continued to fix women's rates of pay at a lower level than men's. No government after the war would have dared to intervene in the matter of the recruitment and pay of women workers; such intervention would have been seen as unacceptable by many in time of peace, even though the writers of the reports clearly hoped that the government would continue to use its power in industry. The concept of state intervention in this field was still alien to many politicians, and, in addition, although the government was prepared to limit women's hours of work and prevent them from working in a few trades, it was not prepared to interfere with the supply of labour except in wartime. If, by some means or other, it had been proved beyond all doubt that outside work really did damage women's health and adversely affect any children born, it is still extremely unlikely that any government would have done anything about this or considered banning all married women's work. Employers depended upon married women's labour, whether they recruited them directly for outwork, weaving, laundering, etc., or used them only occasionally when labour was short. No government would have considered putting women's health, or children's health, *before* the needs of industry. Women's health was an important *public* issue, and one which no doubt many individuals in Parliament considered to be vital, but it was never seen as being more important than either war production or the survival of profitable industries by many of those in government circles who claimed it was an issue dear to their hearts. Even though it appeared to be a national obsession, it did not lead to good wages, comfortable working conditions, free medical care, etc., on a wide scale, all of which men and women needed for the maintenance of health.

On the other hand, it did remain a useful additional excuse for keeping women out of certain jobs during the war, and for accepting their high rates of unemployment afterwards. When the needs of capitalism came into conflict with concern for racial health, the former was invariably the victor. Yet the two could also coexist and even reinforce one another — capitalism depended upon the existence of low-paid female labour, and this was provided by a society which believed that women should not take paid work seriously and should, for the sake of the race, class unpaid motherhood as their true career.

It was, however, through the Health of Munition Workers Committee that the government made its views on the matter of industrial welfare explicit. The Committee was set up to 'consider and advise on questions of industrial fatigue, hours of labour, and other matters affecting the personal health and physical efficiency of workers in munitions factories and workshops'.[95] In the wartime munitions industry the government was prepared to persuade employers to improve working conditions and take the matter of factory welfare seriously; it was not interested in doing this in peacetime, nor was it concerned with conditions in other industries. The government was unashamedly interested in the health of the worker in the factory because it wanted production to increase; the carrot dangled before employers was that of increased profits; workers were supposed to welcome the improved factory conditions and recreational facilities which theoretically resulted.

The Committee, however, took a very broad view of the word 'health', and one which had important implications for women workers:

> Moreover, the health of the industrial worker — man and woman — is but part, essential, plastic, living, of the health of the people as a whole, which in turn raises manifold problems of administration, economics, social relationships and even ethics, which though apparently remote from questions of medicine, are in truth, intimately related.[96]

Although primarily concerned with munitions workers, the Committee members were also interested in factors which were affecting industrial workers in general, and picked upon two particular problems: the advent of the woman worker, which raised 'new issues of physique, of physiological functions, of staying power, of nutrition, of maternity',[97] and the relation of man to the machine. They were most interested in preventive medicine

> which has as its object the removal of the *occasion of disease and physical inefficiency* combined with the husbanding of the physical resources of the worker in such a way and to such a degree that he can exert his full powers unhampered and with benefit to himself and all concerned,[98]

and they also expressed interest in the whole life of the worker, not simply in the prevention of physical injury:

nor is health only a physical condition. It is also mental and moral. Discontent, apathy, monotony, boredom and lack of interest in life may be just as detrimental as physical ailment and may equally involve irreparable loss in industrial fitness, well-being and efficiency.[99]

The 'whole man' and his surroundings needed attention, claimed the Committee, but in fact most attention was paid to women workers. Very little regard was paid to the health of the male workers who were left, or the health of men in industry in general. Why did the Committee concentrate on factory welfare for women?

Women certainly suffered more chronic low-level illness than men (which affected industrial efficiency), they made up the bulk of munitions workers during the war, they were working under particular pressure, and, as many pointed out, since they had lost so much freedom under the Munitions Act they deserved additional protection from the state (although this applied to the men too). But there are other factors to be taken into account. There is something strange about the existence of a committee which was ostensibly concerned with workers' health, and which recognised the damaging effects of poor wages, bad diet, inadequate housing and repeated pregnancy on women workers, yet was only concerned with factory welfare. Undeniably, it was set up by a government which was not interested in ameliorating conditions in the home or guaranteeing good wages; what was wanted was a quick return, in the form of an increased output in munitions, not the transformation of social life. The Health of Munition Workers Committee was supposed to accept the fact of women's vulnerability, without investigating the reasons for it, and work on schemes for improving their health and efficiency *through the factory*.

Women were of primary importance to the Committee because munitions production depended upon their efficient labour. But their health was also a matter for concern because of their reproductive role and domestic responsibilities; the need for efficiency had to be reconciled with the fact that England needed healthy mothers, and this was a matter that the Committee took very seriously, thus:

In considering the conditions of employment of women workers as compared with men, the Committee have recognised that account must be taken not only of physiological differences, but also of those contributions which women alone can make to the welfare of the community. Upon the womanhood of the country most largely rests the privilege first of creating and maintaining a wholesome family life, and secondly, of developing the higher influences of social life.[100]

For, continued the Committee, 'more than ever is their welfare of importance to the nation, and more than ordinarily is it threatened by conditions of employment.'[101] With this fact in mind, the Committee warned employers of the differences between male and female workers:

In considering in particular the *physical capacity of a woman* for withstanding the fatigue consequent upon prolonged industrial employment, it has to be remembered that her body is physiologically different from, and less strongly built than, that of a man. Her muscular system is less developed. At the present time many workers have until recently lived a sedentary or domestic life, and have not been in the habit of taking active and regular exercise. Certain ailments and forms of disability to which women are liable are readily caused or at least accentuated by inattention to these considerations. Among such *conditions in women* are:-

(a) Disturbance of digestion due to unsuitable food, irregular and hurried meals, or fatigue.
(b) Anaemia, with possibly associated disease of the heart and circulatory system.
(c) Headache.
(d) Nervous exhaustion.
(e) Muscular pain and weakness, flat foot etc.
(f) Derangement of special physiological functions.[102]

The aspects of women's work in the munitions industry which the Committee wished to consider were the following:

The physical conditions of work, and the capacity of the woman worker, including the effect on maternity.
The period of employment worked, including night work and its relation to home duties.
The necessities of rest periods, and the provision of meals.
The sanitary conditions of the factory, and the hygiene of the workers.
Questions of management and supervision.

The nature of the concern with women's health at work is all too clear. Women's weakness was seen as being inextricably bound up with their physiology; their femininity made them vulnerable, and working conditions were not supposed to interfere with their biological and social roles. Like other people, Committee members were concerned about the extent to which industrial work interfered with women's tasks in the family to the exclusion of interest in how work affected all people — thus the effect of night work for women was discussed, but the disruptive effect of men's night work upon their families and themselves was ignored. Men's health in the munitions industry was in fact discussed by the Committee, but not at such length, and not in the same terms as women's health, quite simply because men were assumed to be stronger *and* because they had no domestic duties to fulfil. They did not need so much protection, and they were supposed to be more willing to encounter dangerous conditions at work.

What, then, were the Committee's recommendations on the subject of change within the factory? Many of them were in fact welcomed by the labour movement, and had little to do with the protection of women in particular; canteens, rest breaks, seats, cloakrooms and recreational facilities would have benefited both male and female workers. In these matters the Committee recommended more than the government was prepared to enforce; employers were simply encouraged to make such reforms, and told of how much more efficient a less fatigued workforce would be. The government was not prepared to step in to protect women working with TNT or aircraft dope, or make sure that they received financial reward for the risk they ran;[103] there remained a bleak contrast between the brave new world envisaged by the Committee, and actual conditions.

However, there was one recommendation which was taken very seriously by the government and a number of employers, and which was aimed particularly at women. The Committee suggested that firms appoint welfare supervisors to oversee matters to do with the health and welfare of the work-force. Welfare supervision was primarily designed for women and boy workers, and involved a mixture of physical and moral guardianship. Welfare supervisors were supposed to oversee employment and dismissal, watch out for health hazards, organise canteens and recreational facilities; they were also supposed to ensure that women behaved in a discreet way with male workers, and that they lived in respectable lodgings. To make matters more delicate, they were employed not by the state, but by the employers, and thus could be accused of working on their behalf.

A number of people welcomed the idea of supervision, and maintained that women in particular would benefit from it. Noble ideals sometimes lay behind it, even when it was admitted that it was primarily to increase efficiency. One employer, writing for the *Engineer* on the subject, insisted that it was more than a fad, and that it was of benefit to employers and workers alike; his words show the kind of enthusiasm it raised with philanthropic employers:

> The employee is more than a 'hand', more than a ten-fingered mach- ine, and the day has long passed when he was regarded as a useful, adaptable machine that could be hired, worked out, and scrapped. Business economy and efficiency, if not higher motives, demand that the worker shall perform his task under healthful and hygienic con- ditions; that anxiety about sickness and old age shall be removed.[104]

He concluded:

> Work should never be a burden to the normally healthy man or woman, and the aim of welfare work should be to prevent it from being so, and to give leisure and inclination for the pursuit of those more enduring things which make for a fuller and completer life.

But this employer was rare in referring to workers as male, as most people assumed that welfare supervision was primarily for women. The Handbook of the Health of Munition Workers Committee, which was produced as a guide for employers, stated that the supervisors should investigate the reasons for lost time, oversee working conditions, super- vise night work, make home visits, organise canteens, evening classes and recreational facilities, and set up thrift schemes; the writers then added that men needed such supervision less than did women or boys. The Committee decided it would be difficult to apply it to men because many would see it as an intrusion, and that works councils would be more suitable for monitoring the conditions of work. Members did not appear to consider that supervision might also have appeared intrusive to women, even though they finally admitted that 'unwise and unsatis- factory appointments' of supervisors had been made,[105] which had led to many complaints, and that welfare would fail 'in so far as any en- deavour is made to conduct it in a spirit of patronage or superficial philanthropy'.[106]

There were many objectionable features about welfare supervision which the Committee just did not appear to understand. It rested upon the kind of assumptions about women which Dorothea Proud put into words:

Women are habitually less thoughtful than men in matters concerning their own health, and a mixture of mock modesty and ignorance
commonly prevents them from consciously considering themselves
as potential mothers. Whatever changes may occur, the health of
women workers must needs be of paramount importance to the
nation. Their position in industry, even though partially safeguarded
by legislation, is still unsatisfactory.[107]

This attitude (expressed in her book *Welfare Work*) assumes an almost
deliberate ignorance and carelessness on the part of working-class
women, and ignores the fact that all women were denied full knowledge
of their sexuality and the mechanics of reproduction — and continued
'innocence' on this subject was one of the welfare supervisor's aims when
she kept apart men and women workers. In addition, Proud seemed to
feel that women should organise their lives around the possibility of
future motherhood. She wrote:

That women are consciously animated by a sense of their responsibilities towards potential offspring is not to be supposed. That there
is, dormant, some such sense, can scarcely be doubted. It would
probably benefit the whole nation if it were raised to consciousness
and fostered by wise legislation.[108]

The above assumptions went hand in hand with the idea that those who
'knew better' could interfere not only inside but outside the factory,
since all this would be done in the interests of the race. It was hard
enough when the supervisor controlled working conditions, but it was
almost intolerable for working women when she ventured on to the
subject of their 'morals'. The *Queen* carried an article in 1916 about the
duties of a welfare supervisor which is most revealing:

In a sense the behaviour and morals of the workers are in her care. If
any of the hands are too noisy or too free with the men workers,
hers is the delicate task of dealing with this. When the young girls at
the factory telephone exchange were found to idle in their closed
room, it was the supervisor who had glass sides put in (much to their
sorrow!). The supervisor must risk being unpopular until the workers
realise that she is their friend.[109]

One can only imagine the fury with which the glass walls were received,
and wonder how this change was explained on the grounds of 'friendship'

or even protection. Clearly the reasoning behind the action was that it would increase 'efficiency': it is a common idea amongst employers that workers must be seen to be working, and that even if they have nothing to do, they should look busy.

Helen Fraser, in *Women and War Work*, also classed supervision of the behaviour of women and girls as one of the welfare worker's most important duties,[110] and M.C. Matheson (one of Cadbury's co-authors on women workers a decade before), writing for the *Women's Industrial News*, stated her belief that the average mother

> will be glad that someone will support her daughter in her effort not to succumb to evil talk and foul insinuation, to the temptation to join drinking parties or in pleasures that look harmless to the high-spirited girl and are full of peril.[111]

But in fact, women of all ages were treated like ignorant adolescents, and where the welfare worker's supervision ended that of the women's police force began: they watched women outside factories, and attempted to steer them towards girls' clubs instead of conversations with male workers or soldiers. This in turn has clear connections with the supervision of soldiers' and sailors' wives by the ordinary police force, who were supposed to ensure that they did not spend their separation allowances on drink.[112] The same desire to 'guard' women was expressed by Runciman, when he spoke to the ladies who had volunteered to lodge women workers:

> We know that such work can be better done by such organisations as yours than by a government office. You can help in inspecting lodgings and in keeping an eye on the young women and girls in order that their new employment may not bring them into any danger.[113]

These words were from 1915, and in time the state did encourage a more formal guardianship by allowing the emergence of a women's police force, but significantly neither this nor welfare supervision were ever actually organised by the government. Welfare supervisors, who were predominantly middle-class, remained employees of factory owners, and retained an amateurishly patronising approach. The use of untrained middle-class women in the pay of employers was in fact criticised by many of those who wanted welfare work to be an extension of the factory legislation, including Dorothea Proud, who welcomed the concept of welfare work but despaired of the way in which it was being carried out. She thought women were rightfully contemptuous of employers who attempted to improve them morally while paying such low wages that girls were encouraged to depend on men friends for new clothes, and she noted that attempts to separate married women from young girls (who might be 'corrupted' by the former's talk of sex and childbirth) were 'ridiculed as absurd, if not resented as unwarrantable interference'.[114]

Most opposition, however, came from the labour movement and the workers themselves, to whom the whole idea of welfare supervision was abhorrent. It was suspected that welfare would be used to increase output and lower wages still further for female workers,[115] and that the words of the *Yorkshire Observer* would prove to be all too accurate when it claimed that 'if women were treated with courtesy and consideration by the management they would concede a great deal.'[116] As many people pointed out, if wages and conditions were good enough, women should be able to look after themselves.[117] Welfare supervisors did not endear themselves further when they suggested, as some apparently did, that women should not bother to join trade unions[118] — a writer in the *Athenaeum* struck back by saying that one woman trade union leader was worth a hundred welfare workers.[119] Welfare supervision was clearly seen as being associated with scientific management, which led to fears that it would be used to control workers after the war in industries employing the techniques of mass production.

But apart from the economic considerations, welfare workers were disliked for their interference in women workers' lives. There is little doubt as to the extent of their unpopularity.[120] Mary Macarthur referred to welfare as being 'the most unpopular work in the terminology of the factory worker',[121] while Kate Manicom of the *Trade Union Worker* noted the difference in attitude towards men and women workers which the concept incorporated:

> We find no necessity for a Welfare Supervisor to be placed over the men; moreover they would not tolerate such a thing for a moment. So we demand again that if women are to enter industry in work hitherto done by men, they should be treated as workers, not as irresponsible children.[122]

This was an apt comparison; as physical and moral supervisors, welfare workers felt they were entitled to criticise women's behaviour. 'If you go to the picture-house three times a week, you hear about it from her,' complained one girl,[123] and supervisors and superintendents sometimes did not hesitate to tell women to take off their make-up or get rid of their awful hats.[124] Women living in hostels attached to the factories found themselves even more under control; in many places gates were locked and lights put out between 10.00 and 10.30, and neither alcohol nor male visitors were allowed inside.[125] The assumption that working-class women should accept criticism and checks on their personal lives led one writer for the *National News* to say indignantly:

> Factory girls are just as sensitive to home truths as other women. They object to comments on their dress and their domestic arrange-ments from the welfare worker as much as she would object to similar comments from them. One lady made her debut in a factory where very rough girls worked by saying to them 'you want a club, you come from such overcrowded, dirty homes,' and then she was astounded when they threw their lunch at her![126]

There must have existed some welfare supervisors who genuinely wished to improve factory conditions and did not want to interfere in workers' home lives, but these were likely to be regarded with suspicion simply because they were in a minority, and they were, no matter how good their intentions, in the employ of management. The *Woman Worker* spared a thought for this kind of person:

> The present developments seem to us to place the sincere welfare worker in an impossible position. If she truly studies the interests of the girls, her position is made difficult by the employer, to whom her recommendations often mean capital outlay; yet the girls never forget that she is part of the management staff, and therefore sus-pect. Kindness is met by a suspicious 'What's she getting at,' and the woman who tries to raise their physical efficiency by compulsory rest is a 'fusspot'.[127]

But these were rare individuals, and most workers and their representa-tives rightly assumed that welfare workers were not working in their interest.

Outside government circles, even more objectionable schemes were often proposed for the supervision or 'guardianship' of working-class women – schemes which assumed that women workers were inclined to drunkenness[128] and child neglect if not watched carefully, and which tolerated a double sexual standard for men and women.[129] Some in-dividuals moved amongst the women workers criticising their lack of

awareness of the importance of war work, or their poor taste in literature (Lady Scott, in the *Daily Graphic*, proudly announced that she had
introduced them to the joys of the works of Stevenson and Conrad!);[130]
others set up thrift schemes, and deplored the fact that working girls
were spending their new-found money on unsuitable items – they had to
be taught that it was 'unpatriotic' to buy jewellery and gramophones;[131]
another suggestion was that 'women of leisure' should care for working
women's children during the war, and also teach women workers how
to look after their homes properly.[132] At the same time, women were
criticised because they did not always spend all their maternity benefit
on doctors and nurses, and it was suggested that such benefit be spent
for them suitably by 'charitably disposed ladies, or local government
officials', an idea which led the *Woman's Dreadnought* to say acidly,
'Some people cannot endure the thought of a working woman having a
few shillings to spend.'[133]

There are clear associations here with the ideas which lay behind
welfare supervision and the supervision of soldiers' wives. But in addition, welfare supervision was seen as the symbol of an alliance between
the government and employers; while less patronising than any of the
schemes designed by individuals, it was theoretically more dangerous,
and was, because of its interference with private lives, regarded as an
insult to working-class women.

But the interesting thing is that the government and its committees
were clearly in line with the prevailing ideas of the time with regard to
the need for the guardianship and 'protection' of working-class women,
and although representatives of the labour movement condemned this
approach when it was adopted by the state, and of course recognised
the hypocrisy of those who talked of guarding the 'mothers of the race'
while they continued to exploit them, there were strong elements of
patronage in the labour movement's own treatment of working-class
women. They had their own schemes for encouraging thrift or 'baby
saving', and their own convictions that women should devote themselves
to their families. The language used when discussing women's health
and welfare was the same throughout society; as I have shown, speeches
about the health of the race, the importance of preserving working-class
mothers and the need to prevent women from permanently abandoning
their homes or 'allowing' themselves to be physically damaged by work
were not the monopoly of the upper classes, employers and government.
The interests of trade unionists, employers and government were clearly
not the same. The labour movement saw itself as protecting the family
against assaults on its health, and regarded the exploitation of women

workers as an attack on maternity. Employers accepted the idea that women were wives and mothers first and foremost largely because this meant that women would remain cheap to employ; while there were some who genuinely wished to reform working conditions for women's sake, others were happy to improve certain aspects of factory conditions, employ welfare supervisors, and pay women considerably less money. The government, in the meantime, had to take account of public opinion on the matter, but was in general prepared to sanction their exploitation rather than interfere with supplies of labour, or profits.

By accepting not only the sexual differentiation of labour, but the idea that women needed more protection than men in industry, the labour movement was playing into the hands of employers and throwing away a chance to campaign for better conditions and safeguards throughout industry. A united stand for improved conditions for *men and women* would not have solved all the problems of women's poor health, during or after the war. It would, however, have been a step towards helping all workers, and would have been an admission of women's right to work alongside men. Instead, the labour movement continued to accept the idea that women were like a different species, with an inherently weaker constitution, different requirements in industry, and different duties at home. These beliefs did little to foster the health of either men or women, for while it was acceptable for the latter to wear themselves out with childbearing and heavy domestic work at home, men were supposed to accept the strain of long working hours and poor conditions simply because of their extra physical strength. It should also be noted that many of those who spoke most loudly about the need to limit women's employment in industry and encourage their domestic role kept quiet not only about the harmfulness of outwork or the classic 'women's trades', but about the damage done to women by a succession of pregnancies and crudely performed abortions. The focus remained on women's outside work, even amongst trade unionists who should have known better from their own experience. To have taken up these issues would have been to challenge the existing structure of society, and few people in the labour movement, or elsewhere, were prepared to go so far.

There were many ironies in the whole approach to women's health at work and the connection with domesticity, not least in the juxta position of romantic ideas of motherhood with deep suspicions about women's propensity for drunkenness and the possible abandonment of their children. Unfortunately, working-class women were always the victims of this philosophy, whether its proponents were government spokesmen, employers, trade unionists or middle-class do-gooders. The labour movement was bitterly critical of the government's plans for welfare supervision, yet the words of some labour leaders could have been spoken by the government's own advisers, or by welfare workers themselves. In 1917, Mary Macarthur said, 'Women have done some wonderful work, but a baby is more wonderful than a machine gun. I believe that the hand that rocks the cradle will still be a power when the other is only a hateful memory.'[134] This was a ridiculous comparison; certainly a baby was more important than a machine gun, but Mary Macarthur's statement was designed to devalue the importance of women's industrial work and encourage the idea that bearing children was women's most important task. Welfare supervision was patronising, intrusive and potentially dangerous to the working class because of its associations, but was it more patronising to women than many of trade unionists' schemes? As many feminists had seen, the whole concept of protection for one sex was damaging to women's interests, and to *workers'* interests. It is an intriguing thought that had the labour movement been able to influence the government on this subject either during the war or afterwards, women might have found themselves hedged around with far more restrictions; if motherhood had really been taken as seriously as the trade union movement desired, or as the government pretended, life for the woman who did not relish the role of 'mother of the race' would have become much harder when she tried to find paid work.

Notes

1. *Woman's Dreadnought*, 17 Apr. 1915, 'The Baby Saving Crusade'.

2. Adelaide Anderson, *Women Workers and the Health of the Nation* (pamphlet, 1918).

3. Theoretically, employers had to ask for permission from the government to use women on night work, or on certain processes classed as dangerous, and to work them abnormally long hours, but, in fact, since permission was seldom refused, many employers did not bother to ask.

4. Sylvia Pankhurst, *The Home Front* (Hutchinson, 1932), p. 278. See also p. 340, about conditions in aircraft works.

5. For example, *Daily Express* and *Evening Standard*, 19 Sept. 1917, 'Do Women Work too Long?'

6. *Evening Standard*, 19 Aug. 1916, '12 Hour Day for Women'; *The Times*, 24 Oct. 1916, letter from Lilian Barker.

7. For example, *British Citizen*, 8 Dec. 1915, 'Sweated Women First'; see also reports from the War Emergency: Workers' National Committee.

8. *Daily News*, 25 Apr. 1917, 'Girl Munitioners: Causes of Present Unrest and Nervous Trouble'; *Daily Express*, 17 July 1916, 'Airship Dope and Dopers'; *New Statesman*, 3 Feb. 1917, 'Women's Greater Sacrifice'; *Dundee Courier*, 4 Jan.

1917, 'The Deadly T.N.T. Poison'; letters in *The Times*, 14 Sept. 1917; 8 July 1917; 6 Sept. 1917.

9. The *Lancet*, 12 Aug. 1916, 'Observations on the Effects of T.N.T. on Women Workers'.

10. See the interviews made by the Imperial War Museum, plus Joan Williams' typescript, 'A Munition Worker's Career'; also Rosina Wyatt's descriptions of life in John Burnett, *Useful Toil* (Allen Lane, 1974).

11. Health of Munition Workers' Committee, *Final Report*, Appendix B by Janet Campbell.

12. *Woman's Dreadnought*, 22 May 1915, 'Excessive Hours'.

13. D.J. Collier and B.L. Hutchins, *The Girl in Industry* (Bell & Sons, 1918), pp. 7, 8 and 11.

14. Collier and Hutchins, *The Girl in Industry*; also I.O Andrews, *The Economic Effects of the World War upon Women and Children in Great Britain* (Oxford University Press, 1921), and Janet Campbell's work in the Health of Munition Workers' Committee reports.

15. For example, Monica Cosens, *Lloyd George's Munition Girls* (Hutchinson, 1916), and Williams, 'A Munition Worker's Career'.

16. *Woman Worker*, July 1916, letters.

17. *Co-operative News*, 24 Oct. 1914, 'The War and the Future of the Race'.

18. B.L. Hutchins, *Women in Modern Industry* (Bell and Sons, 1915).

19. *Western Mercury*, 8 June 1918, 'Reconstruction'.

20. *Daily News*, 16 June 1917, 'Mothers and Children'.

21. Anderson, *Women Workers and the Health of the Nation*, p. 11.

22. The *Child's Guardian*, February 1918, 'An Armory of Facts'.

23. *New Witness*, 22 July 1915, 'Babies and Shells'.

24. *Daily News*, 4 Sept. 1918, 'Equal Work for Men and Women'.

25. *Daily News*, 11 Sept. 1918, 'The Working Mother'.

26. Lecture, 'The Factors of Infant Mortality', published by the National Baby Week Council, 1918.

27. *North Mail*, 6 Dec. 1916, 'Mothers of the State'.

28. Countess of Warwick, *A Woman and the War* (Chapman and Hall, 1916), chapter on 'Race Suicide'.

29. *Ladies' Pictorial*, 6 Oct. 1917, 'Women's Working Hours'.

30. *Daily Express*, 19 Dec. 1916, 'Safeguarding the Women'.

31. *The Times*, 24 June 1916, 'Women Workers and their Children'.

32. *Daily Mail*, 23 Aug. 1918, 'Women's Wages'.

33. Anderson, *Women Workers and the Health of the Nation*, p. 8.

34. Ibid., p. 10.

35. Basil Worsfold, *War and Social Reform* (Murray, 1919), p. 72.

36. Ibid., p. 162.

37. British Association for the Advancement of Science, *Outlets for Labour after the War*, p. 13.

38. *Sunday Chronicle*, 10 Sept. 1916.

39. *Kentish Independent*, 23 Jan. 1915, 'Women and Employment'.

40. For example, see S.J. Chapman in A.W. Dawson's *Afterwar Problems* (Allen & Unwin, 1919), p. 140, and the welcome given to the Women's Industrial Council's inquiry into 'Industry and Motherhood'.

41. *Trade Union Worker*, January 1916, 'The Woman Worker of Today and Tomorrow',

42. TUC, 1916.

43. *Woman Worker*, February 1917.

44. *Labour Woman*, June 1916, 'Women's Work after the War'.

45. Marion Phillips (ed.), *Women and the Labour Party* (Headley Bros., 1918), p. 20.

46. *Labour Woman*, March 1917, 'Munition Work or Babies'.

47. One correspondent even claimed that if women refused to bear children they became 'nervous wrecks'. *Labour Woman*, May 1916.

48. See, for example, G.D.H. Cole, *Labour in Wartime* (Bell & Sons, 1915), Ch. 8.

49. *Trade Union Worker*, February 1917, 'Women After the War'.

50. *Birmingham Gazette*, 12 June 1916, 'Woman's Part in Industry'.

51. *Labour Woman*, September 1916.

52. Dr Saleeby, *Saving the Future: The War and the Coming Race* (1917) (Imperial War Museum Collection, Box 170, Wel.I.).

53. Saleeby, *Saving the Future*.

54. Harold Scurfield, *Civic Responsibilities with Regard to Child Welfare* (1918) (Imperial War Museum, Box 170, Wel.I.).

55. Ibid.

56. 1917 report of the National Baby Week Council.

57. Ibid.

58. Benjamin Broadbent, *The Duty of Citizens in the Promotion of Child Welfare* (1917) (Imperial War Museum Collection, Box 170, Wel.I.).

59. *New Age*, 12 Aug. 1915 and 26 Aug. 1915, letters from Gladys Biss.

60. *New Age*, 15 July 1915, 'Survey of the Women Workers' World'.

61. *New Age*, 25 Nov. 1915, 'Women in Industry Again'.

62. I say 'glorification', but this did not mean that men wanted to take part in these noble tasks!

63. *Trade Union Worker*, July 1916, 'Co-operative Housekeeping'.

64. *Labour Woman*, February 1918, 'Co-operative Housekeeping and Housing Reform'.

65. *Labour Woman*, January and February 1919, 'Shorter Hours for the Woman at Home', I & II.

66. *Labour Woman*, January 1919.

67. *Labour Woman*, February 1919.

68. Ch. 3, p. 74.

69. Phillips, *Women and the Labour Party*, chapter on 'The Working Woman's House'.

70. *The Engineer*, 22 Mar. 1918. See Ch. 3.

71. Dorothea Proud, *Welfare Work* (Bell & Sons, 1916), pp. 236-7.

72. *Worker's Dreadnought*, 15 Sept. 1917, 'Babies and Patriots'.

73. Lady Randolph Churchill, *Women's War Work* (C. Arthur Pearson, 1916), p. 155.

74. *Common Cause*, 29 Sept. 1916, 'Women's Work after the War'.

75. For example, *Daily Chronicle*, 19 Aug. 1915, 'End of Restrictions'.

76. B.L. Hutchins, *Women in Industry after the War* (Social Reconstruction Pamphlet No. 3), p. 3.

77. *Common Cause*, 3 Nov. 1916, 'The State and the Family'.

78. *Common Cause*, 21 July 1916, 'For the Sake of the Race'.

79. There are of course gaping holes in the logic of this paragraph; if husbands really did stop working when their wives were earning, then women would become the breadwinners; this would make them wholly dependent upon their wages, which would theoretically mean they did not accept inadequate wages. But in any case, the more desperate a person for money, the lower the wages he/she will accept, so in all ways Carol Ring's reasoning is wrong.

80. This approach to the role of mother was clearly made by those who wished to prove how worthy women were of the vote, countering claims that women did little for society. In addition, many feminists emphasised the contrast between women as mothers (pure, and non-sexual beings), and men, who were

sexual predators, and a destructive influence in society.

81. *Labour Woman*, April 1916.

82. *Labour Woman*, February 1917, 'The Mother's Point of View'.

83. *Daily Chronicle*, 20 May 1918, 'Women leave the Gas Industry'.

84. Broadbent, *Duty of Citizens*.

85. As the Committee said: 'In considering women's labour, the relation of their work to the duties which fall to them as mothers and homemakers has necessarily to be born in mind.' *Report of the Women's Employment Committee* (1918), p. 6.

86. *Report of the Women's Employment Committee*, p. 60.

87. Report of the War Cabinet Committee on *Women in Industry*, p. 107.

88. *Women in Industry*, p. 172.

89. Ibid., p. 172.

90. Ibid., Memorandum by Dr Janet Campbell, p. 218.

91. Quoted in Health of Munition Workers' Committee, *Final Report*, 1918.

92. Janet Campbell's Memorandum, p. 223.

93. Ibid., p. 226.

94. Ibid., p. 243.

95. *Final Report*, Introduction.

96. Ibid., p. 7.

97. Ibid., p. 7.

98. Ibid., p. 7.

99. *Handbook* of the Health of Munition Workers' Committee, p. 13.

100. *Final Report*, p. 20.

101. Ibid., p. 21.

102. Ibid., p. 20.

103. A limited number of women were awarded state compensation for ill health caused by TNT, but it was difficult to prove that TNT was responsible to the satisfaction of the authorities.

104. *The Engineer*, 2 Feb. 1917, 'Is Welfare Work Good Business?'.

105. *Final Report*, p. 107.

106. *Handbook*, p. 109.

107. Proud, *Welfare Work*, p. 78.

108. Ibid., pp. 78-9.

109. The *Queen*, 8 Sept. 1916.

110. Helen Fraser, *Women and War Work* (G. Arnold Shaw, 1918).

111. *Women's Industrial News*, July 1917, 'Welfare Work'; also *Economic Journal*, 1916, 'Women in Industry'.

112. For example, see articles in *Woman's Dreadnought*, 15 Jan. 1916 and 15 July 1916.

113. *Woman's Dreadnought*, 17 Apr. 1915, report of the Board of Trade Conference.

114. Proud, *Welfare Work*, p. 86.

115. Under the *Police (Miscellaneous Provisions) Act*, employers were in fact entitled to deduct the cost of welfare provisions from the total wages bill.

116. *Yorkshire Observer*, 17 July 1916, 'Mirrors and Labour Unrest'. Talking about the textile industry, the writer described how much happier women were when they were allowed to hang mirrors on their looms, to look at themselves during the day.

117. *Labour Woman*, November 1916, letter from 'XYZ'; *Labour Woman*, February 1917, letter from 'Observer'; *Women's Industrial News*, April 1917, 'Welfare Work'.

118. *Labour Woman*, February 1917, letter from 'Observer'; *Trade Union Worker*, June 1917, 'The Welfare Supervisor'.

119. The *Athenaeum*, January, 1918, 'The Future of the Woman War Worker'.

120. Marion Phillips was certainly right when she reported that workers complained bitterly about the pretence that welfare supervision was there to help them, rather than to make the business more profitable. *Daily News*, 4 May 1917, 'War and the Welfare Worker'.

121. Quoted by Andrews, *Effects of the War*, p. 159.

122. *Trade Union Worker*, June 1917, 'The Welfare Supervisor'.

123. *Daily Sketch*, 7 May 1917, report on the Conference of Industrial Women's Organisations.

124. Hall Caine's description in the *Daily Graphic*, 6 Nov. 1916, 'The Shell Girl'.

125. *New Witness*, 9 Mar. 1917, editorial.

126. *National News*, 8 Mar. 1917, 'Women after the War'.

127. *Woman Worker*, February 1917, 'Welfare in the West Country'.

128. Such ideas were fuelled by Lloyd George's tirades about drink and the working classes, but staunchly denied by Lord d'Abernon, amongst others, in a lecture on 'Public Health and Alcoholism among Women', reported in the *Child's Guardian*, February 1918.

129. *Woman's Dreadnought*, 5 Jan. 1915. A suffragette deputation protested against the attitudes of people who believed that soldiers needed sexual relief, but who threatened to cut off soldiers' wives' allowances if they failed to live up to certain moral standards.

130. *Daily Graphic*, 9 Nov. 1916, 'The Shell Girl as I Knew Her'.

131. *Southampton Times*, 6 Nov. 1915, 'Women and Thrift'.

132. *New Age*, 15 July 1915, 'Survey of the Woman Worker's World'; *Standard*, 12 July 1915.

133. *Woman's Dreadnought*, 12 Aug. 1916, 'An Insult'.

134. *Daily News*, 15 Aug. 1917, 'Women in Industry'.

6 WOMEN'S PUBLIC IMAGE DURING THE WAR

In this chapter I want to broaden the field of discussion. So far, I have said much about the opinions of employers, unions and government, and other interested parties, on the subject of women's industrial worth, and the interaction of women's duties at home and work. But many of the debates about women took place in less rarefied surroundings, and were on a more general level. It is to the amorphous concept of 'public opinion' that I wish to turn now. What kinds of discussions were going on during the war about women's work or their future prospects, and what kinds of feelings were expressed? My sources here are books and press reports of the time, particularly the latter. Newspapers of various kinds reflected the views of their readers, and also encouraged them to form certain opinions through the articles they produced; then, as now, the press was both a reflector and arbiter of opinion. Editors and journalists usually wrote what they thought their readers wanted to see (within the confines of wartime censorship), and although crusading journalists who supported the underdog were tolerated, no paper could afford to be too much out of step with its regular readership. Fortunately, the press represented a very wide range of political views during these years — far wider than today. Newspapers and popular books do have to be treated with care, for it must be recognised that they were encouraged by the government (or by their own sense of patriotism) to emphasise the positive aspects of women's work; many writers were unashamedly producing propaganda. But this in itself is important, since there must have been many people who believed the reports they read, and made judgements about women on the basis of them. The press also gave particular public figures the opportunity to state their opinions, and letter columns were an interesting barometer of feelings.

Throughout the war, much attention was paid by journalists and writers to women workers, their role in life, their future, and the attitude of 'experts' towards them, not least because the suffragettes had drawn attention to the position of women before the war. The first thing to realise is that during the years 1914 to 1918 the expectation amongst many people was that society would be transformed once peace came; the appalling slaughter was made more endurable through the belief that some good might come of it ultimately. Individuals might speak cynically about the craze for discussing reconstruction, as did one writer (a 'workman') for the *Athanaeum*, who noted:

> The interesting feature of the ideas and proposals being put forward is that while they purport to be measures which are the expression of a 'new spirit in the Nation', and by which the nation is to be rehabilitated after the ravages of the War, at least 90% would have actually been in the range of public discussion had there been no war at all.[1]

But such people were in a minority: many others hoped for radical improvements in the nature of industry and social life as a direct result of the war, and indeed the post-war government was elected on the basis that it would be an agent of reform, for 'ministers had stated again and again that the people, by their conduct during the war, had won the right to a better way of life.'[2] Many believed they already saw signs of the changes to come. Even in 1915, Mary Somerville was writing for the *Women's Liberal Review*: 'Oh! This War! How it is tearing down walls and barriers, and battering in fast shut doors,' and looking forward to the time when 'all work will be noble and inspiring, even factory work, because its conditions and surroundings will be noble and pure.'[3]

Changes were also noted by Dr Shadwell in the *Edinburgh Review*, when he claimed that the war:

> has disclosed deficiencies, waste and weakness, as well as unsuspected sources of strength. It has caused the whole [industrial apparatus] to be overhauled, forced the investigation of standing, but neglected problems, stimulated reform in many directions, and opened the way to a new order . . . there is no going back to the pre-existing state of mind.[4]

Schemes for factory welfare were the cause of much enthusiasm in some articles, and of self-congratulation on the part of the government when speaking to the public: Lloyd George quoted Rowntree in a speech in 1917, saying:

> It is a strange irony, but no small compensation, that the making of weapons of destruction should afford the occasion to humanise industry. Yet such is the case. Old prejudices have vanished, new ideas are abroad; employers, the workers, the public and the State, are all favourable to new methods.[5]

But enthusiasm ranged beyond the bounds of simple factory reform — 'social regeneration' was the ideal. No one could fail to be affected by the psychological atmosphere of the time, wrote M.A. Hamilton a few years later.[6] Optimism was soon to be replaced by bitterness, Hamilton went on: 'Dreams of a new England after the War — today a mocking laughter echoes through them. In 1918 they visited everyone,'[7] but while the dreams lasted (and they began before 1918), there was much discussion about what should be done for England by the state, and how individuals could aid this transformation. Even Sylvia Pankhurst confessed to being caught up for a while in the spirit of optimism, taken in by the 'press romancing of social regeneration' and the 'scheme spinning of [Sidney] Webb'. She spoke for many when she added, 'one is easily gulled when appeal is made to one's heart's desire.'[8]

What part would women play in social regeneration? This question caused much discussion, and invariably the investigation into women's wartime performance also included consideration of their future prospects. But while government reports tended to look at women as a social problem, at the same time there were many who made glowing statements, reported in papers, magazines and books, about the way in which women's position in society had changed, and how the clock could not be turned back. In 1918, Ben Morgan, an engineer, was reported as saying to the Annual Meeting of the National Council of Women that 'The lesson he drew from the future was that women must not retrace their steps from the path of industry which had carried them into a new world,'[9] and a chorus of similarly optimistic statements came from people in all sections of society. Neville Chamberlain took up the theme in one of his speeches, saying:

Among the changes in our social fabric which have been brought about by the war . . . none is more remarkable than the development of women's activities. In previous wars they had been confined to specially feminine tasks such as the nursing and feeding of soldiers and the making of garments and bandages. In this war they had not only done these things, but they had invaded the spheres hitherto considered sacred to men. They had come into the office, the munition factory, even to the tramcars. They had become postmen, policemen and agricultural labourers, and they had done all those things with an efficiency which had surprised and delighted the whole nation.[10]

In this speech the fallacy is clear; it was assumed that because women were doing new jobs an overwhelming social change had taken place, and, to use the words of Mary Stocks in her article in the *Athenaeum*, that 'there is no mending of broken traditions and no re-erecting of shattered illusions.'[11] The future was thus to be different, for as a *Times* journalist wrote, as early as 1916, 'The evolution of the working woman will not stop with the war. Her period of "making good" is to be for all time, and parents will have to educate their daughters accordingly.'[12] Such dreams were not to be fulfilled, and it should be clear from this book that in many ways even more problems were raised by the war, yet such was the belief in the imminence of social change that even people who knew well what kind of industrial conflict might follow the war, nevertheless felt that *something* had already changed in society's, or men's, attitude to women. Mary Macarthur insisted that

> Of all the changes worked by the war none has been greater than the change in the status and position of women: and yet it is not so much that woman herself has changed, as that man's conception of her has changed.[13]

Mrs Fawcett claimed that war 'revolutionised men's minds and their conception of the sort of work of which the ordinary everyday woman was capable',[14] and Adelaide Anderson considered that women's newly discovered mobility and the mixture of classes in the workshop were together 'factors of immense consequence in the economic and social life of the future'.[15]

In fact, men's conception of women often remained precisely the same as it had been before the war, as we have seen, so what led to this feeling that some sort of momentous change had taken place? The press and propagandists played a large part in promoting the idea; newspaper writers talked of the way in which women by 1918 had 'reached a position of freedom and responsibility that in 1914 seemed centuries away', or contrasted the present with the 'dimly remembered days when the place of women was said to be in the home'.[16] Often these writers expressed genuine enthusiasm, but their claims were not backed by evidence. Women themselves may have gained much from the experience of war work, but men's attitudes to them were another matter.

The approach of the press and propagandists must be considered in more detail, not only because articles and popular books encouraged readers to believe that women's circumstances had drastically changed, even where there was little evidence for these claims, but also because judiciously chosen paragraphs from the papers were used then, and are still used now, to give the impression that women had broken through male prejudice. There *were* some reasoned and informed articles about women and their work, many of which I have quoted from already.[17] There were also pieces of sentimental and inaccurate rubbish. There are two important points to be made. First, although many journalists talked of social regeneration and the changes in women's status, as we have seen from the preceding pages, these matters were never fully explored: writers remained very vague about what these changes might mean, if they existed. Readers were apparently supposed to trust that there had been some kind of social revolution simply because a percentage of women were doing the work of men — and, of course, as I showed in Chapter 2, the press gave very exaggerated reports of the extent to which women *were* doing men's work. Secondly, the articles about social change were not even effectively linked with numerous articles about women's war work itself, which were usually descriptive pieces, and were frequently anecdotal. It is true that women achieved much attention because of their work, and that the praise they received in the press was something new. Journalists reported that employers and male workers had changed their attitude to women workers, and at the same time, the very fact that the articles were being written at all encouraged the idea that women deserved to be praised, and that, for once, their work was important. These two aspects together gave the impression that men in general, and their agents in the press, had changed their collective mind about women. Unfortunately, we have seen that in reality the old prejudices and ideals still existed amongst employers, trade unionists, government committee members, etc., and the articles which appeared in newspapers proved to be all too shallow when examined. Writers were looking for good stories, and liked to take for their subject brave, pretty little munitions girls; they were also trying to keep up morale amongst both civilians and troops, and acted as unofficial recruiting agents for industry, when they described war work as being 'good fun'. Working-class women needed the jobs anyway, but could be lured from less popular trades, and middle-class women could be attracted by the lively prose of the journalist. Naomi Loughnan, a middle-class volunteer, recalled that:

> The papers spoke of shells and tool setters, of enormous wages and cheery canteens, happy hostels and gay girl workers . . . we were sick of frivolling, we wanted to do something big and hard, because of our boys and of England.[18]

Newspapers took tales of women's skills and embroidered them, dwelt much on the attractive picture working girls made, and heaped praise upon them for their patriotism. 'Nothing was too good to be said and believed,' wrote Ray Strachey, some years later,[19] and noted that the press 'began to say that "the nation is grateful to the women" — not realising even yet that the women *were* the nation just as much as the men were'.[20] The exaggerated enthusiasm showed how little many had appreciated the hard work done by women before the war, as a number of people, including Adelaide Anderson in the 1916 Factory Inspector's *Report*, pointed out.[21] The astonishment at women's skill or strength could be seen as amusing, and the praise certainly delighted many women who were unused to such attention,[22] but it was not flattering, and it did little to help women's future prospects. Inaccurate information about the extent of women's skills and the willingness of employers to use them can only have disturbed many male workers further and hardened their attitudes towards the interlopers. *Common Cause* was right when it claimed that because of the 'mass of sentimental talk of women's work there [was] bound to be much ignorance as to their exact services and their value'.[23] I have already explained why it was nonsense to talk of women's superior output or better work, but journalists delighted in stories about women's overwhelming success, and reports from employers and managers who professed amazement at women's talent.[24] In spite of the fact that some papers carried a succession of serious articles on pay, prospects, hours, the nature of the work, etc., the majority of writers were not interested in anything so mundane. In the field of non-analytical articles, the approach ranged from the relatively sober congratulations of the *Daily Chronicle*, which informed its readers that:

The spirit in which these women have come forward to take the place of men is beyond praise. They have been a steadying influence on trade disputes. They have shown the utmost courage in moments of danger or panic. Many of them are doing either exceedingly hard or extremely monotonous work. Their physical endurance has equalled their powers of nervous resistance to fatigue. Their morality has been superior to that of the men ... The nation's debt to these heroic women, many of whom have lost their husbands in the war, is so great that it may even be likened to the debt which the nation owes to its soldiers and seamen[25]

to the coy flattery of the *Daily Mail*, one of whose journalists wrote, inconsequentially, of 'Women Engineers':

Overalled, leather-aproned, capped and goggled — displaying nevertheless woman's genius for making herself attractive in whatsoever
working guise — some 18 women are being trained in the Nottinghill
Gate workshops of the Women's Service Bureau,[26]

while another reported, of the sight at a Government Training Centre:

A splendid set of girls were working in the shops, their varied coloured
overalls, simply arranged hair, and bright, fresh English faces all helping to make as wonderful a warworkers' picture as can be imagined.[27]

This latter paragraph appeared in an article designed to encourage women
to take up war work, and there were many similar pieces around at the
time, which said little about the hardship, long hours or variable rates
of pay. The attitude towards women was patronising, and the descriptions of the work were superficial: the work itself was often assumed to
be of less interest than the comradely atmosphere of the factory, or the
attractiveness of the workers. Thus another journalist wrote:

I could not help contrasting the dainty little khaki-class miss, curls
peeping from underneath her spongebag hat, with the setting. She
might have stepped out of a West End Revue. Actually she was a
checker, fulfilling her important and appointed task amidst the
scream and noise and steam, the clanging of a thousand hammers.[28]

Romantic views of war work often meant that real dangers were glossed
over; a writer for the *Weekly Welcome* assured readers (who were potential recruits) in an article about life as a 'munitionette' that 'the yellow
colouring which appears on the skin in no way affects the health, and
will disappear when the work in this department is given up for a week
or so.'[29] This yellow stain in fact came from handling TNT, which was
highly toxic: some were seriously affected by it. Similarly, a girl interviewed by the *Liverpool Post*, when asked whether a twelve-hour day
was not rather long, was reported to have replied, 'It was tiring at first,
but the work is so very interesting,'[30] although many women *did* find
such hours very tiring, and much work was also monotonous, as even
the middle-class volunteers, keen to sacrifice themselves for England,
admitted:

The work is very hard. It may be, perhaps, from sheer lifting and
carrying and weighing, or merely because of those long dragging

hours that keep us sitting on little stools in front of whirring, clattering machines that are all too easy to work. We wish sometimes they were not quite so 'foolproof' for monotony is painful.[31]

A description of this nature hardly ever appeared in the daily press, as opposed to the labour papers or books.

Books are another interesting source in themselves — apart from the careful studies of Kirkaldy or Andrews, there were many which were frankly written for propaganda purposes. Within this category their merit and accuracy varied, much as that of articles in the press did. Gilbert Stone's *Women War Workers* was written to encourage more women to take up patriotic work, yet Stone's own introductory and concluding comments on women's current and future prospects were very perceptive. Boyd Cable and Hall Caine, in respectively *Doing Their Bit* and *Our Girls* (which included a space for a photo opposite the title page, and a caption 'From Our Girls to one of our boys') erred rather more in the direction of glowing description and uncritical enthusiasm. These two latter were designed to show how well women were doing, and some classic comments about picturesque girl workers and workshops came out of this approach, together with unintentionally revealed prejudices about women's skills and 'natural' area of work; Hall Caine wrote innocently:

There is at first something so incongruous in the spectacle of women operating masses of powerful machinery (as indeed any machinery more formidable than a sewing-machine), that for a moment, as you stand at the entrance the sight is scarcely believable.[32]

One wonders whether the noise of machinery really did '[sing] like music in their ears', as Caine reported, and how accurate the description of the 'linnet-like chorus of 3,000 girls' at mealtime was.[33] Yet Caine, for all his romanticised descriptions, also included in his book a denunciation of the traditional views of woman as the drudge or the parasite, and expressed his hope that women would continue to be allowed to do the new jobs under good conditions.[34] His interest was not confined to the pretty pictures which war workers made, and he included more useful material in *Our Girls* beside the hyperbole. The same cannot be said of L.K. Yates, whose book *A Woman's Part* is an extraordinary hymn to the beauty of women's work. Purple passages abound; of 'turning' a shell, she wrote:

The shavings curl off in this process like hot bacon rind and fall in irridescent rings around her: blue, purple, peacock, or gleaming silver . . . But, perhaps the most attractive operation to the visitor to the shell-shop is the fitting and grooving of the shell's copperband, a process which leaves the machine and worker half-hidden in the glory of sunset tints, as the copperscrap falls thickly from the machine.[35]

Picturesque it may have been, but the reality was grimmer, since copperband turning affected women's health, producing sickness and dental troubles. But Yates was involved in writing about a dream world, where 'brighter days' were on their way,[36] and all classes worked together happily:

> They have come from the office and the shop, from domestic service and the dressmaker's room, from the High Schools and the Colleges, and from the quietude of the stately homes of the leisured rich . . .
> Social status, so stiff a barrier in this country in prewar days, was forgotten in the factory, as in the Trenches, and they were all working together as happily as the members of a united family.[37]

Yates was not by any means the only person to make such claims about the amicable mixture of classes – this was a popular myth, as invalid in the workshop as it was in the trenches. Hall Caine, Boyd Cable and other writers reported it,[38] and the press delighted in it, encouraging the idea that munitions work was highly suitable for titled ladies, and that class differences meant nothing to the women who worked together for England.[39] A different picture was presented by those who investigated more thoroughly, and I have explained the class composition of the work-force in Chapter 2. Women themselves reported that relations between the working-class women and the few middle-class volunteers were often strained. I have already quoted Monica Cosens' comment: 'There is no denying immediately a new Volunteer comes into a street [the gangway between machines] there is defiance in the air. She is not gently treated,'[40] and Naomi Loughnan revealed something of the gulf between the two groups when she wrote:

> The ordinary factory hands have little to keep them awake [on night shift]. They lack interest in their work because of the undeveloped state of their imaginations. They handle cartridges and shells, and though their eyes may be swollen with weeping for sweethearts and brothers whose names are among the killed and wounded, yet they

do not definitely connect the work they are doing with the trenches. One girl, with a face growing sadder and paler as the days went by because no news came from France of her 'boy' who was missing, when gently urged to work harder and not go to sleep so often, answered with angry indignation: 'Why should I work any harder? My mother is satisfied with what I takes home of a Saturday.'[41]

Loughnan did not realise that work was different if you *had* to do it, and that quite probably the girl fell asleep because she was tired rather than because she was lazy: working-class women usually went home from night shift to domestic tasks, while middle- or upper-class women could sleep all day. There was an enormous gulf between those who had taken up 'war work' and those who needed to work for a living, and it was hardly surprising that resentment existed: working-class women objected to criticisms of their behaviour and claims that war workers had superior motives in working. They were also likely to be alienated by the attitudes of some of the volunteers when they stated that they did not mind what wages they earned, or that they preferred harsher conditions because 'there was much more romance about "war work" when you weren't made too comfortable.'[42] Such contrasts in outlook could not easily be overcome, but journalists and propagandists were prepared to pretend they did not exist. This was for a variety of reasons: class unity in the war effort was clearly good for morale, it could aid recruitment, and it was a picturesque idea. One has the feeling, however, that many of the writers who repeated tales of duchesses and maids working together for 'our boys' actually wanted to believe that it was happening. It appealed to them as much as it did to their readers.

From 1915 to 1918 women's substitution work, munitions work in particular, was a popular topic for discussion. Caroline Playne wrote later that it 'became a disgrace to be found at home'[43] for the middle-class women, and the press did its best to foster the notion that *all* patriotic women were working together, and to encourage, in Playne's words, a 'self-conscious romanticism' in women who worked. It was at last highly respectable for women to work, and evidence of this was the spate of advertising which appeared in newspapers using women workers as the subjects. 'Munitions workers are the latest to bear most remarkable testimony to the amazing results of "Harlene Hair Drill" in securing Hair Health and Beauty' stated a half-page advertisement in the *Daily News* in 1917,[44] and Ven Yusa, the 'Oxygen Face Cream', was advertised as being 'a boon to *Women War Workers* . . . Women War Workers found that the grit and grime of the munition factories, exacting hospital work,

and exposure to sudden weather changes are injurious to the skin.'[45] Ven
Yusa was the answer. War workers were also benefited by Dr Williams's
Pink Pills for Pale People, and regular consumption of Rowntree's Cocoa.
Advertisers clearly felt that women workers were a good market to aim
at, and also that war work had a good enough image to attract the notice
of the general population.

With all this attention being paid to women's work it was little
wonder that feminists and their sympathisers felt that at last women's
capabilities were being appreciated, and that observers of all political
persuasions frequently stated their belief that attitudes to women were
being revolutionised. There were certainly those who warned that this
optimism was hasty; amongst them was the *Woman's Dreadnought*,
which stated with startling foresight, 'We know that those who cry
"Hosanna" today will cry "crucify" tomorrow!'[46] Others pointed out
that the *kind* of praise was not particularly desirable. It was consistent
with the usual approach to women: surprise if a job was done really well,
admiration if the worker were young and pretty, and amusement at
some of the funny things women did or thought – thus the *Daily Mail*
reported the rueful comment of one employer who said, 'They don't
seem to be happy unless they're making something which explodes.'
One is obviously supposed to ponder on the charming impulsiveness of
such women. Reports were often ridiculously whimsical, as was pointed
out by one speaker at a Hampstead Garden Suburb summer meeting,
who 'considered that newspaper references to women workers showed
the necessity of a new outlook. When girl motordrivers were described as
"petrol nymphs" it was obvious that a changed attitude was needed.'[47]
Many feminists would have agreed with her, but it was all too easy for
them to feel triumphant at the attention women were getting. The
writers for *Common Cause*, the eminently sensible suffragist journal,
whilst fully aware of the problems women were encountering, and would
continue to face after the war, nevertheless pounced with undisguised
glee upon the glowing statements in the press, particularly those which
suggested that women's wonderful work had earned them the vote.

> Suffragists little thought when they suspended their political propa-
> ganda at the outbreak of the war that it would be carried on for
> them so valiantly by a section of the press that has hitherto been
> opposed to their claims[48]

wrote the compiler of 'Notes and News' in 1915, and the editor announced triumphantly early in 1916:

It is impossible to open a newspaper nowadays without finding a more or less complete surrender to the principles underlying the demand for Women's Suffrage. The thinkers were with us long ago; the statesmen of tomorrow are all for us; the Press has, in fact, conceded the position.[49]

Common Cause could not resist reprinting many of the statements which were being made in the daily papers about the wonders of women's work and their worthiness of the vote, including the 'conversions' of Galsworthy and Arthur Conan Doyle to women's suffrage, and the praise of Lord Derby, who rashly 'wondered to whom the greatest credit would be given, to the men who went to fight or the women who were working in a way that many people hardly believed that it was possible for them to work'.[50] On another occasion, *Common Cause* reported the conversion of the manager of an iron works, who had been forced to accept women substitution workers, to women's suffrage,[51] and it is clear that its producers were half-convinced that some kind of change in male attitudes really was taking place. The journal also repeated some of the prevailing myths about class unity, and readily accepted as hard evidence some of the exaggerated descriptions about women's superior production at Messrs Beardmore which were circulating in the daily press,[52] so clearly its editors' optimism sometimes outweighed its good judgement. Undoubtedly, the paper was proud to quote the *Glasgow Herald* as saying, 'We sum up everything in this: the women are magnificent, and the nation is more indebted to them than it can at present express.'[53] *Common Cause* and the leading suffragist spokeswoman, Mrs Fawcett, showed little of the cynicism which was to be found in the *Woman's Dreadnought*, or most of the socialist or trade union papers, when confronted with descriptions printed in the popular press.[54] It was evident to many that there was something wrong with all these conversions to women's suffrage: as Sarah Bailey wrote in *Fortnightly Review*, it was not logical to be converted by women's talent for skilled or outdoor work, for 'the munition worker is not, as such, more or less possessed of those qualities which make for political wisdom and judgement than the charwoman.'[55] Hasty changes of mind were suspicious; they indicated thoughtless enthusiasm which could just as easily evaporate. Similarly, claims by public figures reported in the press that women no longer had a 'separate sphere' now that they were out working[56] meant nothing more than that women were supposed to change *for the duration of the war*. Even while many feminists rejoiced at the change in 'public opinion', and others similarly influenced by current propaganda wondered what kind of new society lay ahead, there were those who looked forward to the time when women would retreat home and 'repair the ravages of war'. Romantic optimism was not confined to those who hoped that women would work side by side with men; B.L. Hutchins warned of the dangers of the post-war glorification of motherhood, and we have seen how powerful the back-to-the-home feeling was, even while women's work was admitted to be necessary. The words of the Countess of Warwick should be noted:

> My own dream and my own vision are of woman as the saviour of the race. I see her fruitful womb replenish the wasted ranks, I hear her wise counsels making irresistibly attractive the flower-strewn ways of peace.[57]

More serious was Mary Macarthur's conviction, as already described, that motherhood was women's most important task; she would not have argued with the views of *The Times*, when it stated, 'Home and motherhood remain woman's great and unique work.'[58] There was even the somewhat strange notion that women's war work would actually make them better wives and mothers. Yates was expressing a widely held view when she wrote, 'Indeed, many of the girls passing through this strange war-time adventure have assuredly gained by their pilgrimage precisely those qualities most needed by the wives and mothers of the rising generation.'[59] This was partly a defence, of course, against suggestions that women were being defeminised or morally corrupted by their war work: propagandists could not allow such ideas to go unchallenged.

The exaggerated praise ultimately meant little, and there were disturbing undercurrents. Myths circulated with or without the aid of the press throughout the war, and there were signs of hostility towards women workers in general, quite outside the resentment of particular unions or workmen to particular female substitutes. To begin with, there was the widespread myth that women workers were overpaid, and that they spent their excessive earnings on fur coats and jewellery. A writer for the *Woman Worker* put such stories in the same category as tales of Russians tramping through Britain with snow on their boots, or reports of the way drunkenness was affecting munitions production (promoted by Lloyd George amongst others), and said that they were fairy stories dreamed up by journalists who were not allowed to write about the truth because of press censorship. But the myth of high wages, obviously untrue, did not appear to have begun with any one paper; it was simply one of those exaggerations which existed and flourished in the climate of the war. Several journalists who were sympathetic to women went out of their way to deny that women workers were over-paid, or that they were working fast and carelessly, or sabotaging machines to get rest (other stories which were circulating); as a writer for the *Umpire* said: 'These criticisms are unfair to the thousands of hardworking women who are putting their best efforts into warwork.'[60] They worked hard for their money, and it was strange, as a female journalist writing for the *Daily News* pointed out, that wealthy leisured women, who bought fur coats themselves, should complain about factory girls buying clothes with their hard-earned wages.[61] The fact that so many writers felt the need to denounce women's critics is proof of how wide-spread some of these misconceptions were. It is apparent from the press reports that there were many people who resented the idea that working-class women might be achieving some financial independence – and this resentment existed as much amongst middle- or upper-class women as amongst men: class prejudice was as strong as sexual prejudice, when it seemed that working women might be stepping out of their proper place. It is also important that rumours of excessive wages coexisted with those about child neglect, high illegitimacy rates and soldiers' drunken wives, all of which were supposed to be evidence of women's abandonment of the home.

Criticism often centred on the munitions workers, rather than any other group of women. There were several reasons for this: they were a distinctive and recognisable group, in streets, cafés and public places, they were undeniably often boisterous and noisy, and they were the ones upon whom the press had lavished most attention – the praise itself caused resentment. They were also the ones most frequently described as earning exceptionally high wages, and could ironically be accused of 'profiting' by the war. Sylvia Pankhurst reported that at one stage some London restaurant proprietors issued orders that munitions workers should not be served:

> Olive Beamish, a suffragette hunger-striker, and one of our East End organisers, went to lunch at Fleming's, in Oxford Street. The manageress came to her sternly: 'You know you cannot be served!' Beamish retired indignant and wrote a letter of protest to the firm. She received a courteous reply, regretting that she had been mistaken for a munition worker. She had been wearing a khaki-coloured raincoat.[62]

Few ordinary munitions workers could afford to eat in restaurants, but they too suffered from criticism when they went around together on

trains and buses, or to shops and cafés. There was little tolerance of
their occasional boisterousness, even though, as *Common Cause* pointed
out, allowances were made for men who had been away fighting, and
returned to let off steam.[63] According to the women themselves they
were even despised by some of the soldiers they met, and certainly male
workers often decided that the ordinary munitions girls were a rowdy
bunch: one man contemptuously referred to the cartridge girls at his
factory as 'scum'.[64]

In fact, thanks to the erroneous ideas about the mixture of classes
in the workshops, women munitions workers were in the worst of all
worlds. While working-class women were criticised for earning too much
money and becoming too precocious, the mythical hoards of middle-
class women were accused of 'playing at war work',[65] not sticking to
their jobs,[66] and searching for 'patriotic glamour' through war work.[67]
Then, when it seemed in 1916 and 1917 that there might be a labour
shortage, and that not enough women were working, there were demands
that the idle must take up work, the slackers must be rounded up, and
that if necessary female conscription should be introduced.[68] These
criticisms were clearly aimed at middle-class women, since most working-
class women were already obliged to work, but at such times the sex,
rather than the class, element was emphasised, and it is interesting to
see how throughout the war women were usually referred to as a solid,
undivided class in many of the more superficial press reports (thus, 'the
women are wonderful', or 'the women are letting us down'), and were
criticised or praised as such — in much the same way as they were regarded as a dangerous group, *en masse*, by so many male trade unionists,
without regard to their varying skills, or levels of motivation and political
activity. This approach was to become even more marked after the war
when women achieved new heights of unpopularity.

The hostility coexisted with congratulatory press reports. Journalists
were concerned with the picturesque, the unusual, the amusing, for the
most part, and their descriptions bore little relation to reality or to many
people's feelings about women and their work. The praise was superficial, and in many ways insulting, since it showed how little the authors
knew of women's pre-war work. It was also for women's *temporary*
work: although there was talk of social change as a result of women's
changing jobs, there is little doubt that most journalists and propagandists assumed that women were not really going to stay in 'men's jobs':
they were 'doing their bit' for the war period only. Women were praised
when they appeared to be putting men's interests to the fore, as during
the 1918 bus strike,[69] but there were warnings about the future as well.

The *Sussex Daily News* expressed what was to be the prevailing view:

> It will be, it is true, a process of dislocation for those many women
> workers to return to domestic life; but this dislocation will be trifling
> compared with the results which could follow their retention in any
> considerable numbers,[70]

and there were mutterings about the need to remove women from 'rough
manual labour and from exhausting or morally detrimental forms of
labour'.[71]

Many women themselves realised the fragility of their supposed
popularity. One wrote to *Common Cause*:

> I feel very strongly that the most urgent task for suffragists at present
> is to safeguard the interests and rights of women workers. I hope
> there may be organised effort on the part of the suffrage societies to
> prepare for the very great problems which will face women after the
> war. To my mind, the very dangerous situation that is arising has
> been unaccountably overlooked by suffragist optimists, who have
> welcomed every sign of women's greater employment, and have not
> investigated sufficiently the conditions and future of the employ-
> ment.[72]

Another woman warned that the women might be even worse off after
the war, thanks to the government's guarantees to the ASE,[73] while
Marian White wrote to the *Woman Worker*:

> We hear a great deal about the industrial rivalry of men and women.
> Men are said to be jealous of women coming into their trades and into
> their unions, and anxiety is felt as to how things will arrange them-
> selves after the war. Do you think we women will be shouldered out
> of our jobs — and some of us need them badly [—] when the war is
> over, or do you think some of us will keep them despite of the men.
> I would never keep a returned soldier out of his job, I hope; but the
> matter will be difficult. Can you give advice or encouragement?[74]

A letter in reply assured her that the NFWW would help, and the author
continued:

> Let every woman be prepared to give up any situation she may hold
> to our soldiers, wounded and otherwise, and by doing so I feel certain

that after the war other spheres of industry will open up where women will be indispensable.[75]

There were no grounds for such optimism. By January 1919 all the congratulations of the preceding years sounded very hollow, and all pretence of approval for women's 'new role' was abandoned.

Notes

1. *The Athenaeum*, April 1917, 'A Working-Man's View of Reconstruction', written in reply to 'An Employer's View of Reconstruction', March 1917.
2. Philip Abrams, 'The Failure of Social Reform', *Past and Present* (1963).
3. *Women's Liberal Review*, Autumn 1915, 'Women in Munition Factories'.
4. *Edinburgh Review*, October 1916, 'The Welfare of Factory Workers'.
5. Quoted by Helen Fraser, *Women and War Work* (G. Arnold Shaw, 1918), p. 141. See also Janet Campbell's Memorandum to the *Women in Industry* report (1918), pp. 218, 252.
6. M.A. Hamilton, *Mary Macarthur* (Parsons, 1925), p. 131.
7. Ibid., p. 167.
8. Sylvia Pankhurst, *The Home Front* (Hutchinson, 1932), p. 42.
9. *Manchester Guardian*, 17 Oct. 1918, 'National Council of Women'.
10. *National News*, 18 Mar. 1917, 'National Work for Women'.
11. *Athenaeum*, January 1918, 'The Future of the Woman War Worker'.
12. *The Times*, 18 May 1916, 'The 1916 Woman: Her Place in the State'; *Daily Express*, 23 Nov. 1915, 'Women Workers after the War'; *Illustrated Sunday Herald*, 19 Dec. 1915, 'The Women Will Not Go Back'; *Athenaeum*, April 1916, 'Women in Industry'.
13. Mary Macarthur in Marion Phillips (ed.), *Women and the Labour Party* (Headley Bros., 1918), p. 18. She made similar comments in the *Daily News*, 23 Jan. 1917.
14. M.G. Fawcett, *The Women's Victory and After* (Sidgwick & Jackson, 1925), p. 106.
15. Adelaide Anderson in S.J. Chapman (ed.), *Labour and Capital after the War* (Murray, 1918), p. 82.
16. *Manchester Guardian*, 3 Aug. 1918, 'Women's War Work', and *Aberdeen Journal*, 12 Nov. 1918, 'Work of Women'.
17. There were also writers who noted the attractiveness of the workers, but hastened to add that this was not really the most important matter, e.g. *The Times*, 16 Nov. 1915.
18. Naomi Loughnan in Gilbert Stone (ed.), *Women War Workers* (Harrap, 1917), p. 38.
19. Ray Strachey, *Our Freedom and Its Results* (Hogarth, 1936), p. 128.
20. Ray Strachey, *The Cause* (Bell & Sons, 1928), p. 344.
21. Quoted in I.O. Andrews, *The Economic Effects of the World War upon Women and Children in Great Britain* (Oxford University Press, 1921): 'It is permissible to wonder whether some of the surprise and admiration freely expressed in many quarters over new proofs of women's physical capacity and endurance is not in part attributable to lack of knowledge or appreciation of the very heavy and strenuous nature of much prewar work for women, domestic and industrial' (p. 41).

22. See B.L. Hutchins, *Women in Industry after the War* (Social Reconstruction Pamphlet No. 3), pp. 4-5.

23. *Common Cause*, 17 Nov. 1916.

24. For example, *Weekly Dispatch*, 21 May 1916, 'Shellmakers in Six Weeks'; *Liverpool Post*, 17 Nov. 1915, 'Munition Making'; *Glasgow Herald*, 22 Sept. 1916, 'War Work'.

25. *Daily Chronicle*, 16 Aug. 1918, 'Our Amazons'.

26. *Daily Mail*, 30 Mar. 1916, 'Women Engineers'.

27. *Daily Mail*, 9 Sept. 1916, 'Single Girls First'.

28. *Illustrated Sunday Herald*, 4 Apr. 1916. See also *The Times*, 14 Oct. 1915, on women ticket inspectors.

29. *Weekly Welcome*, 3 Mar. 1917, 'My First Day as a Munition Girl'.

30. *Liverpool Post*, 17 Nov. 1915, 'Munition Making'. Interesting it may have been, but it was obviously not very difficult, as she was taught in three hours!

31. Naomi Loughnan in Stone, *Women War Workers*, p. 29.

32. Hall Caine, *Our Girls* (Hutchinson, 1917), p. 29.

33. Ibid., pp. 25 and 51.

34. Ibid., p. 94.

35. L.K. Yates, *A Woman's Part* (Hodder & Stoughton, 1918), p. 22.

36. Ibid.: 'Looking out of the door at the stream of bright and happy girls laughing, singing, dancing and running, as only healthy youth can do in the midst of these dark days of war, I seemed to see other and brighter days ahead stretching out into the years of the future, when the work folk would all taste a fuller joy in life' (p. 27).

37. Ibid., p. 9.

38. E.g. Helen Fraser, *Woman's War Work* (G. Arnold Shaw, 1918).

39. *The Lady*, 3 Aug. 1916, 'Women and Munitions'; *Glasgow Herald*, 29 Feb. 1915, 'War Work'; *Daily Chronicle*, 30 July 1915, 'Titled Women as Shellmakers'.

40. Monica Cosens, *Lloyd George's Munition Girls* (Hutchinson, 1916).

41. Loughnan in Stone, *Women War Workers*, p. 33.

42. Joan Williams, 'A Munition Worker's Career at Messrs Gwynn and Sedgewick's' (typescript, Imperial War Museum), pp. 25, 41 and 42 .

43. Caroline Playne, *Society at War* (Allen & Unwin, 1934), p. 137.

44. *Daily News*, 14 Feb. 1917.

45. *Daily News*, 17 Apr. 1917.

46. *Woman's Dreadnought*, 3 Apr. 1915, 'A Contrast and a Caution'.

47. *Daily News*, 7 Aug. 1917, 'Changed Conditions for Women'.

48. *Common Cause*, 23 July 1915, 'Notes & News'.

49. *Common Cause*, 14 Apr. 1916, editorial.

50. *Common Cause*, 21 July 1916, 7 July 1916, 8 Dec. 1916.

51. *Common Cause*, 9 June 1916, 'A Conversion'.

52. *Common Cause*, 28 Apr. 1916, 'Women in Munition Work'; 23 June 1916, quoting from the *Daily Mail*.

53. *Common Cause*, 25 Feb. 1916.

54. M.G. Fawcett, *The Woman's Victory and After* (Sidgwick & Jackson, 1920), p. 118.

55. *Fortnightly Review*, June 1917, 'The War and Women's Suffrage'. See also Strachey, *The Cause*, p. 349.

56. Fawcett, *The Women's Victory and After*, triumphantly quoted the words of Walter Long on this subject, p. 115. Also *The Times*, 18 May 1916, 'The 1916 Woman: Her Place in the State'.

57. Countess of Warwick, *A Woman and the War* (Chapman & Hall, 1916), p. 140; *The Times*, 5 Oct. 1916; Macarthur in Marion Phillips, *Women and the Labour Party*, p. 20.

58. *The Times*, 5 Oct. 1916, 'Women and War Work', III.

59. Yates, *A Woman's Part*, p. 64; also Caine, *Our Girls*, p. 46.

60. *The Umpire*, 31 Dec. 1916, 'Work of the Shell Women'.

61. *Liverpool Daily Post*, 21 Oct. 1915, 'Nation at War Work'; *Daily News*, 5 Jan. 1917, 'Munition Girls' Pay', 6 Jan. 1917, 'Munition Girls' Living Wage', 10 Mar. 1917, 'Furs and Finer'; *Daily Mail*, 13 Apr. 1916, 'Munition Girls Are not too Well Paid'. See also the comments of some of the munitions workers; e.g. Loughnan in Stone, *Women War Workers*, p. 40, and Cosens, *Lloyd George's Munition Girls*, pp. 43-4.

62. Pankhurst, *The Home Front*, p. 379.

63. *Common Cause*, 16 June 1916, 'Our Girls in Wartime'.

64. See tapes held by the Imperial War Museum.

65. *Sunday Pictorial*, 24 Mar. 1918, 'Girls who Play at War Work'.

66. *Daily Mail*, 7 Apr. 1917, 'Changing their Work'.

67. *The Times*, 15 Sept. 1916, 'Women for Men'.

68. *Daily Graphic*, 17 Oct. 1916, 'The Call to Women'; *The Times*, 3 Aug. 1916; *The Times*, 16 Jan. 1918, 'Woman Power'; *Daily Express*, 13 Apr. 1918, 'Call up the Women'; *Daily Mail*, 6 Mar. 1918, 'War Time London'; *Pall Mall Gazette*, 10 Dec. 1917, 'Woman Power'.

69. Many papers believed that the public backed the women strikers for this reason: *Reynolds Newspaper*, 25 Aug. 1918, 'Lessons of the Strike'; The *Star*, 26 Aug. 1918, 'Equal Pay for Equal Work'.

70. *Sussex Daily News*, 25 Apr. 1916, 'Women's Work'.

71. Basil Worsfold, *War and Social Reform*, (Murray, 1919), p. 72. See also *The Times*, 7 Oct. 1918, 'Married Women's Work', and 24 June 1916, 'Women Workers and Their Children', in which the writer stated: 'The sentiment of calling the national guardians back from the factory to the hearth is sound from the racial point of view.' Also, *Daily Mail*, 23 Jan. 1917, letter from Henry Curtis.

72. *Common Cause*, 17 Dec. 1915, letter from M. Sheepshanks.

73. *Common Cause*, 14 Apr. 1916, letter.

74. *Woman Worker*, January 1917.

75. *Woman Worker*, May 1917, letter from A. McGregor.

7 DEMOBILISATION AND THE AFTERMATH

Pre-Armistice Discussions

Most people concerned with industry, whether employers, government officials or workpeople, realised long before the end of the war that the demobilisation of troops and women war workers might prove to be a problem. Discussions about what would become of the displaced women therefore began before 1918.

Theoretically, demobilisation of troops and war workers was a temporary problem, and one which could be solved by good organisation. In fact, unions and workers knew that what happened then would be significant for years to come, and that the actions of the government, employers and labour movement would be crucial to the future. Gilbert Stone, editor of *Women War Workers*, looked forward cautiously, realising (unlike so many newspaper writers) that

> at the best of times the role of a prophet is a risky one, and in wartime, when all the sure foundations of normal life disappear one by one, it becomes one in which opinion gives place to guess work and facts founder in a sea of speculation[1]

but he believed that two facts were plain: 'the one, is that women will go more into the world than heretofore; the other, that many women now engaged in work will have to make way for the men returning from the Front'.[2] He was accurate in these predictions; he was also right when he wrote:

> It must be realized that if women take their full share in this work of reconstruction — a purely business matter, calling neither for patriotism nor sacrifice — she comes to stay. She will have gained her place in the world of work, not temporarily, but for all time. We may tolerate the spectacle of women being taught to use a lathe in order to make munitions and then being dispensed with when the war is over, but if once that lathe continues in times of peace, the woman engineer-artisan will have established her right to continue as such.[3]

Here Stone put his finger on the crux of the matter: if women were to leave their new jobs it would be straight after the war, and they would

173

be classed for ever as temporary, 'patriotic' war workers, who had 'done their bit'; if they were allowed to stay for more than a year afterwards, they would become permanent co-workers with men, and their industrial position would be transformed. The question was, would they stay? Would the government allow them to? Would employers want them? Would unions accept them? Were women themselves willing to stay, and would they fight if they were rejected? These were the issues debated by those involved with women's work, and they were implicit in many of the arguments about equal pay, union membership, etc., which have already been discussed in this book.

I.O. Andrews, writer of the contemporary book *The Economic Effects of the World War upon Women and Children in Great Britain*, decided that there were three different groups in existence when it came to the question of women's future: those who wanted a return to the *status quo* in industry and the home; those who wanted radical changes for men and women in industry; and those who believed that there should be some changes, but that society should remain fundamentally the same with regard to its treatment of women as industrial workers. By far the largest number of observers from all social classes fell into the last category. There were certainly some people who hoped that the clock could be turned back to 1914, but few thought this was really possible, and only in engineering did the government make guarantees about the return of men to their old jobs. The ASE had made a bargain with the government and employers, and was determined that the bargain should be kept through the Restitution of Pre-War Practices Act. Other hard-line unions, as I have shown, often managed to keep women out of particular jobs, or out of unions, and tried to make special arrangements with individual employers. Most unions accepted that there would be some change in the structure of the labour force (this was inevitable, given the number of men killed), but were determined to fight for the best conditions for men, in terms of job opportunities, and wanted women to remain in 'women's' jobs. Men's security was seen as being most important.

There is little need to recap on the reasons for the hostility of the majority of male trade unionists towards women. They feared that women would be kept on in men's places, or used to lower men's wages, and they knew that women would be willing to stay in industry if possible — 'they will not be anxious to go back to the kitchen and laundry,'[4] as the *Trade Union Worker* said. A limited number of men wished to accept this fact, and learn to work *with* women, believing that they deserved a fairer share of interesting and well paid jobs after the war. This is how a writer for the *Trade Unionist* put it:

> It is hardly likely that the women will go back to the same position they occupied before the war. The economic struggle which often took a political turn that characterised the women's movement, has found its chance as a result of the universal upheaval, and the women's movement was too genuine to miss the chance thus afforded.
>
> No fairminded man will be other than glad that the women have come to stay in occupations that they can properly fill, and desire to fill; the men's task in this connection is to be of as much use as possible to enable the women to establish themselves on a right economic basis, fair to themselves and to their male fellow workers.[5]

As others pointed out, many women had lost male breadwinners: it was more logical for the labour movement to attack the employers than the women.[6] Yet although the *Trade Unionist* carried the above article, it was also the paper which triumphantly announced the expulsion of female dockers, and in another article about probable post-war problems, printed in 1916, one of its writers, talking of future unemployment figures, informed readers that 750,000 people should be deducted immediately from the statistics, since this was the number of married women with children who should be back home.[7] The prospect of any future state benefits or concern for married women was in fact particularly galling to many male workers. It may be recalled that one of the vehicle workers' unions objected to the campaign for equal pay on the grounds that many female workers were married, and thus were not breadwinners. This was a common complaint, and fears were for the future as well; one railwayman wrote to the *Railway Worker*[8] about plans afoot to press for alternative work or state allowances for displaced women after the war. Was this fair, he asked, when so many women were the wives of soldiers or munition workers? He then went on to complain about the idea that *single* women needed financial provision made for them, as they had parents to support them; over and over again, the excuse was that all women had someone to support them. This was used to justify the demand that they be forced to leave jobs after the war, without either financial compensation or alternative work to go to. From early in the war there was strong pressure from many quarters to ensure that women would 'go home'. The *Factory Times* carried an article on this subject in 1916 which is typical of one of the strands of opposition to women's continuing role in industry:

> We claim that the solemn obligation to the men who went away will
> necessitate those women going out as quickly as possible, to say
> nothing of the fact that it was universally acknowledged that women
> brought into industry through the war were doing work that is not
> congenial or natural to a woman . . . we must get the women back
> into the home as soon as possible. That they ever left it is one of the
> evil results of the war.[9]

This attitude was vehemently attacked in the *Cotton Factory Times* by
Alice Smith, who asked whether women were expected to give up their
jobs to any man, whether ex-soldier or not, and what physical reasons
there were for women to give up working:

> The plain truth is, that, with the exception of cases where the
> woman has been able to afford some expensive training, the work
> considered most natural or congenial to women has been ill-paid
> labour, not sufficiently remunerative for men to undertake.[10]

She was repeating the argument put forward by feminists and many
people who knew about the problems women encountered in industry, but she knew she was fighting a hard battle, for this was a matter
of ideology, not just economics. The views of the writer for the *Factory
Times* were more widely held.

The Labour Party too accepted that men must come first, although
many of its members discussed possible provision for women. *Labour
Woman* agonised about what would happen after the war — would
women lower men's living standards, and what would become of the
women who had learned new skills and the girls who had taken 'dead-
end' jobs?[11] The question of whether women really wanted to stay was
raised; some people suggested they would be glad to leave, and get
away from the strain — even that they would be happy to go back to
service![12] It was suggested, by women's sympathisers, that the answer
to the problem of undercutting or displacement by women lay in equal
pay, a minimum wage, and an eight-hour day, in the long term, and that
women's own displacement through demobilisation could be coped
with by good government organisation.[13] The TUC adopted a resolution on the demobilisation of women which called for·

(a) Reorganisation of the whole system of unemployment insurance.
(b) An inquiry into firms' labour requirements.
(c) In all government factories and controlled establishments, a

    reasonable period of notice, or wages in lieu of notice.
(d) Workers in munitions, or other trades with excessive overtime, should have 4 weeks paid holiday.
(e) The government should continue to use factories for national production.
(f) Provision of training with maintenance grants for women who could not find jobs.[14]

But this approach depended upon the goodwill and efficiency of the government, neither of which could be guaranteed. There appeared to be no contingency plans, and no ideas for how the labour movement could help women. The words of the Standing Joint Committee of Industrial Women's Organisations are indicative of official Labour Party policy on the subject of women workers:

We . . . urge that every advantage should be taken of the present situation to secure a far higher standard of life for women, and a position of general industrial equality with men. The nation will gain the profit of such an improvement not only in the higher productivity of industry but also in the higher capacity of women as citizens and mothers.[15]

These were fine words, but they meant very little, and they offered women no concrete support. Vague hopes for the future were not enough, given that the writers knew how little most unions were prepared to help or accept women workers.

    The attitude of the government was clearly of vital importance. Unfortunately, its officials and committee members held views similar to those of many trade unionists and employers, believing that women should retire gracefully from war work. (It is worth recalling some of the views of employers already described — for example, the idea that the 'honourable working man' desired to support his wife, and that there were certain 'psychological barriers' to the continuation of women's work after marriage.[16]) The War Cabinet Committee on Women in Industry, looking ahead, came to the conclusion that the state should regulate wages, there should be further regulations controlling employment, and women might be able to extend their field of labour if they did not displace men; members made no recommendations on the subject of the process of demobilisation, since this was not their brief.[17] The Women's Employment Committee, looking particularly at women's future job opportunities, decided ultimately this future was uncertain, given that the state of trade was unknown, and no one could predict whether the pledges made to skilled men would be kept.[18] This Committee too was not concerned with the process of demobilisation, but with long-term trends. In the meantime, the Civil War Workers' Committee, set up by the Ministry of Reconstruction, came to the conclusion that at the end of the war women workers would be a greater problem than discharged men. Members suggested that the government should use labour exchanges to organise employment, and should ensure that munitions workers were given fair notice of dismissal. However, Sidney Webb's proposal for paid holidays for women munitions workers was not enthusiastically greeted: their work was not classed as being sufficiently exhausting.[19] Yet, also, even Sidney Webb, while pressing for training and maintenance for unemployed women, decided that they could 'be usefully trained in domestic management, care of children, dressmaking etc.', and it was left to Marion Phillips to add that industrial training also ought to be provided.[20] Although the Committee of Economists, looking into 'The Probable State of Industry after the War', reported to the government that it was 'undesirable' to expel women from the new industries, it seemed that the government was reluctant to take any measures to *prevent* such expulsion.[21] Indeed, although the problem of demobilised women was much discussed by the government's experts and advisers before the end of the war, the only scheme actually organised was that providing unemployment benefit. This itself was based on traditional ideas about women's financial needs, as it was agreed that women should receive a lower rate than men. Those who drew up the plans had their own ideas about the amount men and women deserved. Writing to Beveridge in 1918, C.B. Hawkins referred to the views of a colleague:

> With regard to paragraphs 3 and 4 however I get the impression that he was really alarmed by the proposal to raise the rate of benefit from 7/- to 15/- for men and to 12/- for women. I get the impression that if the rate were, say 12/- and 10/- he would probably sign the Report, and that he might do so even if the rate of benefit for women only were brought down.[22]

Thus were women's financial interests as usual sacrificed to men's, and there were plenty of other officials around eager to remind the nation of 'the social risks inherent in a widely extended and intensified employment of women in all great industries'.[23]

Demobilisation

The government therefore set up no new machinery for coping with the women who were almost certainly going to be laid off, assuming that the existing labour exchanges and the scheme for out-of-work donation would be adequate. Quite possibly Ministers really did believe that most women would return to their old jobs or withdraw from the labour market.

In fact, only half of those who made up the increase in women's labour chose to withdraw,[24] and the government seemed to be totally incapable of dealing with the immediate post-war employment situation. There was talk of the state encouraging public works and continuing to place contracts with engineering and munitions employers after the war, in order to maintain employment, but in fact the government brought many war contracts to an end in 1918, regardless of the fact that women workers were laid off *en masse*. The government's only practical measures were the promotion of the *Wages (Temporary Regulation) Act*, which was designed to fix wages as at the date of the Armistice for a period of six months, and the unemployment donation scheme for demobilised men and women. Those entitled to the latter had to be contributors under the Health Insurance Scheme before 25 August 1918, or to have proof of employment before that date if aged 15-18 or over 70. The donation was 24s and 20s a week for men and women respectively for 13 weeks; it then dropped to 20s and 15s for a further 13 weeks. The Civil War Workers' Committee came up with nothing better than plans for two weeks' notice, or pay, to be given to women in munitions, free rail passes home, and the extension of the unemployment benefit scheme.[25] Women's lack of work was clearly seen by the government as a temporary problem, and one which would disappear within a few months of the Armistice; the idea that more women might want to work, and that the old jobs might not be available or might seem unsatisfactory, although widely discussed during the war, was clearly not taken seriously by Ministers or advisers. There were still, of course, all too few women who had any influence upon the government; *The Times* wryly noted that no women sat on the Committee on Out of Work Donation, even though by May 1919 three-quarters of those on the dole were women.[26]

The labour movement had warned that the government seemed ill-equipped to deal with demobilisation, and by late 1918 and early 1919 it was revealed to what extent. The *Worker's Dreadnought*, following events with close attention, condemned the government for

falling back on the old idea of training women for domestic service, and
pointed out that in the meantime a Women's Engineering Society had
been set up to recruit unemployed women for work at lower rates.[27]
The standard patterns of women's employment were establishing themselves for the women who found work; those who did not had to face
the fact that the government was not interested in helping them. Depu-
tations were sent to the Prime Minister,[28] but all the government was
prepared to do was set up training schemes for the standard women's
trades (which themselves could not absorb so many unemployed
women), and domestic education for 'war brides'.[29] Before the war
ended, B.L. Hutchins had suggested that as a means of countering unemployment the government should withdraw young workers from
industry by raising the school-leaving age, transfer workers to different
areas, organise rotational holidays, and set up not only public works,
but special training facilities for women.[30] This kind of approach did
not occur to the government, and when public works schemes appeared
they certainly were not aimed at unemployed women.

Women's unemployment did not drop over the six months following
the war's end, and the government decided to try a new 'solution'. It
was suggested that women were not taking jobs because the rate of
benefit was too high, or, to put it in Sir Robert Horne's words:

> The disparity between the amount of unemployment donation pay-
> able to women and the amount they were able to earn in many
> employments before the war, and can now, has created a very
> natural reluctance to go back to work so long as the donation lasts.[31]

The answer, according to the government, was not to improve wages in
those few trades which *were* interested in employing women (notably
domestic service and laundry), but to cut the benefit rates. This was
duly done. The government also decided that there was much 'fraud'
associated with the donation, and that the system should be stricter for
women who claimed; consequently, women's benefit was frequently
suspended if they refused the jobs offered to them by the local labour
exchange. (This had happened before, but to a limited extent.[32]) They
could appeal against this decision, but most appeals were turned down.
In March 1919 a test case was being circulated around labour exchanges
as an example to officials. A girl of 19 who had been earning £1 a week
working in an iron works was made unemployed, and was offered a
job as a domestic servant by the labour exchange. She refused it, saying
she had never done domestic work before. She was disqualified from

benefit by the Court of Referees (the appeal body) on the grounds that she should have been prepared to adapt herself.[33] There was now, as the *Liverpool Post* put it, 'a closer scrutiny of claims'. It reported, of its own area:

> The Court of Referees has refused the continuance of benefit in many cases where women have declined offers of employment. In most instances they have refused the jobs because of the alleged insufficiency of pay. Eligibility to the donation is also withdrawn if it cannot be proved that they normally followed some occupation. By this means, the claims of women who left their homes for war work, but who have since returned to domestic duties, are being eliminated from the register.[34]

Most unemployed women were now in an impossible position. Those who had stayed at home before 1914, or for the first year or two of the war, whether because they had just left school, or because they were looking after children, were not eligible for benefit at all; this included widows and wives of sick men, who may not have needed to work before the war, but did now.[35] Those who *were* eligible nevertheless faced being cut off if they refused any kind of work at all, even if it paid less than the newly reduced benefit of 15s a week. Whether they liked it or not, women were being pushed back towards the staple female trades of laundry and domestic service, where wages were poor and conditions bad, as even the Ministry of Labour admitted.[36] An NFWW deputation to Sir Robert Home complaining that women were being cut off for refusing jobs which paid only 12s a week produced no change in policy,[37] and from February 1919 the labour press was full of examples of women who had been disallowed benefit, examples which are worth looking at. One girl was offered domestic work by her local labour exchange at 10s 6d a week; when she met the employer the wages turned out to be 8s 6d a week, and the hours were 7 a.m. to 5.30 p.m. She refused the job, and was disallowed benefit because she had not bargained with the mistress. Another woman was offered domestic service at £22 per annum (living in); she could not afford to take the work, because she had a mother and four younger sisters to support; her benefit was suspended. A third woman was offered service, and refused it because the job needed someone who would live in: her husband was due back from the army and she wanted daily work. She was informed that she should have given up her rented house, stored the furniture, and taken the job.[38] A widow with one child was receiving benefit, with a dependant's allowance, and was offered laundry work at 17s a week; she refused it, saying it was not enough for two people to live on. She was then offered domestic service, if she would put the child in a home, or wood-chopping at 17s a week, and told she would be reported (and thus disallowed benefit) if she took none of these jobs. She said bitterly that the exchange maintained that these were 'splendid wages, as they don't suppose we did any work before the war'.[39] Fourteen girls had their benefit suspended at Fleetwood, Manchester, after refusing to work at Apex for 6s a week.[40] A soldier's wife lost her benefit after refusing to take work at 8s a week – the week being 7 days, 10½ hours a day.[41] The list of such cases stretches on and on, and the women who appealed against the initial decisions were usually unsuccessful:

> In the Court of Referees the women fare little better. In Manchester alone in a given week, 1,000 appeals were refused and in many districts the chairmen make a point of cross-examining the women as if they were criminals in the dock[42]

reported *Labour Woman*. A rare few succeeded, and their cases were reported triumphantly by *Labour Woman* and *Woman Worker*,[43] although usually the work offered by the labour exchange had to be exceptionally bad to allow women any chance of winning – thus one woman with two children was offered a job as a house parlourmaid, working 7 a.m. to 9 p.m. (leaving the children alone) for 14s a week plus food. Her appeal against suspension of benefit was accepted on the grounds that this was 'unsuitable work'.[44]

Many kinds of low-paid jobs were offered to women, but most vacant positions were in laundry or service. The former would have been less unpopular had employers paid better wages, but by June 1920 the appropriate Trade Board had set the minimum rate of 28s a week, the equivalent of 12s 6d in pre-war terms, and the fight began for a minimum of 35-40s.[45] Domestic service, on the other hand, was seen as being intolerable under almost any circumstances by most women. An informal investigation by the *Woman Worker* outside a labour exchange in February 1919, just before the government attitude hardened, revealed that 5 per cent of the women interviewed were prepared to take such work if conditions improved and wages went up to £40 p.a. for living in, with two half-days free a week, and clothes to be chosen by the maid unless paid for by the mistress (the fact that most servants *had* to pay for their uniforms, the badge of their servitude, was very unpopular); 30 per cent were prepared to accept service if they lived out, did not finish after 6 p.m., had one meal a day provided, and were paid wages of 9d an hour (and double on Sundays); 65 per cent said they would not take the work on any terms.[46]

Unfortunately, many of them were forced to. Placements of domestic servants through the labour exchanges remained low from November 1918 to February 1919, then shot up, so that they were 40 per cent higher in the succeeding six months than they had been during the corresponding period in 1918.[47] By 1920, the position for women was even worse. The *Report* of the Chief Inspector of Factories stated that:

> There is as yet no fulfilment of the expectations that after the war a body of industries and operations offering a hopeful field of fresh employment would lie open to women where their war experience could be turned to account. On the contrary, an automatically operating force has closed all these expected new avenues, and in various occupations hitherto regarded as women's their presence seems, in certain directions, to be threatened.[48]

This included work in the aircraft industry, which had developed during the war with a largely female work-force, and was now recruiting men instead. The slump, which began in 1920, and for which the government was largely unprepared, did not improve matters for women seeking work. State schemes were arranged for men, but not for women.[49] At the same time, the bubble burst in the engineering industry, which had been enjoying a post-war boom: unemployment rates were highest in Coventry and Birmingham, where the expansion had been greatest, and of course a number of those made redundant were women, who had been kept on in some workshops.[50] The slump was the final blow for those women who had managed to hold on to their wartime work or find similar work, and employers were quite prepared to cut the wages of those who remained, now that other jobs were not open to them. In January 1921, the Birmingham and Wolverhampton Engineering Employers cut the basic wage of an adult woman from 43s 6d to 35s 9d, and the Coventry employers followed suit. This was further reduced the following year by the National Employers' Federation; the basic became 16s, plus 20s cost-of-living bonus, which fluctuated according to inflation. July 1921 saw 2 million people unemployed, and a new dole was introduced. To receive it, men and women had to prove to a committee (of one employer, one employee and a chairman) that they had previously been employed in insurable work, that they were looking for work, and that they needed the money (they were means tested). The system of withholding benefit from women who would not go into service continued, and it has been estimated that only 4 per cent of unemployed women received benefit at this time.[51] The government *Report on Domestic Service* in 1923 included advice to the public to report any 'false' claims for benefit from former domestic servants. As a final blow, in February 1922 married women were automatically excluded from benefit.

The slump worsened women's position, but the events of 1918-20 had already shown that not only was the government not prepared to help women keep their jobs, but that employers too were reluctant to keep on many of the women they had employed during the war, particularly those in 'men's trades'. There were a handful of cases where women were retained in trades covered by the Restitution of Pre-War Practices Act, and which the ASE fought successfully, managing to have the women removed.[52] But a questionnaire sent out by the Women's Industrial League revealed that out of 764 firms using women for the first time during the war, 228 would like to have retained them, 97 would have done so had there been no union opposition, and the remaining 439 were not interested in keeping them, citing as their reasons Home Office restrictions on night work, women's unsuitability for heavy labour, the extra supervision required, etc.[53] Even this seems to be an unusually high proportion in favour of women, however, as there was no rush to use them in trades where unions would have found it difficult to keep them out (as the ASE would have done without government legislation), had employers made a concerted effort to use them. More typical was the view expressed in the *Hardware Trade Journal* in 1919:

In general (though there are exceptions), it is found that both as regards quality and quantity of work and wages and earnings in a normal week, women do not compare favourably with men; as regards time-keeping (apart from natural causes of absence), they are not so reliable as men; in length of service the fact that a large number of them give up working in factories on getting married (which is of course not the case as regards males) causes their length of service to be generally less than that of men, although in other respects, there would not appear to be any evidence that they are generally more given than men to changing their employment; in aptitude for training it is considered that women are at least equal to men.[54]

The writer proceeded to say that they would be glad to have women on simpler or less skilled work, but that their wages should be lower than men's, or the trade would be adversely affected by foreign competition. Equal pay, he claimed, would result in the women being squeezed out, and would lower the standard of work.[55] Similarly, the *Engineer*, once keen to get employers to use women, decided that they were not so useful in peacetime:

> We think . . . that the question of the ability of women may be left out of the argument; it may be accepted without reserve. But it by no means follows that because women can do men's work therefore they should be allowed to do it. Nor does it follow because women are willing and steady workers that therefore they should be employed in factories. This is not the place to renew all the familiar economic and sociological reasons against factory life for women, but we may say this, that the employment of women is only desirable where the supply of men is deficient, and when that state arrives the question will settle itself.[56]

These statements come as no surprise if one has read what employers had to say during the war, and looked behind the propaganda of the Ministry of Munitions and the press. Women were still distrusted as employees, and in any case employers who might have used them wanted to avoid any industrial disputes with irate male workers. A few enthusiastic employers had promised to set up 'women's factories' when the war ended, but these too did not materialise — the slump put paid to expansion on these lines. Generally speaking, as the Factory Inspector's *Report* noted, all too little attention was paid by employers to the women who had worked for them, and few considered special training schemes once the war was over.

The Public Debate on 'Woman's Place'

Looking back from the 1930s, the feminist Irene Clephane remarked upon the change in attitude to women which occurred in the press between 1918 and 1919:

> From being the saviours of the nation, women in employment were degraded in the public press to the position of ruthless self-seekers depriving men and their dependants of a livelihood. The woman who

had no one to support her, the woman who herself had dependants, the woman who had no necessity, save that of the urge to personal independence and integrity, to earn: all of them became, in many people's minds, objects of opprobrium as violent as that meted out in the ensuing years to the returned 'heroes' who found themselves metamorphosed into worthless wastrels when they too fell into unemployment.[57]

The contrast was noted at the time. Women workers were supposed to go back to their 'proper place',[58] which meant paid or unpaid domestic work or the women's trades. When they did not immediately leave their wartime jobs (and some did manage to stay in them for a few months longer) or when they claimed unemployment benefit, the change in the tone of the press reports was extraordinary. Women, who had 'formed one of those rather numerous groups who were severally assured that they had "won the war" or "saved the country" '[59] were now 'limpets', 'bloodsuckers' or 'bread snatchers', *Common Cause* reported bitterly, while *Solidarity* too was scathing about the irony of the situation, and the turn-around of the 'prostitute press':

> These women, who now find themselves faced with the choice of unemployment and starvation, or employment and semi-starvation, are those 'splendid women' who so 'gloriously helped to save this country from the ravaging Hun'! Laughable, isn't it – if you happen to be in a position to see the joke.[60]

As Ray Strachey said (like Irene Clephane, several years later), 'public opinion assumed that all women could still be supported by men, and that if they went on working it was from some sort of deliberate wickedness.'[61]

Opinion was not entirely hostile, as I shall show, but certainly resentment of women workers was now seen as acceptable, and from December 1918 the superficial praise changed to spiteful criticism in many newspapers. Women did have their defenders – although sometimes the defence was slightly ambiguous and lukewarm – who often wrote in the same papers which at other times criticised them, but these journalists knew that they were fighting against strong anti-feminist feeling.

Early in December 1918, the *Chronicle* described the kind of women who were signing on at one particular labour exchange. One woman, working in munitions, was reported to have averaged 37s 6d a week during the last months of the war, but did not expect to earn that much again:

'But I feel so pleased the war's over that I'll take any old job again.'
'Domestic service?'
'Except that,' she laughed.[62]

This was one of the last times that the scene was described in such a neutral fashion, for women's failure to take up jobs in domestic service resulted in much criticism from the press, and, it seems, the public. At the turn of the year 1918-19, the *Telegraph* was becoming sarcastic when it referred to unemployed women. Their reporter wrote:

A little investigation [at the labour exchange] showed that since they have 'been in munitions' women have acquired to a remarkable extent a taste for factory life. Many of them of course, might return at once to the domestic service from which they came, but, for the moment at any rate, they literally scoff at the idea.[63]

From this time onwards the attitude worsened. 'When are munition girls to grow tired of their holiday?' demanded the generally sympathetic *Daily News* in January, 'Housewives who want servants and laundry men who want workers are anxious to know.'[64] In the same week the *Daily News* complained about the dearth of female servants in Bristol, where it was said that women were turning down 'good wages' and large houses were standing empty,[65] and carried an article entitled 'Out of Work "Holiday" ' which informed readers:

There have been cases before the Labour Exchanges of women who have tried to get a long holiday by refusing to say what their previous occupation was, and declaring they were factory hands. After the bulk of the women who have had experience in non-wartime trades and occupations have been drafted back to their old employments, these cases of the doubtful factory hands will be carefully investigated.[66]

The *Evening News* jumped into the fray with its article 'The New Rest Cure' on 4 January. The writer of this piece reported that the government was kindly giving women 25s a week, and continued:

Of course, it was understood that no one who refused a suitable job should continue to draw unemployment money, but for those who wish to take a holiday at the National expense there was an easy way out of the difficulty, and the holiday makers were not long in finding it.[67]

Women's 'way out' was to claim that they were factory workers, for whom there was little available work, rather than domestic servants, laundry women, seamstresses, etc. which they 'really' were. The writer went on:

> These women are not wearing out their shoe leather to any great extent looking for work. Many of them would do their best to avoid a job if they saw it coming. A holiday on 25s a week is quite good enough for them.

Twenty-five shillings a week was not a great deal of money, but even so it was more than many of the jobs women were offered were paying; the *Evening News* did not take up this point, nor did it look at the poor conditions experienced by those in 'women's trades', or indeed at the reasons for women's unemployment. They were simply assumed to be lazy scroungers.

Other papers carried similar articles. The *Evening Standard* too decided that women were in no hurry to find work, and that they were asking excessively high wages for domestic service.[68] Why won't women become servants, or go back into the laundry trade? demanded the *Express*,[69] while others persisted in describing women's unemployment as a 'holiday'.[70] Women were increasingly taken to task for not facing up to the reality of the situation, and told they could not expect jobs outside their traditional trades. The *Southampton Times*, for example, said sternly:

> After nearly 6 months of Armistice [in fact 4½ months], women still have not brought themselves to realise that factory work, with the money paid for it during the war, will not be possible again. They still demand employment of this sort, but there has been a great tightening of the strings lately, and a woman does not necessarily get benefit because the work is not forthcoming. Women, for instance, who left domestic service to enter the factory are now required to return to the pots and pans.[71]

But the emphasis of newspaper articles changed subtly over 1919.

Papers which originally concentrated on lambasting *unemployed* women and asking why they did not take the jobs offered to them[72] started demanding that women still in employment be dismissed to enable ex-soldiers to find work. As usual, there was little investigation into the kinds of work women were actually doing, and no realisation that men might not *want* the majority of jobs held by women. As the year progressed, women were not only castigated for being lazy and work-shy, but for staying at work while war heroes were unemployed. In addition, the criticism levelled at married women, for working when (a) they should be dependent upon their husbands and (b) they should be looking after the home, spread to single women as well, who were now commonly supposed to be working for nothing more than 'pin money'. As a journalist for the *Southampton Times* wrote:

> While it would be a shame to turn women out of their jobs at short notice in cases where such procedure would mean absolute hardship, and, perhaps, starvation, there is no reason to feel sympathetic towards the young person who has been earning 'pin money' while the men have been fighting, nor the girls who left women's work, to which they could return without difficulty, to take the places of soldiers who have now come back.[73]

Ideas of state responsibility for women's unemployment were rejected; indeed, a number of writers called upon the government to set a good example and dismiss their remaining female employees on 'men's work'.[74]

Nor were newspapers averse to hurling abuse at the departing war workers for the role they had played during the war itself — including the very women who had been praised for their sense of patriotism and fairness when they struck for equal pay a year earlier. Thus a *Leeds Mercury* journalist wrote, with unashamed smugness:

> Without appearing ungallant I may be permitted to place on record my unfeigned pleasure on hearing today that by October 3rd nearly all women 'bus conductors, underground [workers] etc. in the employ of the Traffic Combine will have departed from the service. Their record of duty well done is seriously blemished by their habitual and aggressive incivility, and a callous disregard for the welfare of passengers. Their shrewish behaviour will remain one of the unpleasant memories of the war's vicissitudes.[75]

Perhaps any woman not fitting into the stereotype of meek, docile femininity, no matter how unsuitable such characteristics were for a bus conductress, was bound to be called 'shrewish'.

The press was backed by a succession of letters from the public expressing their hostility. As early as December 1918 the *Saturday Review* printed a barely comprehensible letter from E. Austin Hinton, who complained about the praise lately showered upon women:

> It is almost incredible that a nation which prides itself on its reserve and well-balanced judgement should be afflicted with such a mental aberration as makes it create an atmosphere of what one is pleased to call 'self-sacrifice' (mawkish sentimentality would be a more correct term), round the girl who for the last 4 years has been protecting herself from the Hun, or taking up what she calls 'war work' for the sake of a love or flirtation and associated giddiness, which the freer and more licensed life has made it possible to indulge.[76]

This letter was an outpouring of resentment for women's apparent freedom, and was based on no real cause for complaint. Other letter-writers took up more down-to-earth points, and complained, as the press did, that women would not take the jobs offered to them and that they preferred 'to loaf idly about the streets, receiving money which tax payers have to provide'.[77] Unfortunately, ex-servicemen too believed what they read in the papers, and complained that women were taking their jobs. One man wrote to the *Hull Daily Mail* saying that men would never work while women were employed, and that although there were jobs for them in domestic service, 'they would sooner fill a man's place while he walks the street looking for a right to live.'[78] The assumption remained that women did not really need to work; as the *Manchester Dispatch* stated in March 1919, the unemployment figures might look bad, but in fact they were not — a closer look at the register revealed that many unemployed women had worked for the first (?) time during the war, and these must be wives who ought to return home.[79]

Women did have some defenders at this time, although as I have said a number of them wrote for papers which at other times criticised women bitterly, a fact which is hard to explain. We have already seen that the *Daily News* carried a number of hostile articles early in 1919; at the same time some defensive reports also appeared, although their tone makes it clear that the writers knew they were flying in the face of public opinion. As demobilisation approached in late 1918, the paper had stated that munitions workers had 'a claim upon the

community that is second only to that of the soldiers'.[80] This statement might subsequently have meant very little, as many other people
made similar ones at the time, but in fact throughout 1919 a number of
journalists for the *Daily News* stood by this view, and defended women
(either cautiously or more aggressively) from the charges of being work-
shy and selfish. One such piece began, like so many other articles, by
discussing the idea that it was necessary to get women 'back to work':
'One of the big problems awaiting solution is that of getting back to
their ordinary duties the woman factory hands, laundry workers and
domestic servants, who during the war went into munition factories
and are now unemployed.'[81] The writer referred to the fact that from
all quarters came the complaint that women would not return to work
while they were receiving 25s a week, but he then went on to give the
'other side' of the story — that the work was hard and long, the wages
low, and servants especially had little freedom. He finished by saying
that women would take the work if they were offered good wages and
conditions.

Later in January, Mary Macarthur was given space in the same paper
to defend women — she was, she wrote, concerned to give the true facts
of the case, since women's image varied from month to month. She
informed readers that munitions workers did not want to be idle, and
that laundry work, which was hard and disagreeable, paid 'starvation
wages' (20s 8d a week was quoted). Her views were supported by a
letter from a woman worker the following day, and an article from M.P.
Willcocks, who gave women's reasons for disliking domestic service, and
made an unusual suggestion for the time, that women who were short
of servants should do the work themselves — although it has to be asked
by any feminist why women alone should be responsible for housework![82]

Other national dailies and local papers also ran articles which defended women workers, first from the idea that they were shirking employment, and later from the suggestion that they should leave paid
work to men. Various writers pointed out the difficulties of ex-muni-
tions workers, who knew no other trade, asked why women should be
blamed for their own unemployment, noted the low wages and poor
conditions of the jobs offered, maintained that women did not want to
take away men's jobs, and that it was unfair to use the claims of ex-
soldiers to turn out women (particularly since many of the men who
replaced women had reportedly never been in the forces), and finally
upheld the right of both married and single women to work.[83] The
writers often pinpointed accurately the misconceptions and unfair

assumptions made about women in industry. The *Daily Chronicle*, for example, carried an article which carefully balanced the claims of men and women:

> There is much justification for the protest made by the National Union for Equal Citizenship against the indiscriminate way in which women are being dismissed from every sort of employment. We have more than once declared our view that the claims of the disabled soldier must come first, and that women who have taken up jobs to keep them open for soldiers must expect to relinquish them when the soldiers return. Whilst this is true, it is unfair to the ex-Serviceman to use his needs as an excuse for recklessly turning out women from work for which they are suited.[84]

The writer went on to say that women should not be dismissed simply because they were women, but by mid-1919 women were indeed being expected to leave because of their sex: it became almost irrelevant whether or not they were 'taking' a soldier's job, as another article in the *Chronicle* complained: 'Other things being equal, women have as much right to work as men. To turn them recklessly into the streets, not on account of inefficiency, but their sex alone, is a policy as disastrous as it is unjust.'[85] One woman wrote a letter on this subject to the *Hull Daily Mail*:

> As to women workers, why is it all the insults are thrown on the women? Why not throw some for the masters? I myself am working in a man's place, but still, if I give it up, my employer will start another girl in my place ... If our men come back, I, like others, am willing to give it up for them, as it is only fair that they should have it back again. I have been employed in this place for 4 years, and then have to be insulted in the street, whilst on my way to work — 'When are you going to throw your —— job in, and let your men come back?'[86]

Where were the men who wanted her job? she asked, answering bitterly, perhaps they were drawing the dole rather than working.

Those who defended women's right to work included John Murray, who wrote in the *Newcastle Journal* that the women registered as unemployed in Tyneside either could not afford to stay home, or did not wish to, and that both groups deserved respect.[87] G.R. Malloch discussed the same issue in the *Evening Standard*, and maintained that financial independence was the key to women's full independence, whether or not they were married.[88] These views were unpopular, as those who upheld them knew. Women's 'natural aptitude' for housework was now used against them, and validated their unemployment. As a journalist on the *Liverpool Daily Post* wrote:

> One would think to hear some people talk that the whole problem of women's unemployment is to be solved in the near future by a general 'back to the kitchen' movement on the part of the ex-munition workers. Certainly the ordinary man in the street holds that view, but it is not a true one. It is simply a belated survival of the old myth that woman's sphere is the home, and if she does not happen to possess one of her own she had best make herself useful in someone else's.[89]

Edith Shackleton took up the same matter in the *Manchester Dispatch*:

> There is an alarming revival of a strange fallacy that iₐ a woman does not work neither need she eat, an ugly acceptance of the idea that men and women must necessarily be antagonistic in industry.
> Every day one comes across evidence of it — now in some minor discourtesy of some man towards working woman, again in some savage public demand that women should give up their jobs and 'go home' because there are so many men out of work.[90]

Where were all these homes women could go back to, she asked, and was it better to have starving women than starving men? She added grimly that men had no moral right to call for women's dismissal unless they were willing to take financial responsibility for all female kin.

Curiously enough, although by 1921 it was clear that women's and men's unemployment was due to economic circumstances, rather than the selfishness or laziness of the former, their unpopularity remained, and the *Daily News* felt the need to bring public feelings into the open. An article by W. Keith faced up to the fact that the current attitude to working women was based not on any real social or economic crimes they might have committed, but was simply *dislike* — which was itself rooted in resentment at the way they did not want to return to their pre-war position. Wrote Keith:

> Women are almost as unpopular today as ex-soldiers [another irony]. It is an unpleasant truth hidden from us for such reasons as

modesty, tact and tactics. But the attitude of the public towards women is more full of contempt and bitterness than has been the case since the suffragette outbreaks . . . The flood of praise poured out on women during the war has had its inevitable backwash. The women who saved the allies are not fit to receive unemployment benefit. They did dirty work during the war. No wonder we resent their refusal to do housework now.[91]

These were the debates carried on by the popular press and the public, but what points were taken up by the papers representing groups with a particular interest in the future of women workers? I have no space here to go through the views of many such groups in detail, and no further information on individual trade unions' views should be needed here: hostility increased amongst those which had shown resentment towards women during the war, if they still felt threatened by them. Many of the male-dominated unions no longer troubled themselves with the position of women as long as they had been removed from their particular trades. Several papers were representative of the views of people with particular political views, and these show a range of concerns. The opinions which interest me most are those of the general labour movement, the women within that movement, feminists and radical socialists.

The views of the right wing of the labour movement, as expressed by the *Democrat* (which was unassociated with any particular trade union) were depressingly similar to those I have already discussed in this chapter: the most important matter was seen as justice for men. Certainly women's employment problems were mentioned: it was appreciated that they were reluctant to go back to low pay and poor conditions, said one writer, but the problems must be treated 'firmly and sympathetically', and women must be allowed neither to drift, nor to rely too much on state aid.[92] This fear that benefits might demoralise the workers was echoed in a later article on unemployment in general, when the author announced soberly, 'By a system of state donations a premium is being put on idleness. Men and women are finding it more profitable for them to do no work, and are acting accordingly.'[93] It was quite clear from the articles which appeared throughout 1919 that although women's right to education and equal pay for equal work were accepted, there was no desire to disturb the *status quo* of male breadwinner and female dependant; female unemployment was not seen as a major problem. The old ideals were held up; in an article on education, E. Gittens stated, 'Education does not unfit a woman for home duties and the rearing of children; rather it teaches her to bring to bear on them a keenness of intelligence that cannot but be all for the good.'[94] In another article, on the question of equal pay, the writer began with fine egalitarian sentiments:

This premise [of female dependence] today is altogether wrong. It has been proved by statistics that at least 2/3rds of the women in this country must remain single and consequently must provide for themselves. Moreover, the old theory, always economically unsound, that ruled that however badly off a husband was his wife should not be allowed to use her labour to contribute to the exchequer has been wiped out,[95]

but he finished with the traditional reasons for wanting equal pay:

Many trades, which by reason of their peculiarities are suited only to the stronger male, are laid open to female competition [if women are paid less]. If, however, the wages of either were equal, woman would by sheer force of competition be driven into the trades most suited to her, thereby making her work more efficient.

The logic behind this last statement is not altogether clear; what *is* clear from these articles is that women's primary role was seen as wifehood, and that they should stay in their own trades and not interfere with men's industrial position.

When it came to the particular matter of women war workers, the *Democrat* was increasingly hostile, and incorporated as many myths and half-truths about the nature of unemployment as did the daily press. In June 1919 it carried a full-page cartoon on the subject. A young woman sits at an office desk, holding a cup of tea, and looks startled at the entrance of a soldier, who points at her accusingly. The caption reads: 'What is tea for you is bread for me,' and underneath, in brackets, is the Democrat's explanation — 'Many girls are filling, for the sake of pocket money, positions that should now be occupied by breadwinners.'[96] The same issue carried an article entitled 'Married Women and Industry: Make Room for the Discharged Soldiers', which began: 'One of the avenues that offers some scope for the placing in employment of men discharged from the army is that of the reduction, as far as it can fairly be done, of woman labour.'[97] The author insisted that the girls who had worked so gallantly, and who needed to support themselves (perhaps including the one in the cartoon?) should not be the ones to go, and nor should women be elbowed into low-class jobs, but —

> There is, however, a large body of married working women whose hus-bands can comfortably keep them and who never worked before the war. These women find the extra income they can earn is a very use-ful household asset, and intend to retain it if possible. These are the women who in these hard times, might give place to the returning men.

The same line was pushed repeatedly; the following week an article ap-peared stating that now was the testing time for real patriotism amongst girl war workers:

> Unfortunately, however, there are many cases in which the attrac-tions of pin money have proved too strong for good resolutions. There are even more in which the freer life of the employed girls has bred a disinclination to go back to the old conditions . . . In many cases, unhappily, the girl has made up her mind to remain as long as possible, with no thought for the fact that she is occupying a post which means the bread and butter of some discharged soldier and his dependents.[98]

The phantom of the pocket-money worker — the girl who should be liv-ing on her parents, or the wife who should be supported by her husband — loomed again. There was no investigation into the kind of jobs women were doing, or whether men would want them, even if they were avail-able; many who should have known better assumed that *most* women workers during the war had taken over 'men's jobs', and that most of those who stayed on were still doing such work. The stated aim was to return them to the home — because this was a matter of justice for de-mobilised men, because women had special duties there (housework and child-rearing), and because they belonged there. H.J. Jeffrey, writing of women's role, stated:

> The home is still woman's most rightful sphere, the sphere in which she can best apply her powers if only she be content to do so. For exceptional women there are parliament, the learned professions, the common market place of life. But the average woman is wiser than to seek these things. She prefers to quietly study social matters from the point whence she can best see them; that is, in relation to her home and its well-being.[99]

Employment was seen as being a trivial matter in comparison.

Such views clearly overlapped with those of the Labour Party, which professed to believe in the equality of the sexes,[100] and to a certain extent upheld women's right to work, yet certainly believed that men were the breadwinners and women had their most important duties at home. Those opinions were shared, as I have shown, by many women in the Labour Party, and in the labour movement — thus the response from such women to the conditions of 1919-20 was fairly predictable. They defended women workers from slander, and supported women's right to work, but at the same time they were not interested in putting women's cause before men's, and still upheld the idea of the nobility of wifehood and motherhood (even though individuals argued about the inevitability of such a role).

As with other interested groups, their views on women's employment, or lack of it, during the years immediately following the war have to be seen in the context of their views on woman's social role. During 1919-21, *Labour Woman* campaigned for shorter hours for the housewife at home, and urged that co-operative laundries and kitchens be set up, but did not criticise the fact that women alone were responsible for housework. The paper was taken to task for its schemes to improve the structure of domestic service in the homes of the rich by one correspondent, who asked it to turn its attention instead to the plight of the woman worker, and consider

> a new type of household where the mother is a skilled worker and requires time for her own work. It is a very bad economy to make women who are highly skilled in other directions into houseworkers, and a great deal of nonsense is talked about the injury to home life when mothers don't spend their whole time in domesticity.[101]

Likewise, although *Labour Woman* criticised government inefficiency, low wages and the fact that women were being deprived of unemployment benefit, it was reluctant to criticise male-dominated unions for their attitude to women, and once again it was left to a correspondent to demand justice. Winifred Moore wrote in saying that it seemed to her that organised labour was determined to throw women out, and that unions believed no woman had the right to work while men were unemployed. She appealed:

> Give women a chance, a fair field and no favour; work towards equal pay; make them full members of the unions — and then all work

together to do away with the real cause of unemployment — the capitalist system of industry.[102]

By 1922, the Labour Party was still campaigning for displaced women to be provided with work and maintenance, had reiterated the need for equal pay for equal work, and demanded that restrictions on women's right to vote, enter professions and be assessed for tax independently be removed. Significantly, the Labour Party Conference also decided that those women still in wartime jobs should only stay if they were paid at trade union rates, and that unions should be persuaded to accept all women working in the trades they covered.[103] The matter of women working in men's trades was still a vexed question, and it was here that Labour women had divided loyalties.

At the same time, the *Woman Worker*, organ of the NFWW, defended women's right not to take the badly paid, exploitative work on offer, campaigned to raise wages, criticised the LCC for dismissing married women cleaners, and maintained that men's prospects would not be improved by making women leave their jobs,[104] but nevertheless, like the Labour Party women and many other women trade unionists, held fairly traditional ideas about women's place and needs. Demands were made for training schemes, but it was often accepted that these would be in domestic subjects and the standard 'women's trades', and in fact Mary Macarthur of the NFWW was also the Honorary Secretary of the Central Committee on Women's Employment, which, when given £500,000 by the government, proceeded to set up precisely such classes.[105] Schemes were suggested for improving the status of domestic service through training courses[106] (which the *Worker's Dreadnought*, believing that service should be abolished, complained about bitterly[107]), and there were strong elements of the 'home as woman's true sphere' philosophy in evidence. Julia Varley (Workers' Union), expressing her interest in the idea of re-training munitions girls to be domestic servants, was reported as saying, 'Our aim . . . is to turn a C3 nation into an A1 nation, and we want to do what we can to create home makers.'[108] Clearly she subscribed to the classic notion that a good servant made a good housewife.

There was also a lingering dislike of the idea that married women with children should be working. At an International Women's Conference in 1920 Mary Macarthur found herself disagreeing with one of the French workers' representatives, Madame Bouvier. The latter was fighting for mothers to have the right to take their babies to work with them, while Mary Macarthur believed that nursing mothers should stay at home. At the concurrent International Labour Conference, Madame

Bouvier won most support when the same issue was raised, and the *Woman Worker* considered this to be a 'blot upon the Conference'.[109] At the NFWW's own conference in 1920 many delegates deplored the fact that women worked when they had children to look after, and one Mrs Prosser stated that women who went to work in spite of children and home let the health and morals of the former suffer. At this conference, mothers' pensions were supported on the grounds that women would stay at home once they had no financial inducement to work; as Miss Stephen said, 'If the mothers had pensions they could stop at home, and that would reduce unemployment.'[110]

Significantly, the same issue came up at the TUC in 1919, couched in familiar terms:

> The question of the position of the mothers of our race is one of the most important that this Congress or any other gathering of thoughtful men and women could be called upon to consider. If we have got to have an A1 nation, we must protect the mothers in the way suggested in this solution. We have got to encourage motherhood, and therefore this proposal ought to receive your hearty support. I honestly believe that the institution of pensions for mothers would go a long way towards checking the race suicide that is now going on.[111]

These words were spoken by another woman trade unionist. Many of these women from the trade union movement or the Labour Party did consider themselves to be either feminists or supporters of women's rights, but there is a big difference between their attitude to women's post-war position and that of the Women's Industrial League, or the readers of *Common Cause*. Middle-class feminists did concern themselves with the status of motherhood and the health of the race, as discussed in Chapter 5, but on the issue of women's right to work they were far more outspoken than their sisters in the labour movement. Ruth Adam, in her recent book *A Woman's Place*, refers to a letter from the Women's Industrial League to the *Daily News* in 1919, in which Lady Rhondda asked why women should be dismissed, and Mary Macarthur's reply that it would be little comfort to the unemployed woman if her father or husband were dismissed instead of her. Ruth Adam states her belief that 'this split in feminist ranks stood for the difference between the middleclass career woman and the workingclass wage earning ones.'[112] But to my mind there is more to the rift than this. The suffragettes and suffragists had long been fighting for *women*, and they recognised that women were still oppressed, whether or not they had the Vote. Women in the labour movement, however, had been reared in a different tradition — the tradition of male-dominated trade unionism and the fight against capitalism. This rested on right of *men* to work, and incorporated the belief that men were the breadwinners while women were an economic threat. Even women trade unionists who fought so hard for women workers found it hard to accept that women had an *equal* right to work, and that their destiny need not revolve around husband and family. Middle-class feminists were not content to see women's work being classed as less important than men's, and there was a strong feeling that working-class women were being betrayed by those they had trusted when the Labour Party gave its support to the Pre-War Practices Bill, just as they had been let down by many trade unions during the war.[113] Feminists were angry and disappointed by the treatment women received after 1918; as one writer stated in *Common Cause*:

> The whole situation is affected by the assumption which still seems to lurk at the back of most men's minds, that it is not as necessary for women to work as it is for men, and that if they cannot get work all they have to do is to 'go back to their homes'.[114]

They insisted that women who had worked in factories were totally un-fitted for domestic work, and anger even prompted the suggestion that women abandon such niceties as the equal pay campaign and attempt to get into different trades as quickly as possible. Maud Selbourne wrote in *Common Cause*:

> It [the current situation] confirms me in my belief, which I have often stated in public, that women should leave 'equal pay for equal work' to be insisted upon by men. They are giving up their chief weapon when they agree not to undercut men. And they should do so only when they receive 'quid pro quo'. If the men are willing to give them equal opportunities, they should agree to equal pay. But if the men are trying to prevent their entry into skilled trades, the only way in which they can obtain admission is by working for less money than men do.[115]

This may be seen as an unfair suggestion, for women as well as men, but it must be remembered that even if they did undercut men, women were likely to earn more money than they could in the conventional women's trades, and would have more interesting work.

Foremost in the campaign to make women workers more acceptable to industry was the Women's Industrial League. This organisation, headed by Lady Rhondda, was viewed with considerable suspicion by all sections of the labour movement, and warnings were issued to working women by *Solidarity* and the *Woman Worker* not to be lured by the WIL propaganda, not least because it took up the slogan of 'equal pay for equal output', seeing this as less threatening to women's interests.[116] The League received a lot of publicity, partly because it contained some famous names, but also because it was well organised, and members kept up a stream of letters to the press. It early attacked the Pre-War Practices Bill,[117] suggesting that new processes should be excluded from its jurisdiction, and stated its overall aims as equal employment, training and educational opportunities, equal pay and working conditions, and adequate representation on all official committees and public bodies.[118] It criticised the Labour Party's failure to take up women's cause,[119] but insisted that members *did* want women to join trade unions as they did not want women to be used as cheap labour, and also supported the idea that men should have their old jobs back.[120] A League official staunchly defended women's right to work in an interview with the *National News* in 1919:

No, I do not believe the fairy stories about injuring their health. Of course, labour of a heavy nature must not be undertaken, but I have seen a lot of cases in which the regular hours and adequate pay have turned pale anaemic girls into bright, healthy examples of womanhood, with a consequent gain to the nation.

Go into domestic service and the laundries? I'm afraid they will do no such thing. They want better conditions than employment of that kind usually offers, and apart from that the public loses sight of the fact that there are now large numbers of women who must have sufficient money not only to maintain themselves, but a family.[121]

The League's demands seem eminently reasonable now, but at the time the feminist campaign had little chance of success, though it received much attention.[122] Faced with the apathy of the government,[123] the hostility of many unions, the lack of interest amongst employers and extensive public resentment of working women, League members could do very little: they wielded no political power, and they were cut off from female sympathisers in the labour movement. They could not even persuade the government that the maintenance grants paid to women on training courses should be equal to men's, or that they should have training in trades other than domestic service and the traditional 'women's' jobs. When the League complained, Sir Robert Horne replied that he sympathised, but that the government was under an obligation to cater for discharged soldiers first, and, on the issue of maintenance, men's grants were higher than women's because they needed more money to support themselves. This was of course the standard excuse.[124]

Finally, in this résumé of post-war opinion, it is interesting to look at the views of the radical socialists, once the economic depression began. Like the middle-class feminists, many continued to discuss women's role at a time when so many other people were content to demand simply that women 'go home'.[125] Their views are those of a minority (as are those of the feminists), but they are important, because they show what lay in the minds of some of the more progressive thinkers. Their existence also proves that it is not unfair for me, now, to look critically at the approach of trade unionists, employers, the government or the 'general public'. It could be argued that anyone who condemns past generations for their lack of interest in women's problems, or lack of concern with changing women's role, is demanding the impossible — that people from another age possess the consciousness of the feminists of the 1980s. But the views of certain individuals and organisations during and after the First World War reveal a full understanding of women's social and economic position: the political ideas existed in the early twentieth century, but they were unacceptable to the majority of people, even those who realised that there was much wrong with the existing state of things.

Although less involved with women's cause than the feminist movement, radical socialists included many who were less inclined to accept the prejudices of the mainstream labour movement on the issue of women workers, particularly after the inspiration provided by the 1917 revolutions in Russia. Kathleen Wadsworth, in *Socialist Review*, raised one vital question when she asked why men were allowed to have work and marriage, while women were not,[126] and *Solidarity* took up the cause of working women with a vengeance through the columns of 'Everywoman', by 'Bee'. She criticised the continuation of restrictions on women's work, which were still legal, in spite of the farcical Sex Qualification (Removal) Act, and said that it was ridiculous that an excess of chivalry prevented women from entering certain jobs, in view of the dirty and degrading work they were often forced into.[127] As she wrote, 'Woman may have the vote, but she has realised by now how little equality that has brought her.' Married women were, she noted, used as a convenience; they were called up for work when needed, and then, when their labour was no longer necessary, 'Married Women must go' was used as a convenient slogan to fool men into believing that un-employment was due to them.[128] She also criticised men for standing by while women did ill-paid, hard work, and protesting only when women came near their trades, and added, 'It is the man who is most ruthless where his own desires are concerned, who is most often the protector of women's purity and virtue,'[129] an interesting comment on men's be-haviour towards women in both the social and industrial sphere.

'Bee' also gave a timely reminder that the fight was against capitalism, not against those who had become used as cheap labour, and demanded that both sexes should unite against the system, not men unite against women.[130] This point was also made by the *Communist* and *Out of Work* (produced from 1921 by the London District Council of the Un-employed). From the start, these two papers treated men *and women* as workers, not as workers and their wives, and appealed to women to take a greater part in the National Unemployed Movement. 'A Letter to Women' appeared in *Out of Work*, but it was clearly addressed to men as well; an important role is played by the wife and mother, said the writer, but men must realise that women can be powerful outside the home as well — 'There are many women who are keen to do something active, but are unable to owing to the narrow margin allowed to women.'[131] While many trade unions closed in upon themselves, and denied women an equal right to work, the socialists who produced these papers con-tinued to try and mobilise women. Their attacks on women's social and industrial position could be bitter, and readers replied in the same vein. One such letter came from Lily Webb, and expressed sentiments with which *Labour Woman* and *Woman Worker* would have disagreed strongly:

The time is now right for woman's entry into the economic and political struggle and she must shake off her apathy and realize the necessity of organisation. The sympathies and aspirations of women should not be confined within a domestic area, to desire this is to make her merely a serf, a slave of the hearth. How can such a woman ever become the mother of men and women of broad views and gen-erous impulses? Working women today are mentally and physically weakened by the narrow and close environment of the home. Given an opportunity of interesting themselves in matters political and with a wide field of development woman will become man's rival for intel-lectual attainment.[132]

This was not just men's struggle, she continued, but women's as well.
The *Communist* took the same line, with Stella Browne and Cedar

Paul writing regularly about women and Communism, both of whom recognised that 'The movement for the emancipation of the workers has not always been guided by persons friendly to the emancipation of women.'[133] They desired for women economic independence and an end to parasitism, but, interestingly, there were arguments in the paper's columns and, presumably, the movement about birth control. Stella Browne claimed that women had the right to control their own bodies, and was criticised by 'Clete', who wrote, 'Stella Browne's exclusively feminist opinions make an unbiased statement on Birth Control appear exclusively masculine,' and proceeded to say that woman's 'control of her own person and environment' was not possible while women were living under capitalism. S. Francis also requested that Stella Browne spend less time talking about the domination of women by men or the evils of childbearing, and more about the immediate fight (i.e. against capitalism).[134] Clearly, although women's right to work and their need to escape from domestic slavery were recognised in such circles, socialist feminists found that wider issues were less well understood by their male companions.

The Imposition of the Status Quo

Mrs Fawcett, suffragist, gave regular interviews to the press about women workers. In 1917, she was reported by the *War Illustrated* as saying:

> I cannot help feeling that the character of the women who have shared in this truly national work has been uplifted and strengthened. They have known the sweets of economic independence and the joy of service to a cause they love. They have gained in dignity and self-reliance, and the country has found in their labour an asset which will not be neglected in the future as it has been in the past.[135]

The sentiments are romantic, and the prophesy turned out to be wrong, but what of the idea that women workers were 'changed' by their war experience? I have poured scorn on the optimistic forecasts of journalists and women's rights supporters, and shown that there was no basis in reality for their hopes of post-war change and social regeneration, but had the views and character of working-class women been altered, as was frequently suggested?[136] This is an important matter. If women were content with leaving work on marriage, being full-time homekeepers, or being confined to the 'women's trades', then to blame workmen,

unions, government and employers for their conservative attitude to
women's work and training would not necessarily be fair.[137] But to my
mind many women *had* been altered by the war, but like numbers of
women before and since that time they lacked the power, confidence
and organisation to bring about change in their industrial or home lives.
They were also used to sacrificing themselves for their men, and continued to feel that their interests came second.

There is evidence from both feminist and non-feminist observers that
women blossomed during the war, in spite of the strain the population
lived under and the fact that men were killed and mutilated abroad.
Women's determination to do well at work and their growing sense of
independence were noted by those who were not interested in feminism
and propaganda; thus Adelaide Anderson wrote:

> heightened pride in enhanced valuation of their services, new and
> varied interest in work, access to opportunities for training, as well as,
> in certain cases, receipt of men's pay for men's work, also strength-
> ened their powers of body and mind, and gave utterance of a manag-
> ing foreman to the writer: 'there is more to this than people think;
> women have been too much kept back'.[138]

A Birmingham manufacturer reported, in Kirkaldy's study:

> I think a great proportion of the women at present employed in muni-
> tions and other factories, having tasted the sweets of freedom and
> good wages, will be loath to go back to the humdrum, unpaid, house-
> hold toil. Where this inclination against a return to women's home
> sphere will lead us, we cannot foresee; but it does exist, I know.
> Typical cases which have come under my personal observation show
> that women prefer factory life. They like the freedom, the spirit of
> independence fostered by their new-found earning power, the social
> life. The children, they say, are better off than before, better fed,
> housed and clothed. These women will not want to return to their
> domestic duties after the war. The widening of women's sphere and
> outlook is a phase which has been greatly accentuated by war condi-
> tions; and, although it will be modified when peace comes, it will
> never go back to what it used to be.[139]

To a certain extent, both these comments over-simplify women's position; women were not universally praised or well paid, and they had not
given up domestic work just because they were also doing factory work,

but the observations remain important, and similar points were made by others who were not interested in propagandising or romanticising like I.O. Andrews, who reported that 'as a class they have grown more confident, more independent, more interested in impersonal issues'.[140] War conditions did have important psychological effects. Many women were doing new jobs, learning new skills, coping with finances and family alone, receiving higher wages than they could have expected to earn before the war (in conjunction with separation allowances for women married to soldiers), and were photographed and praised by the press and propagandists. Women were *expected* to work outside the home, and to make a good job of their trades, while those whose husbands were away had a new form of independence. They could buy food for themselves and their children instead of the main breadwinner; they could organise their days around their own working lives, instead of their husbands'. Lady Bell, in her important article 'Women at the Works — and elsewhere' phrased it thus: 'She had not always to be thinking of someone else. She herself was now the person to be first considered, and she gave that consideration fully.'[141] In addition, instead of being shut up in their own small homes, married women who had earlier been obliged to give up work now found themselves with many other people, working together, with the important topics of war, food prices, working conditions, transport and wages to discuss. Single girls too found the work a way of escaping from home and earning money and independence, and the excitement of doing something new led to exuberance, as a 'housewife', who was delighted by the apparent change in women's status, but startled by it, testified:

> There is something rather upsetting to one's old-fashioned idea of 'woman's place' on meeting groups of young girls and women arm in arm and singing 'It's a long way to Tipperary' — while the searchlights are busy in a dark sky, and the ordinary timid wayfarer anxiously hurries home.[142]

It is interesting to look at the experiences of the women interviewed by the Imperial War Museum in the 1970s. They made up but a tiny percentage of those women who were working during the war, and many of them were very young at the time, but they came from a cross-section of the working class (from poverty to the relative prosperity of a small shopkeeper's family), and their memories are valuable to anyone who is interested in women's opinions of their work and its significance. Some went to work for the first time during the war, usually straight from school, others had worked in the classic women's trades before the war, such as weaving, tailoring, dressmaking and domestic service. The feelings they express about their work are not entirely uniform, since they had different experiences, and worked under a variety of conditions, but certain opinions come across very clearly. They took up war work for a number of reasons — because they wanted extra money (the propaganda about high wages had made an impact), for reasons of patriotism, to get away from home, or for a combination of these — and few of them realised the danger of working with explosives, particularly the younger ones.[143] But nearly all of them enjoyed aspects of their wartime work. They spoke of making good friends, of working together in a crowd (and going around together after work), of discovering independence, of learning interesting jobs, and of earning better wages than they could have hoped to receive either before or after the war. Although most of the work was completely new to them they were eager to learn, and some of them progressed to more complex work or positions of authority. Hundreds of thousands of men died or were wounded during these years, but still many women said that they were almost untouched personally by the events of the war, either because they were too young to really understand what was happening, or because they had no relatives or close friends killed or injured. But many of them felt they were 'doing their bit' by working, and were pleased to be useful.[144] It is poignant now to hear how much war work meant to many of them for whatever reasons. They were 'happier then' in those 'happy times'. Did they enjoy war work? One woman was asked; she replied, 'Yes, every minute of it. It was a very happy time and well, everything was very happy, the atmosphere on work and with the people you worked with.' Another said that the war itself was useless, but as far as women's experience was concerned, she felt they had gained new freedom, and that it was like being let out of a cage. There was a definite feeling that the war had in fact changed their lives: 'it allowed women to stand on their own feet. It was the turning point for women.'[145] One woman added that she would go and do the same work again now, if she had the chance. This is not to say that they did not realise that they were often used as cheap labour, patronised, ostracised, or obliged to put up with poor conditions and long hours. But these aspects have to be seen in the appropriate context. First, the women themselves felt there were compensations: they were doing important work, learning about life and making friends; they also met helpful men amongst the labour force, and some of them learned of the importance of trade unions.

Secondly, the work was in distinct contrast, for all its disadvantages, to the jobs available either before or after the war. Pre-war work had offered little to these women; it was poorly paid and had seemed inescapable. The situation for middle-aged women had been even worse; several of the interviewees reported how their mothers had been forced into doing the most menial and low-paid work before 1914, and had enthusiastically taken the opportunity to go into munitions when women were recruited. Conditions, wages and jobs during the war were far better than they had been before.

Although a few of the women interviewed had the opportunity to stay on after the Armistice, most were laid off – 'they threw us on the slag heap,' as one woman put it,[146] and sometimes saw themselves being replaced by cheaper boy labour.[147] The years that followed were hard times: 'Things were bad after the war, very, very bad. I mean, people of this day and age can't have any conception of what it was like. It was really bad.'[148] They realised there was little they could do about it, although at least one woman was amongst those munitions workers who marched to Parliament to protest.[149] They either went back to the 'women's trades' or became unemployed.

Women in general did not find it easy to accept the idea that they should 'go home' or return to the traditional female jobs. But it was not possible for them to hold out for better jobs once they were threatened with the suspension of unemployment benefit. They had to take the work offered or face acute poverty, but even so many of them avoided domestic service for as long as possible.[150] Acceptance of the inevitable did not mean that the post-war circumstances were welcomed. The experience of better work, more money and new horizons can only have made the years after 1918 seem even less tolerable.

Women's position in industry by the early 1920s was possibly worse than it had been before the war. The good-humoured contempt which had characterised much of the criticism of women until 1914 was replaced by outright hostility, and a determination to keep them out of men's jobs at all costs. Once it was realised (even if it was not openly admitted) that women really could do men's jobs if necessary they were more dangerous to working men. Similarly, once it became obvious that they were willing to step outside the sphere of the home and could respond with enthusiasm to industrial opportunities, it was more important than ever to make sure that they did not abandon their true female role – as unpaid houseworkers and low-paid workers. Many people, even at the height of the need for women's labour, had continued to maintain that women had different needs and duties, and that their very psychology was different from men's. An article appeared in the *Daily*

Express on this theme in 1917; the writer discussed the differences in attitude between a young girl and a young man to the process of leaving home:

> That is one of the great psychological differences between men and women. A man's instinct is to go out and take pot luck, trusting to chance, but a woman dreads leaving familiar environments for unknown conditions ... Woman's love for her home is instinctive. For man it is a spot to come back to at night or after his wanderings, for woman it is ever the centre of her thoughts and plans, even though most of her hours may be spent away from it. She clings to it as naturally as she extends her arms to a child, and to her the break threatens to sever some vital part of her life.[151]

Of course this feeling that women ought to regard their homes as the centre of their existence (no matter how dreadful those homes might be) also had repercussions for middle-class women, but the working-class woman, oppressed by both class and sex, had fewer escape routes. Middle-class women who had gone out to work during the war and then found themselves confined to the home afterwards could at least pay others to do their housework and find other, more interesting unpaid occupations to do. Working-class women did not have this choice, and were not supposed to need it. Lady Bell wrote movingly and bitterly of the particular plight of working-class women after the war:

> The working woman, whatever her natural bent and aptitudes, has no possibility of choosing [an alternative way of life]. If she wishes to succeed there is only one subject which she may take up. She must be a skilled housewife. And in this capacity she is incessantly called upon to satisfy the examiners, who are in this case the whole community, inquiring into what she does with her life. She cannot escape from the searchlight of investigation for ever playing upon her, and must unavoidably display to the demands on her from all and sundry, for it is always there accusing or justifying her. It is her House. She cannot hide it. Her house testifies whether she is of clean habits or the reverse, whether she is tidy or a slattern, whether she does her cooking at home or buys her food outside, whether her children are well cared for or neglected; and she will be judged or condemned accordingly, without being allowed to appeal to some other set of endearing qualities which if she were better off would equally justify her existence.[152]

The home was often a trap, or a heavy burden, for working women, yet it was supposed to be at the centre of their lives. It was used as an excuse for not taking their paid work seriously, and no matter how good a worker a woman might be, she always had to prove that she was also a good wife and mother, and a good *housewife*. This idea remained during the war, for women were seen as essentially *temporary* workers in wider fields of industry, who would return to their 'true sphere' once no longer needed in 'men's jobs'. That this sphere included badly paid domestic and industrial work was not a matter for debate; there was no doubt about the fact that it was *not* men's work, therefore it had to be women's.

Women had been offered a broader experience by wartime conditions, but they were not allowed by government, employers, unions and workmen to capitalise upon this. On the subject of women's work the 1919 Inspector of Factories *Report* stated that:

> Today there is little call to a strenuous and sustained effort, entailing full use of powers and facilities. Instead, interesting work is taken out of their hands, and they are being forced back into the routine of their hitherto normal occupation.[153]

The 1921 census showed that the proportion of 'gainfully employed females' (over ten years old) was slightly lower than it had been in 1911: 30.8 per cent, as opposed to 32.3 per cent.[154]

Notes

1. Gilbert Stone (ed.), *Women War Workers* (Harrap, 1917), p. 310.
2. Ibid., p. 311.
3. Ibid., p. 319.
4. *Trade Union Worker*, October 1916, 'The Scientific Management Craze'.
5. *Trade Unionist*, February 1916, 'After the War'. This was also the hope of some socialist papers, like the *Woman's Dreadnought* (later *Worker's Dreadnought*) and *Solidarity*, both of which promoted the idea that in the event of unemployment rates rising, priority should be given to those adults with most dependent children. See *Woman's Dreadnought*, 10 Apr. 1915, 'What is Patriotism?', and *Solidarity*, September 1917, 'An Appeal to Women Workers'.
6. *Trade Union Worker*, October 1916, 'Women's Work after the War'.
7. *Trade Unionist*, June 1916, 'Unemployment after the War'.
8. *Railway Review*, 19 May 1916, letters.
9. *Cotton Factory Times*, 7 July 1916, 'Should the Women be Cleared out' — an article written in response to one in the *Factory Times*, which was in turn prompted by the words of an NUR official, who said that he saw no reason why the women should necessarily have to leave.
10. *Labour Woman*, February 1916, 'Working Women and the Problems of the

War', June 1916, 'Women's Work after the War'.

11. *Labour Woman*, September 1916, letter from Mary Stone.

12. See, for example, *Labour Woman*, November 1916, letter from 'A House-wife'; February 1917, 'The Mother's Point of View'.

13. *Labour Yearbook*, 1916; Marion Phillips (ed.), *Women and the Labour Party* (Headley Bros., 1918), chapter by Mary Macarthur; the Report of the Standing Joint Committee of Industrial Women's Organisations on *The Position of Women After the War*.

14. Beveridge Papers, III, 48; Report of the Standing Joint Committee.

15. Report of the Standing Joint Committee, p. 20.

16. See, for example, *Machinery Market*, July 1918, 'Trade after the War'; *Engineer*, 1 May 1917, 'Women in Industry'.

17. War Cabinet Committee on *Women in Industry*, Ch. V.

18. *Women in Industry*, Ch. IV.

19. Bev., III, 48, draft interim report of the Civil War Workers Committee, and Minutes of the Committee's meeting, 13 Dec. 1917.

20. Ibid.

21. Committee of Economists, draft interim report on *The Probable State of Industry after the War*, p. 31. See also Bev., III, 48, p. 15.

22. Bev., III, 48, Part II, letter, 22 Jan. 1918.

23. S.J. Chapman (ed.), *Labour and Capital after the War* (Murray, 1918), chapter by Adelaide Anderson, p. 85. See also Sir H. Bell, quoted in A.W. Kirkaldy, *Industry and Finance*, vol. I (Isaac Pitman, 1917): 'The withdrawal of multitudes of women from their proper function cannot fail, it may be feared, to be detrimental to the future wellbeing of the nation' (p. 7).

24. See Bentley Gilbert, *British Social Policy* (Batsford, 1970) and A.C. Pigou, *Aspects of British Economic History* (Cass & Co., 1947).

25. I.O. Andrews, *The Economic Effects of the World War upon Women and Children in Great Britain* (Oxford University Press, New York, 1921).

26. *The Times*, 31 May 1919, and *Daily News*, 26 May 1919.

27. *Worker's Dreadnought*, 16 Nov. 1918, 'Victory, Short Pay, Unemployment'; 21 Dec. 1918, 'Unemployed Women: the Usual Expedient'; 22 Sept. 1919, 'Workshop Notes'.

28. M.A. Hamilton, *Mary Macarthur* (Parsons, 1925).

29. *Manchester Guardian*, 18 Dec. 1918, and others.

30. B.L. Hutchins, *Women in Industry after the War* (pamphlet).

31. *Worker's Dreadnought*, 8 Mar. 1919, 'Between Ourselves'; *Woman Worker*, March 1919, editorial.

32. *Woman Worker*, February 1919, 'We Want Work – Coventry and the Unemployed'.

33. *Daily Sketch*, 25 Mar. 1919, 'Unemployed Women'.

34. *Liverpool Post*, 15 Mar. 1919, 'Unemployment on the Increase'.

35. *Woman Worker*, April 1919, editorial.

36. *Labour Woman*, March 1919, editorial.

37. *Daily Chronicle*, 27 Mar. 1919, 'Women's Wages Come Down with a Run'.

38. *Labour Woman*, April 1919, 'The Unemployed Woman'.

39. *Woman Worker*, March 1919, letter.

40. *Woman Worker*, June 1919, 'Unemployment Notes'.

41. *Portsmouth Evening News*, 13 May 1919, letter; *Daily News*, 8 Apr. 1919, 'Some Bad Cases of Sweating'.

42. *Labour Woman*, March 1919, 'Demobilised Women Workers'.

43. For example, *Woman Worker*, June 1919, 'Unemployment Notes'.

44. *Woman Worker*, May 1920, 'Before the Umpire'.

45. *Woman Worker*, March 1920, 'Our Laundry Workers', June 1920, 'A Crisis

in the Laundry Trade', July 1920, 'The Laundry Trade'.

46. *Woman Worker*, February 1919, 'We Want Work'.

47. A.C. Pigou, *Aspects of British Economic History*, p. 35.

48. *Report*, 1920, p. 16.

49. J.J. Clarke, *Social Administration Including the Poor Laws* (Pitman & Sons, 1922), Ch. XXX.

50. Henry Clay, *The Post War Unemployment Problem* (Macmillan & Co., 1929), and Richard Hyman, *The Workers' Union* (Clarendon, 1971).

51. Sheila Lewenhak, *Women in Trade Unions* (Ernest Benn, 1977), Ch. XII.

52. For example, *Engineering*, 7 Mar. 1920, 'Restoration of Pre-War Practices in Workshops'; *Keighley News*, 17 Jan. 1920, 'Women Engineers Barred'.

53. *The Times Engineering Supplement*, January 1920.

54. *Hardware Trade Journal*, 27 June 1919, 'Women's Work on Hardware and Metals'.

55. *Hardware Trade Journal*, 27 June 1919.

56. *Engineer*, 14 Nov. 1919, 'Women in Industry'.

57. Irene Clephane, *Towards Sex Freedom* (John Lane, 1935), p. 201.

58. Ray Strachey, *Our Freedom and its Results* (Hogarth, 1936), p. 129.

59. *Women's Industrial News*, April 1919, 'The Women's Reward'. *Common Cause*, 5 Sept. 1919, 'Are Women Wanted?'.

60. *Solidarity*, February 1919 and April 1919, 'The Woman Worker in all Spheres'.

61. Ray Strachey, *The Cause* (Bell & Sons, 1928), p. 371.

62. *Daily Chronicle*, 7 Dec. 1918, 'First Day of Out-of-Work Donation'.

63. *Daily Telegraph*, 30 Dec. 1918.

64. *Daily News*, 8 Jan. 1919, 'Demand for Servants'.

65. *Daily News*, 6 Jan. 1919, 'The Dearth of Servants'.

66. *Daily News*, 10 Jan. 1919, 'Out of work "Holiday"'.

67. *Evening News*, 4 Jan. 1919, 'The New Rest Cure'.

68. *Evening Standard*, 9 Jan. 1919, 'Slackers with State Pay'.

69. *Daily Express*, 19 Feb. 1919, 'Workless Women'.

70. *Glasgow Bulletin*, 27 Feb. 1919, 'Women's "Holiday"'.

71. *Southampton Times*, 20 Mar. 1919, 'Unemployment'.

72. As well as the above, see *Morning Post*, 7 Apr. 1919, on stopping unemployment benefit, and *Manchester Evening Chronicle*, 25 Mar. 1919, 'Work for Women', on weeding out genuine work-seekers from the dodgers.

73. *Southampton Times*, 12 July 1919, 'Women's Peace Work'.

74. *Morning Post*, 25 Sept. 1919, 'Women in Men's Posts'. See also telling quotation from the *Daily Graphic* in David Mitchell, *Women on the War Path* (Cape, 1965), p. 266.

75. *Leeds Mercury*, 23 Apr. 1919, 'Women Workers Departing'.

76. *Saturday Review*, 7 Dec. 1918, letter.

77. *Aberdeen Free Press*, 4 Feb. 1919, letters.

78. *Hull Daily Mail*, 14 Feb. 1919, letter. See also article in the *Portsmouth Evening News*, 25 July 1919, about the National Federation of Demobilised Sailors' and Soldiers' Associations, which demanded that women return to their domestic duties.

79. For example, *Daily Express*, 19 Feb. 1919, letter on whether 'women really need work'; also *Manchester Dispatch*, 27 Mar. 1919, 'The Women in the Case'.

80. *Daily News*, 29 Oct. 1918, 'Disbanding the War Workers'.

81. *Daily News*, 4 Jan. 1919, 'Out of Work Girls'.

82. *Daily News*, 22 Jan. 1919, 'Women "Shirkers"'; *Daily News*, 23 Jan. 1919, letter from Ellen Wilkinson; *Daily News*, 23 Jan. 1919, 'The Truth about Domestic Service'.

83. *Daily Chronicle*, 25 May 1919, 'Training Centres for Ex-munition Workers' on the difficulties of women workers; the *Pioneer*, 5 Apr. 1919, 'The Unemployed Woman', which gave examples of poor wages and hard work; *Manchester Guardian*, 19 Dec. 1919, letter about women being replaced by non-soldiers; *Leicester Daily Post*, 27 June 1919, 'Women in Industry' (report of a conference); *Glasgow Weekly Record*, 15 Mar. 1919, 'Scandal of the Girl Slacker', which defended shell girls from employers' insinuations: they could not be blamed, said the writer, for choosing to live on benefit which itself was only worth 12s 6d a week in pre-war terms, and it was not surprising that they refused to work for less than 30s a week, which was little enough, compared with money spent on society weddings and fox hunts; *Fortnightly Review*, October 1919, 'The Woman's Part', which claimed that domestic service was not the right trade for those used to greater freedom; *Daily Chronicle*, 17 Jan. 1920, 'Unemployed Women', which urged the nation to realise women's awful plight; *Daily Herald*, 29 Nov. 1919, 'Hard Case of the Workless Women'; *Manchester Daily Dispatch*, 13 Jan. 1919, 'Unemployment Problem', which described the jobs which paid less than benefit; *Manchester Guardian*, 9 Feb. 1920, 'The Demobilised Woman', which asked why the unemployed woman did not receive as much attention as the ex-soldier; *Daily News*, 26 Sept. 1919, 'Our National Debt to Women'.

84. *Daily Chronicle*, 19 Dec. 1919.

85. *Daily Chronicle*, 4 Nov. 1919, 'The Attack upon Women'.

86. *Hull Daily Mail*, 30 Apr. 1919, letter.

87. *Newcastle Journal*, 18 June 1919, 'The Employment of Women': he also noted that employers' prejudices against women were hardening.

88. *Evening Standard*, 3 Feb. 1920, 'Married Women's Right to Work'.

89. *Liverpool Daily Post*, 21 Jan. 1919, 'The Revolt of Women'.

90. *Manchester Dispatch*, 20 Sept. 1919, 'Sex War in Industry'.

91. *Daily News*, 11 Mar. 1921, 'Dislike of Women'.

92. *Democrat*, 10 Apr. 1919, 'Unemployed Women'.

93. *Democrat*, 1 May 1919, 'The Unemployment Donation'.

94. *Democrat*, 1 May 1919, 'The Education of Girls'.

95. *Democrat*, 5 June 1919, 'The Woman Worker', 13 Feb. 1920, 'Female Labour'.

96. *Democrat*, 13 June 1919.

97. *Democrat*, 13 June 1919, 'Married Women and Industry'.

98. *Democrat*, 20 June 1919, 'Girl War Workers'.

99. *Democrat*, 16 Jan. 1920, 'Woman in Social Life'.

100. See the Labour Party *Manifesto*, 1918; 'Labour has always stood for equal rights for both sexes, when other parties were ignoring or persecuting women.'

101. *Labour Woman*, July 1919, letter from Rosalind Nash. Also, *Labour Woman*, January 1919, 'Shorter Hours for the Woman at Home'.

102. *Labour Woman*, November 1920. See also, *Labour Woman*, January 1922, 'The Girl who serves the Meals', on low wages; and *Labour Woman*, April 1922, 'The Unemployed and Hungry Woman Worker'.

103. *Labour Woman*, March 1922, 'The Employment of Married Women'. See also the varied response to the report on Married Women's Work, produced by the Standing Joint Committee of Industrial Women's Organisations. The representatives of the Union of Post Office Workers decided that they could not accept any proposals which would increase the number of people seeking work, and stated that the Union's policy was not to retain married women in the postal service. The Association of Women Clerks and Secretaries decided that priority should be given to women who were dependent solely upon their own earnings.

104. *Woman Worker*, June 1921, 'The Case of Married Cleaners'; March 1921,

'A Shelter at Shoreditch'.

105. *Woman Worker*, January 1920, 'Unemployment: A Constructive Scheme', March 1920, editorial.

106. See also the *Democrat*, 10 Apr. 1919, 'Servants' Minimum Wages', and 1 May 1919, 'Domestic Service: Its Decline and Fall'.

107. *Worker's Dreadnought*, 15 Mar. 1919, 'Questions of the Day: Domestic Slavery'.

108. *Daily Sketch*, 30 Dec. 1918, 'The Future of the Shell Girls'.

109. *Woman Worker*, February 1920, conference report.

110. *Woman Worker*, August 1920, 'Home Affairs'.

111. TUC Conference 1919, Mary Carlin's words.

112. Ruth Adam, *A Woman's Place* (Chatto & Windus, 1975), p. 73.

113. See Mrs Fawcett in Dawson, *After War Problems*, p. 198.

114. *Common Cause*, 5 Sept. 1919, 'Are Women Wanted?'

115. *Common Cause*, 21 Nov. 1919, letter.

116. *Solidarity*, January 1919, 'News and Views'; *Labour Woman*, February 1919, editorial.

117. See also *Daily Sketch*, 24 July 1919, on Women's Freedom League; *Daily Herald*, 16 June 1919, 'An Appeal to Trade Unionists'; *The Times*, 4 June 1919, 'Pre-War Practices Bill'.

118. *Croydon Times*, 7 June 1919, 'Women in Industry'.

119. *Leeds Mercury*, 20 Feb. 1919, letter from Amy Lillington. The Labour Party was defended by Marion Phillips in the *Daily Express*, 21 Feb. 1919.

120. *The Times*, 20 June 1919, 'Mr. Lloyd George's Promise'; *Glasgow Herald*, 12 June 1919, 'Rival Women's League'; *Liverpool Courier*, 31 Mar. 1919, letter from Miss H. Jollie.

121. *National News*, 23 Feb. 1919, 'Army of Workless Women'.

122. Attention lasted well into 1920; see *Manchester Guardian*, 15 Mar. 1920; the *Electrician*, 28 Nov. 1919.

123. In spite of the fact that Lloyd George claimed to recognise the justice of their cause: see the memorial presented by the Women's Industrial League, and the Prime Minister's reply.

124. *Daily Telegraph*, 16 Feb. 1920, 'Women Workers' Demands'.

125. Not all socialists, of course, since we have seen how traditionalist were the views of the Guild Socialists. Whether trade unionists or socialists were classed as 'left' or 'right' in the political spectrum was not a reliable indication of their approach to the role of women in society.

126. *Socialist Review*, July-September 1919, 'Marriage and Vocation'.

127. *Solidarity*, 11 Feb. 1921, 'Everywoman'.

128. *Solidarity*, 11 Apr. 1921, 'Everywoman'.

129. *Solidarity*, 25 Feb. 1921, 'Everywoman'.

130. *Solidarity*, 18 Feb. 1921, 'Everywoman'.

131. *Out of Work*, no. 22 (n.d.).

132. *Out of Work*, no. 23 (Jan. 1922); see also nos. 32 and 33.

133. The *Communist*, 19 Aug. 1922 and 26 Aug. 1922. An interesting discussion of the views of socialists and the labour movement is contained in Sheila Rowbotham, *A New World for Women: Stella Browne — Socialist Feminist* (Pluto, 1977).

134. The *Communist*.

135. *War Illustrated*, 6 Jan. 1917, 'The War's Effect on Women's Work'.

136. Middle-class women had a different kind of experience in munitions factories, which was often bound up with feelings of patriotism and self-sacrifice. See Monica Cosens, *Lloyd George's Munition Girls* (Hutchinson, 1916), pp. 1-2, and Naomi Loughnan in Stone (ed.), *Women War Workers*, p. 25.

137. This is a debatable point. Presumably one does not think better of America's slave-owners, of Russia's serf-owners, or even ordinary employers, because slaves, serfs or workers did not appreciate the extent of their own exploitation. Thus recognition of society's, or men's, exploitation of women does not depend upon women's own consciousness of their oppression.

138. Adelaide Anderson in S.J. Chapman, *Labour and Capital After the War*, p. 77.

139. A.W. Kirkaldy, *Industry and Finance*, vol. I (Isaac Pitman, 1917).

140. I.O. Andrews, *The Economic Effects of the World War upon Women and Children in Great Britain* (Oxford University Press, New York, 1921), p. 9. A number of women noted similar characteristics, for example Strachey, *Our Freedom and its Results*; Caroline Playne, *Society at War* (Allen & Unwin, 1930); Strachey, *The Cause*; *Woman Worker*, March 1920, editorial; *Labour Woman*, February 1917, 'The Mother's Point of View'.

141. *Fortnightly Review*, December 1919, 'Women at the Works – and Elsewhere'.

142. *Labour Woman*, November 1916, letters.

143. See interviews held by Imperial War Museum, London, particularly Caroline Rennles, Elsie MacIntyre, Isabella Clark, Lilian Miles (00566/07, 00673/09, 00854/04, 00774/04).

144. Interviews with Jane Cox, Annie Howell, Dorothy Haigh, Isabella Clark, Lilian Miles, Elsie Farlow and Bessie Davies – the latter said that colliery explosions in her home area had affected her more than the war (00705/06, 00613/08, 00734/07, 00774/04, 00854/04, 00773/03, 00828/02).

145. Isabella Clark, Lilian Miles, Jane Cox, Elsie Farlow (00774/04, 00854/04, 00705/06, 00773/03).

146. Caroline Rennles (00566/07).

147. Beatrice Lee (00724/06).

148. Jane Cox (00705/06).

149. Caroline Rennles (00566/07).

150. See, for example, Rosina Wyatt's desire to avoid service, in John Burnett, *Useful Toil* (Allen Lane, 1974), p. 132.

151. *Daily Express*, 5 Mar. 1917, 'Into the Unknown'.

152. *Fortnightly Review*, December 1919, 'Women at the Works – and Elsewhere'.

153. *Report*, 1919, p. 9.

154. Pigou, *Aspects of British Economic History*, p. 20.

8 THE POSITION OF WOMEN WORKERS IN THE TWENTIES

There are several ways in which one can view the effects of the First World War upon the position of women workers. Some would say that these years constituted a watershed in women's history, and that the changes which occurred were drastic and far-reaching. Others would say that it led to few fundamental changes in the position of women in general, or of working-class women in particular. In fact, neither view is adequate. Society had not been 'transformed', yet many people had been changed by their war experiences, and certain aspects of industrial technology had been stimulated by the war's requirements. In this brief look at the twenties I would like to set the war in context, and add something about the work women were offered during these years, together with some of the attitudes towards such work. This is no more than a postscript, and I have not ventured into the years of the Depression and the thirties, which belong to a different study.

The entry of women into the professions, clerical work and the retail trade was almost certainly encouraged by their work in these jobs during the war, and a number of employers were happy to recruit women in these expanding fields during the twenties. For young middle-class women, employment opportunities were improving, but the position of working-class women was quite different. In 1924, the Ministry of Labour *Gazette* reviewed the current *Report* of the Factory Inspectorate:

> With reference to the general condition of women's employment the Report states that the reversal of the process of substitution which was so striking a feature of war-time industry is now practically complete. Women have returned to women's industries, and very few of them are to be found even in those sections of men's trades for which war-time observation and experience showed them to be peculiarly well-fitted.[1]

The factory inspectors may have seen them as 'well-fitted' for certain trades, but, as Janet McCalman has pointed out in her recent article on women workers, had employers and managers really believed women substitutes were adequate, they would have kept them on.[2] They did not. The trades women reluctantly returned to included domestic service,

216

the declining cotton industry and the clothing industry, but in addition there were new industries willing to recruit female labour, and changes in some of the old established trades also led to alterations in women's work. Such recruitment was based on the idea that women would be cheap unskilled, or semi-skilled, machine minders, ideally suited to tedious tasks. Women's numbers increased in the pottery industry, light metal trades, boot and shoe, printing, bookbinding and the new electrical goods industries. Contrary to views expressed at the time, this hardly affected male employment rates, as neither employers nor male workers classed much of this work as being fit for men. But technological change often did go hand in hand with the use of female labour. The cotton-spinning industry is a good example of this. Mule spinning, performed by skilled male workers (who set their own machines) with the assistance of two 'semi-skilled' assistants (the 'big' and 'little' piecer), was steadily being replaced by ring spinning, performed by those classed as 'semi-skilled machine minders', the worker usually being 'the semi-skilled female operative so familiar in industry generally since the introduction of automatic machinery of which the ring frame is a typical example'.[3] It was suggested by some that as unemployment amongst men was high, they might like to consider ring spinning, but it remained a female trade. The wages were low, and men were not prepared to work and campaign for better rates. Here, and in other industries affected by technological change (particularly engineering), skilled men were loath to become mere minders at any price. If women had refused the work offered to them by new or changing industries, it would have gone to *other* men, not the displaced craftsmen.[4]

As semi-skilled operatives, women were still low-paid and short-term workers. It was anticipated that they would leave when married, and the average age of women factory workers remained low. As Sylvia Anthony, in her 1932 book *Women's Place in Industry and the Home*, pointed out, in 1921 70 per cent of women workers were under 35, and 50 per cent of them were under 25.[5] Once again, allowances have to be made for the women not included in such figures, but the youth of the factory workers is beyond dispute. Blainey produced another set of interesting statistics in 1928. Thirty-five per cent of women workers were still in domestic service, 12 per cent in textiles, and 11 per cent in the clothing trades; the 'old' industries were still the major employers.[6] Technology and consumer demand combined to affect women in old and new industries. For example, shoes were now more fashionable than boots; shoes were usually the women's branch of the trade, and machinery coped well with the flimsy styles of the twenties. Electrical goods were increasingly in demand, and this new industry recruited women readily. In engineering, women were employed on light press machines, small automatic lathes and light assembly work;[7] production increased and prices were cheaper as a result. In old and new trades there was still pressure to stay home if married; the clothing trade depended upon the labour of female outworkers, and the Nottingham lace trade employed single women in factories and married workers as homeworkers.[8] There was little need for an official marriage bar when such strong social pressure was brought to bear on wives by husbands, relatives and employers at once.

There are many familiar features in the facts of women's employment during the 1920s. They were low-paid,[9] confined to few trades, encouraged to leave work on marriage, and excluded by unions or employers from trades classed as 'skilled'; even when their work was quite complex, it was not seen as being 'skilled'.[10] Indeed, suggestions were even made that some of the 'dead end' jobs done by boys should go to girls, to whom monotony and lack of prospects would not matter. With the decline in mule spinning, for example, fewer piecers (assistants) were promoted to skilled work, and thus the men remained on relatively low wages for years. The recruitment of girls would have solved this problem, according to some; they could continue happily in such work until marriage, and the smaller number of male piecers would have a better chance of promotion — it was not envisaged that women might want promotion as well! Interestingly enough, both employers and workmen objected to this scheme:

> Most of the authorities consulted on the question of women as piecers were agreed, however, that this would be undesirable on general social grounds. They argued that the spinning room was not a fit place for women; the temperature of the room is high, the operatives work in very scanty clothing, and in most mills the provision for changing of clothing is either inadequate or absolutely non-existent[11]

reported Jewkes and Gray in the early thirties, showing how little arguments had changed since the war. They added that the reluctance of the employers was probably due to the desire to avoid spending money on improving facilities, but it is interesting that such employers did still refuse to recruit women, even though female labour would have been cheaper. They were not worth the trouble. Sylvia Anthony, a feminist writer of the time, reported another attempt to get employers to use girls for 'blind alley' occupations, as described by *The Times*:

Major M.C., speaking at a luncheon of the London Master Printers' Association . . . said that . . . they could have to consider the introduction of a class of labour at a lower rate than the skilled rate. The Trade Unions are realizing the difficulty of dealing with boy labour when the age of 21 was reached, and were prepared to regard with sympathy an extension of the amount women and girls could do . . . In theory they ought not to employ in the trade more boys than they could find work for when they grew up, but it must be admitted that they had been taking boys into 'blind-alley' occupations. If girls were employed instead, they could still afford to keep them when they became adults.[12]

Debates also continued about the nature of 'suitable' work, and the necessity of protective legislation for one sex. Another feminist, Winifred Holtby, looked back with bitterness at the history of such debates:

From the 1830s to this day there are people who declare that women need, for their own welfare, these special restrictions. The humanitarians, moved by the sight of woman's suffering, the sentimentalists, who regard her chiefly as a potential mother, the male trade unionists, jealous of their own standards, and certain sections of the women themselves, such as the Standing Joint Committee of Industrial Women's Organisations, which, in spite of the middle-class origin of its most articulate members, claims to represent the organised opinion of working women, maintain that differential sex legislation has not harmed women, that, for instance, in the textile industries of Lancashire, the most highly skilled and highly paid women themselves demand it, that women caught between starvation and oppression cannot be reached as free agents, and that after conditions have been alleviated for women, the improvements are extended to men.[13]

Many middle-class feminists still fought against the whole concept of protective legislation, objecting to the possible effect on women's job prospects, and the tacit acceptance of long hours and dangerous conditions for men and boys. Yet they were aware that most of society still classed such legislation as desirable and necessary; as J. Blainey said of the 1926 Factory Bill, it 'appears to follow blindly in the steps of what has gone before, and continue the present unscientific and prejudicial attitude to the whole question',[14] and there were many who pointed out, as they had done during the war, that protection was given to women who might rival men, not to those in the classic women's trades.[15] Eleanor Rathbone, in Ray Strachey's book *Careers and Openings for Women*, claimed that objections came from 'oldstyle' feminists, and *Labour Woman* attacked the 'ultra feminists' for their views, maintaining that 'It is useless to start by assuming that men and women are the same in every way. Women have special handicaps,'[16] but a large proportion of middle-class feminists in the twenties and thirties fought against both the legal restrictions on women's work and the maintenance of the 'custom' of excluding women from certain trades. Ray Strachey herself emphasised the fact that the exclusion of women did not help men's battle, that it was in any case impossible to remove women from the labour force completely, and

> the consequence has been on the one hand to prevent women from having a free chance to sell their labour on the open market, and on the other to create a large class of ill-paid workers who are a standing menace to the wage rates, and even to the chances of employment of men, in every field into which they make their way.[17]

In many senses, therefore, women's work in the 1920s was of a similar nature to pre-war employment, even though technology had altered particular jobs, and the arguments surrounding it were familiar. But when one turns to the matter of the *feelings* expressed about women's work and role, additional features emerge. Two factors were important in influencing opinion. First, there was a definite post-war backlash; many men wished to see women back in their peacetime role as decorative objects, or wives and mothers, not as uniformed workers. The desire for women to return to 'femininity' seems to have been stimulated by more than simple economic fears about the possible displacement of male workers, important though this aspect was. Men who fought for months or years had almost certainly been worried about the faithfulness of wives and girlfriends, and about the long-term effects of women's wider economic opportunities. For a combination of reasons, they wanted their mothers, wives and girlfriends 'back home', and this feeling also existed amongst those who had never fought, but who had curbed their impatience at seeing women in a multiplicity of jobs simply because they knew such work was for the war period only. The 1920s saw much propaganda about the joys of domesticity and the role of the housewife. It may be said that this was not new, but there were certain additional features. There was an element of fear behind the propaganda, fear that, having experienced higher wages and different jobs, women would seek to escape from their domestic role. This may seem bizarre, in view of the limited range of jobs available to working-class women by the early twenties, but there was a strong feeling, encouraged by the press, and held by many people of both sexes, that women had achieved a major breakthrough in employment opportunities and legal rights — that the victory had been won. This belief was fostered by the fact that single middle-class women did have a wider choice of employment, and had gained a greater degree of sexual and economic independence. What if such young women wanted to remain 'career women', not become home-loving wives? They had to be shown how important child care and housework were to society. The propaganda on this subject was fired at women of all classes, including those who had little chance of escaping from domestic drudgery. When *Labour Woman* takes up such themes, one wonders whether there was a conscious or unconscious desire to soothe those married women who had sought jobs in vain. Increasingly, housewifery was described as though it were a science, requiring intelligence and dedication. Women were no longer supposed to act as guiding lights to husbands and children in the Victorian manner; they were supposed to take pride and pleasure in a spotless and modern home, and to take seriously the trade of housewifery. This leads me to the other important influential factor during these years. British industry was turning to consumer goods for the mass market. It needed women to buy electrical goods, mass-produced clothes (now easily washable at home) and processed foods; thus it needed women who would spend a large proportion of their lives shopping, and who were interested in equipping their homes with new goods. Ann Oakley and others have pointed out that, ironically, as houses became easier to clean (with vacuum cleaners, hot water, proper bathrooms and less cluttered rooms) higher standards of cleanliness were required. Many working-class homes did not have vacuum cleaners, hot water, etc., but to keep up with these new levels of cleanliness, women were supposed to work even harder. The manipulation of the domestic ideal in the twenties (and the fifties) is a fascinating subject, and not one I can discuss in any depth here, but it is worth looking at some examples of what was said about women's role during the twenties.

One piece of background information to bear in mind throughout the following pages is the nature of the government's training schemes, which kept domestic work well to the fore of working-class women's lives. For example, the Central Committee on Women's Training and Employment (which had been the Queen's Work for Women Fund at the beginning of the War) ran three employment training schemes for women. These were the Scholarship Scheme, which gave grants for training in non-industrial occupations like teaching, midwifery, nursery nursing and cookery; the Home Crafts Scheme, which organised training for women to go into domestic service; the Home Makers Scheme, which gave women general domestic training; grants were also given to help buy uniforms for domestic service.[18] The economic convenience of promoting domestic work, whether paid or unpaid, must be taken into account when looking at this time of relatively high female unemployment.

Pressure on women to accept and enjoy life as full-time housewives came from many quarters. Cynthia White, in her book on women's magazines, describes the speedy acceptance of the domestic ideal by journals in the twenties. As early as 1920, a journalist was writing in *Woman's Life*:

> The tide of progress which leaves woman with the vote in her hand and scarcely any clothes upon her back is ebbing, and the sex is returning to the deep, very deep sea of femininity from which her newly-acquired power can be more effectively wielded.[19]

White points out that even magazines like the *Lady*, which had previously carried a substantial number of features on employment, now cut such articles drastically: 'Throughout the fiction, the chat, and the answers to correspondents in this and other magazines, there was a substantial effort to curb restlessness on the part of wives, and to popularise the career of housewife and mother.'[20] This material was aimed at women of all classes, and coexisted with a steady stream of criticisms of feminism, as typified by a comment made by a writer in *Forum*, an American journal: 'The cry for equality is merely a delusional projection of the female wish to be a man,'[21] a statement which echoed countless others of earlier years. Any possibility of expansion in women's job opportunities was opposed by those who protested that outside work was harmful to marriage and children. This belief led to such books as Charlotte Haldane's *Motherhood and its Enemies*, which determinedly attacked the idea that the family gained any economic benefits from working wives (who would 'waste, through lack of knowledge and experience of housekeeping, almost as much as [they] may earn'[22]), and urged, amidst much pseudo-scientific 'evidence', women to bear children, as 'every woman who refuses motherhood is curtailing her psychological as well as her physiological development in a manner which may have serious consequences to herself.'[23] Interestingly, Haldane also attacked women war workers (of all kinds, military and industrial) for their 'masculinity':

The newspapers began to be filled, side by side with pictures of peer-esses in delightfully graceful nursing uniform, and actresses appearing at hospital concerts, with photographs of the 'war-working' type of 'woman' — aping the cropped hair, the great booted feet, and grim jaw, the uniform, and if possible the medals of the military men.[24]

Such comments, although indicative of the kind of ridiculous lengths to which some people were prepared to go in order to discredit women's work, were hardly typical, and it is probably true that Charlotte Haldane's tirades convinced very few, even supposing that there were many who could be bothered to read her book.

Far more significant was the continuing acceptance by the labour movement that women's duties and interests lay in the home. Even papers which had discussed all aspects of women's paid work during the war, and explored questions of pay, conditions and unionisation, now became very quiet on the subject, and gave little space to the problems of the female work-force or female unemployed. The *Daily Herald*, in its weekly feature on 'Woman's Life and Work', concentrated on dressmaking, cookery, housework and fiction. One week, the authors discussed the existence of a diploma in housewifery for girls in America, lamenting the lack of domestic training English girls received. The writer continued:

> But it isn't only domestic training. Wifehood does not consist only in being able to keep a house clean and meals well cooked. That is the smallest, most elementary part of it. Most intelligent girls can learn to keep a house clean in a very short time . . . and most girls, by buying a decent cookery book, can manage to make dinners for their men.
>
> But what of all the incidental mending that crops up — the care of house linen, the care of personal clothing? What of the nursing that has to be done when the man is ill, when babies come along and have to be cared for? What of the shopping that has to be done?[25]

The occasional piece on paid jobs appeared on these pages, but such aspects of women's lives were put well to the background. The assumption was not only that all the *Daily Herald*'s female readers were obliged to look after their husbands and children, but that they would be *pleased* to devote the bulk of their time and energy to making fancy dress costumes for their children, cleaning the brass, and 'Keeping Him Tidy'. Nor were writers reluctant to attack those who wanted sexual equality,

wilfully confusing, as they did so, 'equality' with 'similarity'. 'L.E.'
wrote:

> An elementary understanding of biology shows that equality between
> men and women is as impossible as equality between a chicken and
> a potato. Both are excellent things in their own way, but they are
> utterly different. A woman is one manifestation of the life force, a
> man another.[26]

An elementary understanding of biology should also have shown that
unlike chickens and potatoes, men and women were of the same species!
In her article, 'L.E.' proceeded to describe women rather as though they
were millstones round the necks of their husbands:

> Woman is the steadying, stabilising element, man the adventurer. Man,
> with his greater strength and pioneer spirit, can initiate; woman, with
> her steady endurance and power of patience, prevents him from mak-
> ing blunders, holding him back into more practical channels.

Labour Woman is another paper which devoted much space to women's
domestic duties. Although the occasional article criticised society's neglect of men's health, and the belief that all women had men to support
them,[27] a lot more time was spent on baby competitions, housewives'
competitions and 'mothercraft' — a page entitled 'Motherhood and
Mothercraft' became a regular feature in 1927, and 'Keep the Pot Boil-
ing' was designed to 'instruct housewives in the science that underlies
all principles of cookery'.[28] All this was interlaced with sentimental
drawings of working-class mothers, one example being the cover of the
May 1927 issue: a woman irons in the foreground, a baby lies in the
background, and the caption is 'Preparing for May Day'. It is a depressing thought that women's role in the preparations for a day designed to
celebrate comradeship and revolutionary struggle should be *ironing*!
Equally insidious was the fiction, which also promoted the image of
women as worker's wives and mothers,[29] and only occasionally was the
average woman supposed to be interested in politics. Marion Phillips
urged that all effort be made to re-elect Labour MPs in 1923; this was a
matter of such importance that 'the proudest of housewives can afford to
let her housework slide a little for the weeks of the general election'.[30]

Some attention was paid in *Labour Woman* to women's employment
problems, but less as the decade progressed. Articles which began by
attacking the government's neglect of women ended by asking for more

domestic training schemes, which may have been better than nothing, since maintenance grants were higher than unemployment benefit, but which increasingly appear to have been seen as an end in themselves. One such article praised the Central Committee on Women's Training and Employment for its Homemakers Centres: 'it is felt that these classes increase the general skill of a woman in all the qualities which she is likely to need in her home life later on. They are, indeed, a training in citizenship.'[31] It is interesting that male citizens did not need such classes. Demands for government action were couched in the following terms:

> Three things are needed. First, the organisation of our education system, to provide education and maintenance of young girls between 14 and 16. Secondly, a great extension of the Homemakers' classes for girls between 16 and 18, who at the most perilous years of adolescence are without employment, and for the most part without anything to live on. Thirdly, further grants for the development of Homecraft and Homemaker schemes for adult women.[32]

This was suggested in spite of the fact that the National Conference of Labour Women demanded equal opportunities in jobs and training.[33] Little was done to further this aim, and throughout the labour movement men's unemployment was still regarded as a more serious problem. In 1925, a resolution was put forward at the Conference suggesting that, because of the economic situation, preference should be given for jobs to those who were dependent on their earnings 'over married women whose husbands can afford to support them and those with private means'.[34] The resolution was condemned by Miss Stephen of the ILP, who considered it 'the most reactionary one they had had put before the Conference', and it was ultimately withdrawn, but it is significant that it appeared on the agenda at all, and there is little doubt about the fact that many men and women in the labour movement and the Labour Party thought that married women ought to withdraw from employment. On the broader issues concerning women's lives, the Labour Party also remained wary; protective legislation was still accepted, and birth control was regarded nervously. It should not be an end in itself, commented *Labour Woman* mysteriously, and was not a political issue,[35] whilst Ramsay MacDonald, faced with the demand that women should have information on the subject, at the 1926 Labour Party Conference, said sternly, 'Was it a question of health, or was it, to put it more bluntly, neo-Malthusianism?'[36] In dwelling on Labour Party attitudes here I am not seeking to put the blame on the party for working-class women's position in the twenties, but simply showing how extensive particular views were. A relatively radical group of people, concerned with workers' oppression and women's legal and political rights, nevertheless accepted the inevitability of women's domestic role, and did not take the matter of their employment very seriously. The concern with motherhood and domesticity which had underpinned many of Labour's arguments during the war was expressed more loudly during the twenties, although the language had changed; the working-class woman was no longer the struggling mother of the race, she was the proficient housewife. Even less interest in any ambitions working-class women might have had to move into well paid or skilled work was shown by most other factions of society, whose members were unlikely to approve of any training courses or maintenance grants, and who were untroubled by the thought that working-class women might need to work for money, or that they might tire of monotonous tasks and domestic responsibilities. Only feminists continued to criticise society's expectation of women in general, and noted the stultifying effect this had on the lives of working-class women in particular.

Looking at the 1920s in general, therefore, one can see that certain classic beliefs and attitudes remained, and these can be traced back to the nineteenth century. The potential which had shown itself during the war was ignored, and women were still valued for their cheapness, dexterity, tolerance of boredom and lack of ambition. Women's unemployment was not classed as a major problem by successive governments, and the fact that a large proportion of society expected married women to retreat from paid work meant that there was no general outcry when their unemployment benefit was stopped or when the government failed to provide them with industrial training.

In 1930, a Home Office report was published, entitled *A Study of the Factors which have Operated in the Past and those which are Operating now to Determine the Distribution of Women in Industry*, stimulated by questions about whether protective legislation damaged women's job opportunities. The report came to the conclusion that trade union restrictions, women's strength and the interruption caused by marriage were responsible for the division of work into men's and women's trades, while the fact that women could not do night work and had to work shorter hours was irrelevant. This conclusion is debatable, since the writers of the report themselves cite instances of women's displacement, and employers often gave factory legislation as one of the reasons why they did not employ women — if they could get men to do shift work, what was the point of employing women who could not? But the important thing is that the whole report echoes those of pre-war years: the conditions of employment they described were similar, and there was the same ready acceptance of the devastating effect of marriage upon women's job prospects. There was also the same underlying feeling that women themselves contributed to their poor industrial position, since they lacked ambition and were eager to leave upon marriage. There was no discussion of the fact that a number of women had expressed interest in better paid, more skilled work during the war, and the twenties were seen as years when order re-established itself.

The report stated: 'The rapid and easy return to the pre-war position indicates, however, that the division of work between men and women in industry tends to settle itself naturally on the lines indicated in the previous pages.'[37] With this comment, the experiences of women during the war, and the bitter months of unemployment which followed, were dismissed.

Notes

1. *Ministry of Labour Gazette*, September 1924, 'Factories and Workshops: Chief Inspector's Annual Report'.

2. *Labour History*, November 1971, 'The Impact of the Great War on Female Employment in England', Janet McCalman.

3. John Jewkes and E.M. Gray, *Wages and Labour in the Lancashire Cotton Spinning Industry* (Manchester University Press, 1935), Ch. IX.

4. Jewkes and Gray, *Wages and Labour*.

5. Sylvia Anthony, *Women's Place in Industry and Home* (Routledge & Kegan Paul, 1932), Ch. IV.

6. J. Blainey, *The Woman Worker and Restrictive Legislation* (Arrowsmith, 1928), Introduction.

7. See, for example, the London School of Economics, *New Survey of London Life and Labour* (King and Son, 1931 and 1935).

8. *Oral History*, vol. V, no. 2 (Autumn 1977), Sandra Taylor, 'The Effect of Marriage on Job Possibilities for Women and the Ideology of the Home, 1890-1930'.

9. Low pay existed in white-collar jobs as well, where women were always paid less than men. *Daily Herald*, 1 Jan. 1927 reported on one such case. Counter clerks at the Post Office started on the same wages whether male or female, but men's maximum was £6 1s 3d while women's was only £3 12s 8d. The union proposed that the latter should go up to £5 0s 6d.

10. 'Women workers in the engineering trades are not "skilled" in the craft sense of the word, but many of them acquire great skill and speed in particular processes' (LSE, *New Survey*, p. 143).

11. Jewkes and Gray, *Wages and Labour*, Ch. XII.

12. *The Times*, 4 Dec. 1928, quoted by Anthony, *Women's Place*, Ch. IV.

13. Winifred Holtby, *Women Workers in a Changing Civilisation* (Bodley Head, 1934), pp. 78-9.

14. Blainey, *The Woman Worker*, p. 43.

15. E.g. Erna Reiss, *The Rights and Duties of English-women* (Sherratt & Hughes, 1934).

16. *Labour Woman*, January 1925, 'Protective Legislation for Women'.

17. Ray Strachey, *Careers and Openings for Women* (Faber & Faber, 1935), p. 35. This is, of course, an exaggeration, but Strachey is using the often expressed beliefs of male trade unionists against them — if women really were a menace, why not do something to change conditions and prevent them from being such?

18. *Ministry of Labour Gazette*, September 1923, 'Women's Training and Employment'.

19. Cynthia White, *Women's Magazines 1693-1968* (Michael Joseph, 1970), quoted p. 99.

20. White, *Women's Magazines*, p. 101.

21. *Forum*, February 1927.

22. Charlotte Haldane, *Motherhood and Its Enemies* (Doubleday, 1927), p. 144.

23. Haldane, *Motherhood and Its Enemies*, p. 214.

24. Haldane, *Motherhood and Its Enemies*, p. 94.

25. *Daily Herald*, 15 Jan. 1927, 'Woman's Life and Work'.

26. *Daily Herald*, 22 Jan. 1927.

27. *Labour Woman*, August 1925, 'Working Women and the Industrial Crisis', January 1926, 'Women and Unemployment Benefit'.

28. *Labour Woman*, May 1927; see also July 1924, August 1924 covers.

29. Two stories stand out. One, 'Ethel Finds a Place' (April, May, June 1923) is about a woman who becomes a servant and is dismissed because she agitates for a domestic servants' union. Instead of moving away to find a job in an area where she is not branded as a trouble-maker, she marries Jack, who proposes thus:

'You've got to stay and see the union through, old girl . . . and as I see it, the best way to keep the Domestic Workers' Union is for you and me to form another union. Is it a go?' And it was! That is how Ethel left domestic service.

Cynics might say that Ethel had not really left domestic service at all, but that she had certainly found her 'place'. It is typical of *Labour Woman*'s fiction that the problem is solved through marriage, and wider issues are left untouched. Another story, 'Fraternity' (June 1926), involves Mrs Bryce, who has been worn out by housework and children, and decides to commit suicide. She goes to borrow money for the gas meter from her neighbour, childless Mrs Trent, is drawn into conversation, and admits what she is about to do. 'How can you be sad with children?' asks Mrs Trent, weeping. Mrs Bryce changes her mind. A year later she is to be found happy, healthy, and fully appreciated by her husband. In some miraculous way, overwork and too many children have ceased to be a problem.

30. *Labour Woman*, December 1923, 'Women's Work in the Elections'.

31. *Labour Woman*, January 1923, 'The Government Neglects Unemployed Women'.

32. Ibid.

33. *Labour Woman*, June 1924.

34. *Labour Woman*, July 1925.

35. *Labour Woman*, March 1924.

36. *Labour Woman*, November 1926.

37. Report, p. 25.

9 FINAL COMMENTS

To conclude, it might be useful to list some of the points I have been making over the preceding pages, and consider the broader issues this book touches upon.

The women who were employed on 'men's work' during the war did these jobs well or adequately, yet they were recruited reluctantly, and most of them were made redundant as soon as possible. These events are not a recognised part of the standard mythology which surrounds the war; the classic view is that women were recruited eagerly by employers, and that they left willingly, of their own accord, when they were no longer needed. Nor do the events I have described agree with the interpretations of many labour historians, who have frequently claimed that employers would always use women (at cheaper rates) rather than men, if given the opportunity. Sexism frequently cut across class barriers. Feelings about women's 'proper place', their domestic responsibilities and their inherent industrial capabilities affected all classes: even the evidence of their war work failed to shake ideas about their 'true role'. But I am not suggesting that sexism has been the only factor affecting economic relations or the structure of society. During the war, as now, capitalism coexisted with a patriarchal system. Sometimes the two reinforced one another, sometimes they were in opposition; the relationship between them does not fit into any convenient pattern. To illustrate this interaction, it is worth re-examining two of the examples used earlier in the book.

Employers and Married Women's Labour

Many employers expressed the belief that married women belonged at home, yet they used them as a source of cheap labour. One sometimes has the impression that the failure of working wives to devote themselves to their domestic duties was seen as a good reason for paying them low wages. As well as claiming that women would not know what to do with good wages, or that higher rates of pay would be unfair to male breadwinners, it was on occasion implied by observers of all classes that good rates and interesting work would encourage women to desert their domestic responsibilities. Thus employers could have claimed that

229

they were fulfilling a valuable social function by paying women low
wages and encouraging them to reject ill-paid work and stay at home!

I have tried to show that society's conviction about the proper
feminine role (which there is little doubt that most employers readily
accepted, to judge by the lives of their own wives and daughters) was
extremely convenient for those who wished to employ cheap labour,
since the existing system offered them both single and married women
who were obliged or prepared to work for low wages. There are additional features worth considering. For example, apart from the occasional claim that low female wages were essential for the protection of
the family (for the reasons outlined above), how did employers, who
would not allow their wives and daughters to work, rationalise their use
of cheap female labour? Did they realise their own hypocrisy? This is
not a question I can answer. In order to do so, one would have to look
at the private lives of employers and managers, and contrast them with
the stated aims and policies of the firms with which they worked on the
subject of women's labour. I feel it is important to know more about the
lives and ideas of those who have been in positions of industrial power;
the public and private should both be analysed when looking at forms
of oppression. Labour historians have become increasingly used to the
fact that men and women cannot be studied through their labour and
trade union activities alone, and that their home and family lives are
equally important; this approach should be extended to research into
industrialists and entrepreneurs.

Working-class Men and Married Women's Labour

It is of key importance that union leaders and workmen largely accepted
the dominant ideology regarding women and the home. The existing
social structure was economically useful to employers, but it was also
actively supported by many working-class men, who fought against
women's equal participation in industry and reacted strongly against
any suggestion of a shared domestic role. Why? It is not enough to say
that they were motivated by purely economic fears since the best weapon
against unscrupulous employers would have been an undivided working
class. It was recognised by many men that while women were paid less,
and treated as casual workers who would leave work when married,
there would be a ready supply of potential blacklegs, yet they persisted
in attempting to remove married women from the labour market (an
impossible task) and in refusing to consider enlisting women's support

in industrial campaigns. The desire to maintain the sexual *status quo* was strong. Men gained certain advantages from it. Working-class men must have taken comfort from the fact that in their own homes at least they were in charge, and from the idea of regarding women as their inferiors. They also had the satisfaction of having someone to cook and clean for them. It is an interesting fact that many men who were reluctant to do domestic work around their own homes not only avoided it because they were tired after a day's work, but because they classed such labour as being fit only for women. They felt their status was diminished if they cooked or washed dishes. This feeling was all too evident when men were unemployed. In spite of their extra free time, many men would not do housework; wives, whether or not they had paid work to do, were left to do the domestic work alone. There was obviously a suspicion that housework was in some way feminising, and effeminacy was to be dreaded; masculinity meant superiority. To paraphrase one of the writers quoted earlier in this book, women might wish to be men, but what man would wish to be a woman? Working-class men gained advantages from their gender only because they chose to support the sexual division of labour – even though this was economically damaging to them. I cannot explain the reasons for this acceptance, since the domestic advantages are surely outweighed by the economic disadvantages. All I am trying to show here is that the two forms of exploitation, through sex or class, can complement each other or come into conflict with each other. The important thing is that they coexist, and no analysis based upon the acceptance of the effects of one *or* the other alone is satisfactory.

Many of these assumptions about domestic work are still made today. Paid work is still classed as being more important than unpaid, and lower wages mean lower status. Jobs which involve nursing, looking after children, cleaning or cooking fetch low wages quite simply because they are chiefly done by women, and because they are regarded as being an extension of women's natural, unpaid, duties. In addition, many people have the bizarre idea that making objects which can be sold for money is in some way 'productive' (i.e. worthy of higher wages), while nursing, cooking, etc. are 'unproductive', no matter how essential they are. This idea has been used as an excuse for paying women lower wages in these trades, and for looking down on much of the work women do. I have been talking about the right to paid work, but this does not mean I fail to accept the importance of domestic work. Far from it. Women's right to paid work will only be a burden until men accept domestic responsibilities. The end to women's role as unpaid domestic servants would have repercussions throughout industry and society.

This book is about the war period, but, as I said at the beginning, women's work, and men's attitude towards women, should not be seen in isolation. The four years of war cannot be separated from the rest of history, and women's work cannot be detached from the broader issues concerning work roles, sexual stereotyping and economic relationships inside and outside the family. Any one of the preceding chapters could be expanded tenfold to incorporate further information and debate. I hope that other people will take up some of the themes I have touched upon, for in my view, it is essential that we understand the nature of women's economic and psychological oppression in the past, as well as the present.

SELECT BIBLIOGRAPHY

I Books and Pamphlets

Adam, R. *A Woman's Place* (Chatto & Windus, London, 1975)

Anderson, A. *Women in the Factory* (John Murray, London, 1922)

—— *Women Workers and the Health of the Nation* (an address to the Royal Institute of Public Health, published as pamphlet, 1918)

Andrews, I.O. *The Economic Effects of the World War upon Women and Children in Great Britain*, 2nd edn (Oxford University Press, New York, 1921)

Anthony, S. *Women's Place in Industry and the Home* (Routledge & Kegan Paul, London, 1932)

Banks, J.A. & O. *Feminism and Family Planning* (Liverpool University Press, Liverpool, 1964)

Bell, Lady F. *At the Works* (Arnold, London, 1907)

Black, C. (ed.) *Married Women's Work* (Bell & Sons, London, 1915)

—— *Sweated Industry and the Minimum Wage* (Duckworth & Co., London, 1907)

Blainey, J. *The Woman Worker and Restrictive Legislation* (Arrowsmith, London, 1928)

Booth, C. *Life and Labour of the People of London*, vol. IV (Macmillan, London, 1893)

Boucherett, J., & Blackburn, H. *The Condition of Working Women and the Factory Acts* (Elliot Stock, London, 1896)

British Association for the Advancement of Science *Draft Interim Report of the Conference to Investigate into Outlets for Labour After the War* (BAAS, London, 1915)

Bruce, M. *The Coming of the Welfare State* (Batsford, London, 1961)

Burnett, J. *Useful Toil* (Allen Lane, London, 1974)

Butler, C.V. *Domestic Service* (Bell & Sons, London, 1916)

Cadbury, E., & Shann, G. *Sweating* (Headley Bros., London, 1907)

Cadbury, E., Matheson, M.C., & Shann, G. *Women's Work and Wages*, 2nd edn (T. Fisher Unwin, London, 1909)

Caine, H. *Our Girls* (Hutchinson, London, 1917)

Chapman, S.J. (ed.) *Labour and Capital After the War* (Murray, London, 1918)

Churchill, Lady R. (ed.) *Women's War Work* (C. Arthur Pearson, London, 1916)

233

Clarke, J.J. *Social Administration including the Poor Laws* (Pitman & Sons, London, 1922)

Clay, H. *The Post War Unemployment Problem* (Macmillan, London, 1929)

Clephane, I. *Towards Sex Freedom* (John Lane, London, 1935)

Cole, G.D.H. *A History of the Labour Party since 1914* (Routledge & Kegan Paul, London, 1969)

— *Labour in Wartime* (Bell & Sons, London, 1915)

— *Organised Labour* (Allen & Unwin, London, 1924)

— *Trade Unionism and Munitions* (Clarendon Press, Oxford, 1923)

Collier, D.J., & Hutchins, B.L. *The Girl in Industry* (Bell & Sons, London, 1918)

Cosens, M. *Lloyd George's Munition Girls* (Hutchinson, London, 1916)

Davies, M. Llewelyn *Maternity* (reprinted, Virago, London, 1979)

Dawson, A.W. (ed.) *After War Problems* (Allen & Unwin, London, 1919)

Dilke, Lady E.F.S. *The Industrial Position of Women* (pamphlet, 1893)

— *Trade Unions for Women* (pamphlet, 1891)

Drake, B. *Women in the Engineering Trades* (Fabian Research Department, London, 1917)

— *Women in Trade Unions* (Labour Research Department, London, 1921)

Ewart, A.E. ('Boyd Cable') *Doing their Bit* (Hodder & Stoughton, London, 1916)

Family Endowment Committee *Equal Pay and the Family* (Headley Bros., London, 1918)

Fawcett, M.G. *The Women's Victory and After* (Sidgwick & Jackson, London, 1920)

Fox, A. *A History of the National Union of Boot and Shoe Operatives* (Blackwell, Oxford, 1958)

Foxwell, A.K. *Munition Lasses* (Hodder & Stoughton, London, 1917)

Fraser, H. *Women and War Work* (G. Arnold Shaw, New York, 1918)

Gilbert, B. *British Social Policy* (Batsford, London, 1970)

Haldane, C. *Motherhood and Its Enemies* (Doubleday, New York, 1927)

Hamilton, M.A. *Mary Macarthur* (Parsons, London, 1925)

Hammond, M.B. *British Labor Conditions and Legislation During the War* (Oxford University Press, New York, 1919)

Harris, J. *William Beveridge* (Clarendon, Oxford, 1977)

Hewett, M. *Wives and Mothers in Victorian Industry* (Rockcliff, London, 1957)

Higenbottom, S. *Our Society's History* (Amalgamated Society of Woodworkers, London, 1939)

Hinton, J. *The First Shop Stewards' Movement* (Allen & Unwin, London, 1973)

Hirst, F. *The Consequences of the War to Great Britain* (Oxford University Press, Oxford, 1934)

Holtby, W. *Women in a Changing Civilisation* (Bodley Head, London, 1934)

Hutchins, B.L. *Women in Modern Industry* (Bell & Sons, London, 1915)

—— *Women in Industry After the War* (Social Reconstruction Pamphlet no. 3, published by the *Athenaeum*, undated)

—— & Harrison, A. *A History of Factory Legislation* (King, London, 1926)

Hyman, R. *The Workers' Union* (Clarendon, Oxford, 1971)

Jefferys, J. *The Story of the Engineers* (Lawrence & Wishart, London, 1945)

Jewkes, J., & Gray, E.M. *Wages and Labour in the Lancashire Cotton Spinning Industry* (Manchester University Press, Manchester, 1934)

Kirkaldy, A.W. *British Labour* (Isaac Pitman, London, 1921)

—— *Industry and Finance*, vol. I (Isaac Pitman, London, 1917), vol. II (Isaac Pitman, London, 1920)

Labour Year Book, 1916

Lamb, T.A. *TNT Tales* (Blackwell, Oxford, 1918)

Lewenhak, S. *Women and Trade Unions* (Ernest Benn, London, 1977)

Lloyd, E.M.H. *Experiments in State Control* (Clarendon, Oxford, 1924)

Lloyd George, D. *Memoirs* (Oldhams, London, 1938)

London School of Economics, *New Survey of London Life and Labour*, vol. II (King & Son, London, 1931), vol. IX (King & Son, London, 1935)

Macdonald, J.R. *Women in the Printing Trades* (King & Son, London, 1904)

Mitchell, D. *Women on the Warpath* (Cape, London, 1965)

Neff, W. *Victorian Working Women* (Allen & Unwin, London, 1929)

Orton, W. *Labour in Transition* (P. Allan & Co., London, 1921)

Pankhurst, E.S. *The Home Front* (Hutchinson, London, 1932)

Peel, Mrs C.S. *How We Lived Then* (John Lane, London, 1929)

Phillips, M. (ed.) *Women and the Labour Party* (Headley Bros., London, 1918)

Pigou, A.C. *Aspects of British Economic History* (Cass & Co., London, 1947)

Pinchbeck, I. *Women Workers and the Industrial Revolution* (Routledge London, 1930)

Playne, C. *Society at War 1914-16* (Allen & Unwin, London, 1930)

Pollard, S. *A History of Labour in Sheffield* (Liverpool University Press, Liverpool, 1957)

Pollock, M.A. (ed.) *Working Days* (Cape, London, 1926)

Pribicevik, B. *The Shop Stewards' Movement and Workers' Control* (Blackwell, Oxford, 1959)

Proud, D. *Welfare Work* (Bell & Sons, London, 1916)

Reiss, E. *The Rights and Duties of English Women* (Sherratt & Hughes, London, 1934)

Rowbotham, S. *A New World For Women: Stella Browne – Socialist Feminist* (Pluto, London, 1977)

Rowntree, S. *The Human Needs of Labour* (Thomas Nelson, London, 1918)

— *Poverty* (Macmillan & Co., London, 1901)

Solden, N. *Women in British Trade Unions* (Gill & Macmillan, Dublin, 1978)

Standing Joint Committee of Industrial Women's Organisations *The Position of Women after the War* (Standing Joint Committee, London, n.d.)

Stone, G. (ed.) *Women War Workers* (Harrap, London, 1917)

Strachey, R. *Careers and Openings for Women* (Faber & Faber, London, 1935)

— *The Cause* (Bell & Sons, London, 1928)

— *Our Freedom and Its Results* (Hogarth, London, 1936)

TUC reports of annual conferences.

Vynne, N., & Blackburn, H. *Women Under the Factory Act* (Williams & Norgate, London, 1903)

Warwick, Countess of *A Woman and the War* (Chapman & Hall, London, 1916)

Webb, B. *Diaries 1912-24*, ed. M. Cole (Longmans, London, 1952)

Webb, S. *When Peace Comes* (Fabian Tract 181, London, n.d.)

Webb, S. & B. *Problems of Modern Industry* (Longmans, Green & Co., London, 1902)

White, C. *Women's Magazines* (Michael Joseph, London, 1970)

Wilson, E. *Women and the Welfare State* (Tavistock, London, 1978)

Women's Industrial League *Memorial to the Prime Minister on the Future Employment of Women in Industry, and his Reply* (published as pamphlet, 1918)

Worsfold, D. *War and Social Reform* (Murray, London, 1919)

Yates, L.K. *A Woman's Part* (Hodder & Stoughton, London, 1918)

Yates, M.L. *Wages and Labour Conditions in British Engineering* (Macdonald & Evans, London, 1937)

II Contemporary Newspapers and Journals

ASE Monthly Journal and Report
The *Athenaeum*
Common Cause
The *Communist*
Daily News
Democrat
The *Economic Journal*
The *Engineer*
Fortnightly Review
Labour Woman
Ministry of Labour Gazette
Out of Work
The *Socialist*
Socialist Review
Solidarity
The Times
Trade Union Worker
Trade Unionist
Woman Worker
Woman's Dreadnought, later *Worker's Dreadnought*
Woman's Industrial News

III Articles

Abrams, Philip, 'The Failure of Social Reform', *Past and Present* (1963)
Alexander, Sally, Davin, Anna, & Hostettler, Eve 'Labouring Women: A Reply to Eric Hobsbawm', *History Workshop* (Autumn 1979)
Davin, Anna, 'Imperialism and Motherhood', *History Workshop* (Spring 1978)
McCalman, Janet, 'The Impact of the Great War on Female Employment in England', *Labour History* (Nov. 1971)
Oral History, vol. 5, no. 2 (Autumn 1977), whole issue

IV Unpublished Theses

Kozack, M. 'Women Munition Workers During the First World War, with special reference to Engineering', unpublished PhD thesis,

University of Hull
Thom, D. 'Women Munition Workers at Woolwich Arsenal in the 1914-18 War', unpublished MA thesis, University of Warwick

V Special Collections, Published and Unpublished

Fawcett Library: unpublished documents of the Women's Service Bureau, and newspaper cuttings
Imperial War Museum: assorted documents in the library, and the recordings held by the Department of Sound Records
Labour Party Archives
London School of Economics: Beveridge Collection
TUC Library: Gertrude Tuckwell Collection of newspaper cuttings

VI Government Papers

Home Office Memorandum, *A Study of the Factors which have Operated in the Past and those which are Operating now to Determine the Distribution of Women in Industry* (1930), Cmd 3508
Chief Inspector of Factories, *Reports*
Ministry of Munitions, Reports and Memoranda of the Health of Munition Workers Committee (*Final Report*, 1918, Cd 9065)
— Catalogues of the exhibitions of women's work, 1916, 1917, 1918
— *Handbook on the Health of the Munition Worker* (1917)
— *Notes on the Employment of Women on Munition Work* (1916)
— *Women's War Work* (1916)
Ministry of Reconstruction, *Report of the Women's Employment Committee* (1919), Cd 9239
— *Report of the Civil War Workers Committee on Substitute Labour* (1918), Cd 9228
— *Report of the Women's Advisory Committee on the Domestic Service Problem* (1919), Cmd 67
— Reports from the War Cabinet Committee on *Women in Industry* (1919), Cmd 135 and 167
Censuses, 1891, 1901, 1911

INDEX